SMITH

Austin
BUFFUM

Mike
MATTOS

BEST
Practices
at Tier 3

**Intensive
Interventions
for Remediation**

Elementary

Solution Tree | Press
a division of
Solution Tree

555 North Morton Street
Bloomington, IN 47404
800.733.6786 (toll free) / 812.336.7700
FAX: 812.336.7790

email: info@SolutionTree.com
SolutionTree.com

Visit **go.SolutionTree.com/RTIatWork** to download the free reproducibles in this book.

Printed in the United States of America

Library of Congress Cataloging-in-Publication Data

Names: Rogers, Paula, author. | Smith, W. Richard, author. | Buffum, Austin
  G., author. | Mattos, Mike (Mike William), author. | Solution Tree.
Title: Best practices at tier 3 : intensive interventions for remediation,
  Elementary / Paula Rogers, W. Richard Smith, Austin Buffum, Mike Mattos.

Other titles: Best practices at tier three
Description: Bloomington, Indiana : Solution Tree Press, 2020. | Includes
  bibliographical references and index.
Identifiers: LCCN 2019049364 (print) | LCCN 2019049365 (ebook) | ISBN
  9781943874392 (Paperback) | ISBN 9781943874408 (eBook)
Subjects: LCSH: Education, Elementary--United States. | Response to
  intervention (Learning disabled children)--United States. | Remedial
  teaching--United States. | Effective teaching--United States.
Classification: LCC LA219 .R64 2020 (print) | LCC LA219 (ebook) | DDC
  372.21--dc23
LC record available at https://lccn.loc.gov/2019049364
LC ebook record available at https://lccn.loc.gov/2019049365

Solution Tree
Jeffrey C. Jones, CEO
Edmund M. Ackerman, President

Solution Tree Press
President and Publisher: Douglas M. Rife
Associate Publisher: Sarah Payne-Mills
Art Director: Rian Anderson
Managing Production Editor: Kendra Slayton
Senior Production Editor: Christine Hood
Content Development Specialist: Amy Rubenstein
Copy Editor: Kendra Slayton
Proofreader: Elisabeth Abrams
Editorial Assistants: Sarah Ludwig and Elijah Oates

Acknowledgments

This book is dedicated to the work and legacy of Rick and Becky DuFour. Their mentorship, friendship, and guidance provided the foundation of all that is in this book. Gone, but never forgotten.

We sincerely thank the staff, students, and parents of the following schools. We have been honored to work with them. They are examples of the dedication, leadership, and commitment to all children that inspire us daily.

Hallsville Independent School District
Hallsville, Texas

Sanger Unified School District
Sanger, California

Pine Tree Independent School District
Longview, Texas

Solution Tree Press would like to thank the following reviewers:

Paul Goldberg
Assistant Superintendent
Schaumburg School District 54
Schaumburg, Illinois

Suzanne Osborne
SPED Teacher
Pepperell Elementary School
Lindale, Georgia

Jennifer Plucker
Director of Professional Learning
Mackin Professional Learning
Burnsville, Minnesota

Kimberly Rodriguez Cano
Educational Consultant
President, Cano & Associates, LLC

Gerald Williams
Solution Tree Associate
Payette, Idaho

Visit **go.SolutionTree.com/RTIatWork**
to download the free reproducibles in this book.

Table of Contents

Reproducible pages are in italics.

About the Authors

Paula Rogers retired in 2015 after a career in public education as the deputy superintendent for instruction, accountability, and human resources for Hallsville Independent School District (ISD), a midsize district in East Texas with five Title I campuses. Paula led the implementation of professional learning communities (PLCs) districtwide, beginning in 2004. As a result of this work, the district earned the highest level of accountability awarded by the state of Texas, and AllThingsPLC.info named it as a model professional learning community.

Paula has seen the powerful results of building a team that embraces the collective responsibility for all students reaching high levels of achievement. Being part of this team of educators and seeing the results in student outcomes are the most rewarding experiences of her educational career. Prior to Hallsville ISD, Paula served as the Assistant Superintendent and Director of Federal Programs and Special Education in Pine Tree ISD in Longview, Texas.

Paula now works with schools across the United States and in Canada as they implement PLC at Work® and RTI at Work™ practices. She passionately believes in these practices and the outcomes for students that are a result of their implementation.

Paula is a contributing author to the book *It's About Time: Planning Interventions and Extensions in Elementary School* edited by Austin Buffum and Mike Mattos, published by Solution Tree.

She has experience as a general education teacher, a special education teacher, and an educational diagnostician. Paula holds a master's degree in education from Stephen F. Austin State University and certifications in general education, special education, and school administration.

To learn more about Paula's work, follow her @Tools4Teams on Twitter.

W. Richard Smith was deputy superintendent of the Sanger Unified School District, which serves more than thirteen thousand students with a large population of minority and high-poverty students. He has been involved in public education for more than forty years. Richard has presented on the power of professional learning communities throughout the nation. During his time in Sanger Unified, more than three hundred districts from across California and the United States visited Sanger to see its collaborative culture firsthand. He has taught at the elementary and high school levels and has served as a special education resource teacher. He was principal of four elementary schools and was a high school administrator for nine years. He also worked at the district office level for fifteen years.

When Richard joined Sanger in 2004 as assistant superintendent for human resources, the district was one of ninety-eight in California to be named a program improvement district due to low performance. Two years later, Sanger became one of the first districts to rise above this status and is now one of the highest-performing districts in the Central Valley. Among all eighteen schools, Sanger has won multiple state and national awards, fifteen California Distinguished School awards, ten Title I Academic Achievement awards, and two National Blue Ribbon Schools awards.

Richard was named the 1998 Crystal Award Winner for the Clovis Unified School District for his leadership and work at the high school level. In 2010, he was named a distinguished alumnus by the Kremen School of Education and Human Development at California State University, Fresno. California State University, Fresno, honored Richard as the 2014 Top Dog Distinguished Alumni Award winner.

Austin Buffum, EdD, has fifty years of experience in public schools. His many roles include serving as former senior deputy superintendent of California's Capistrano Unified School District. Austin has presented in over nine hundred school districts throughout the United States and around the world. He delivers trainings and presentations on the RTI at Work model. This tiered approach to response to intervention is centered on PLC at Work concepts and strategies to ensure every student receives the time and support necessary to succeed.

Austin also delivers workshops and presentations that provide the tools educators need to build and sustain PLCs. Austin was selected 2006 Curriculum and Instruction Administrator of the Year by the Association of California School Administrators. He attended the Principals' Center at the Harvard Graduate School of Education and was greatly inspired by its founder, Roland Barth, an

In the book *Taking Action: A Handbook for RTI at Work* (Buffum et al., 2018), the authors define the word *intervention* as follows:

> An *intervention* is anything a school does above and beyond what all students receive to help certain students succeed academically. If all students receive a particular instructional practice or service, it is part of the school's core instructional program. But if the school provides a specific practice, program, or service to some students, it is an intervention. Intervention and remediation are not merely provided for academic skills. Behavior, attendance, and health services can be interventions as well as enrichment for students who have already mastered essential grade-level standards. (p. 27)

There are three levels of intervention that occur in the RTI at Work process: (1) prevention, (2) intervention, and (3) remediation. When students receive additional help as part of the core instruction delivered at Tier 1 prior to the end-of-unit assessment, we call this kind of intervention *prevention*. When students receive additional support following an end-of-unit assessment, we call this kind of intervention simply *intervention*. When students receive additional help to address the gaps in foundational skills and knowledge from prior school years, we call this kind of intervention *remediation*.

The purpose of this book is to provide specific, proven instructional practices and processes that will improve a school's Tier 3 intensive interventions—*remediation*. But before we dig deeply into these practices, it is critical that we build clarity on some essential vocabulary and how Tier 3 remediation fits into a larger multitiered system of support.

The RTI at Work Pyramid

After working with hundreds of schools and districts around the world, we have found the use of lots of RTI jargon but a general lack of specificity on what the terminology means. In *Taking Action: A Handbook for RTI at Work*, Austin Buffum, Mike Mattos, and Janet Malone (2018) carefully rethought and revised the traditional RTI pyramid in order to help clarify this terminology. We refer to our visual framework as the RTI at Work pyramid. See figure I.1 (page 4).

At first glance, you probably noticed that our pyramid is upside-down. We have found that some educators misinterpret the traditional RTI pyramid as a new way to qualify students for special education (see figure I.2, page 4). States, provinces, and school districts visually reinforce this conclusion when they place special education at the top of the pyramid.

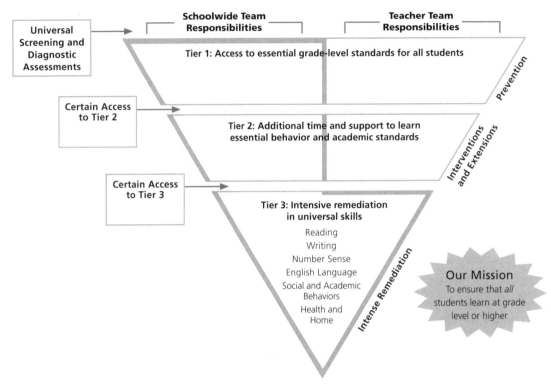

Source: Buffum et al., 2018, p. 18.

Figure I.1: The RTI at Work pyramid.

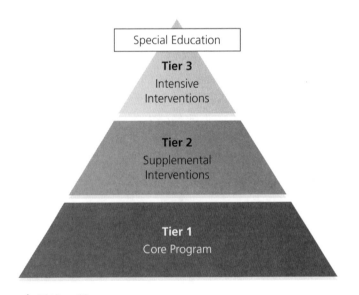

Source: Buffum et al., 2018, p. 19.

Figure I.2: RTI pyramid with special education at the top.

To challenge this detrimental view of the traditional pyramid, we intentionally inverted the RTI at Work pyramid, visually focusing a school's interventions on a single point—the individual student (see figure I.3).

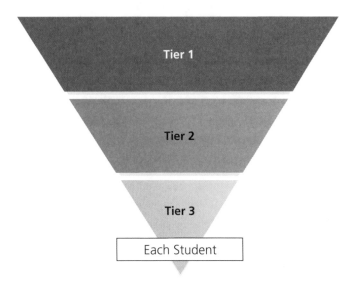

Source: Buffum et al., 2018, p. 19.

Figure I.3: Inverted RTI at Work pyramid.

Tier 1 is represented by the widest part of the pyramid because it constitutes the instruction that all students should receive. This is the school's core instructional program (see figure I.4).

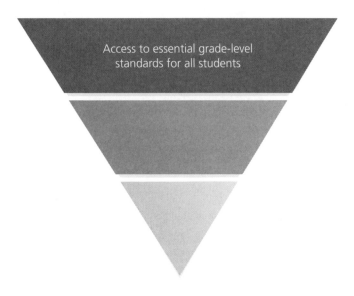

Source: Buffum et al., 2018, p. 20.

Figure I.4: Core instruction program.

Many traditional RTI approaches advocate that the key to Tier 1 is effective first instruction. We don't disagree with this. However, Buffum et al. (2018) write:

> This teaching must include instruction on the skills, knowledge, and behaviors that a student must acquire during the current year to be prepared for the following year. Unfortunately, many schools deem their most at-risk students incapable of learning grade-level curriculum, so they pull out these students and place them in Tier 3 interventions that replace core instruction with remedial coursework. So, even if the initial teaching is done well, if a student's core instruction is focused on below-grade-level standards, then he or she will learn well below grade level.
>
> If the fundamental purpose of RTI is to ensure all students learn at high levels—grade level or better each year—then we must teach students at grade level. Every student might not leave each school year having mastered every grade-level standard, but he or she must master the learning outcomes deemed indispensable for future success. (pp. 20–21)

Despite the best of efforts, every unit of study ends with *most* students having learned the essential learning outcomes and a few students still struggling. Because schools are dedicated to the idea that *all* students must master essential learning outcomes, it next provides additional time and support to help these students master essentials without missing critical new core instruction. This additional time and support are the purpose of Tier 2 (see figure I.5).

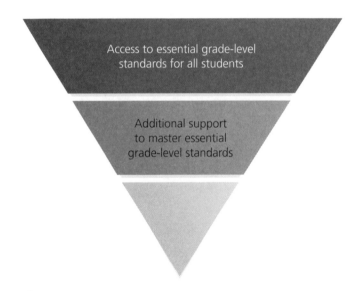

Source: Buffum et al., 2018, p. 21.

Figure I.5: Supplemental help to master grade-level curriculum.

This is a crucial point! Traditional RTI approaches often define Tier 2 by either the size of the intervention group or the duration of the intervention. These recommendations are based largely on early RTI research focused on primary reading interventions. Our experience shows us that this approach has limitations when applied across all grades and subjects. Instead, we recommend that the defining characteristics of Tier 2 are the learning outcomes being targeted. Supplemental assistance should focus on providing targeted students with the additional time and support needed to master specific skills, knowledge, and behaviors identified at Tier 1 to be essential for a student's future success. Classroom teacher teams should be actively involved at Tier 2, as these outcomes directly relate to their areas of expertise. Because supplemental interventions are focused on very specific learning targets, placement into Tier 2 interventions must be timely, targeted, flexible, and most likely aligned to classroom assessments.

Equally important, for students that do master essential curriculum during core instruction, Tier 2 time can be used to extend their learning. To be clear, there is an important difference between *extension* and *enrichment*. *Extension* is when students are stretched beyond essential grade-level curriculum or levels of proficiency. We define *enrichment* as students having access to the subjects that specials or electives teachers traditionally teach, such as music, art, drama, applied technology, and physical education. We strongly believe that this curriculum is essential for all students (Buffum et al., 2018). Tier 2 time should be used for extension, not enrichment.

Providing all students access to essential grade-level curriculum and effective initial teaching during Tier 1 core instruction, as well as providing additional time and support to students at Tier 2, will result in success for most students. However, some students lack foundational skills needed to succeed at their grade level. These universal skills of learning include the ability to:

1. Decode and comprehend grade-level text

2. Write effectively

3. Apply number sense

4. Comprehend the English language (or the school's primary language)

5. Consistently demonstrate social and academic behaviors

6. Overcome complications due to health or home (Buffum et al., 2018, p. 22)

These foundational skills are much more than a student needing help in a specific learning target, but instead:

> Represent a series of skills that enable a student to comprehend instruction, access information, demonstrate understanding, and behave appropriately in a school setting. If a student is significantly behind in one of these universal skills, he or she will struggle in virtually every grade level, course, and subject. And usually a school's most at-risk students are behind in more than one area. Therefore, for students who

> need intensive remediation in foundational skills, the school must have a plan to provide this level of assistance without denying these students access to essential grade-level curriculum. This is the purpose of Tier 3. (Buffum et al., 2018, p. 22)

See figure I.6.

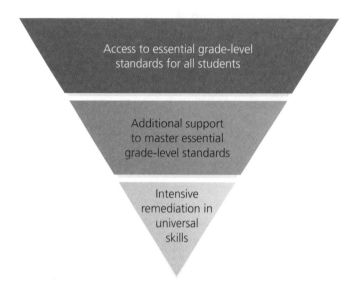

Source: Buffum et al., 2018, p. 22.

Figure I.6: Intensive remediation in foundational skills.

Universal skills are developed over time, not overnight. For this reason, schools need highly trained staff to provide Tier 3 remedial interventions, targeted specifically to each student's areas of need, during the regular instructional day.

Finally, RTI is considered a multitiered system of supports because, as noted by Buffum et al. (2018):

> Some students need all three tiers to learn at high levels—this is why it is called a multitiered system of supports. Schools don't just move student from tier to tier. Instead, the tiers are cumulative . . . value added! All students need effective initial teaching on essential grade-level standards at Tier 1. In addition to Tier 1, some student need supplemental time and support in meeting essential grade-level standards at Tier 2. In addition to Tier 1 and Tier 2, some students need intensive help in learning essential outcomes from previous years. Students in need of Tier 3 intensive help in remedial skills most likely struggle with new essential grade-level curriculum the first time it is taught. This means these students need Tier 2 and Tier 3, all without missing new essential instruction at Tier 1. (p. 23)

Creating this level of support cannot be done effectively by an individual teacher in his or her own classroom. Instead, it requires a schoolwide, collaborative effort in which the entire staff take collective responsibility for student learning. It also requires continuous collaborative processes to create a guaranteed and viable curriculum and develop the ongoing common formative assessments needed to target Tier 2 interventions. At Tier 3, it requires the school to call on all its resources in an all-hands-on-deck effort to rescue those students needing intensive remediation at Tier 3. This is why structuring a school to function as a professional learning community is the key to effectively implementing RTI.

To make this point as clear and explicit as possible: Being a PLC is an essential prerequisite to successful RTI implementation. Specifically, we advocate for the Professional Learning Community at Work (PLC at Work) process, originally developed by Richard DuFour and Robert Eaker (1998). While this book includes many references to the PLC process, for a deeper dive into the specifics, we highly recommend the book *Learning by Doing: A Handbook for Professional Learning Communities at Work* (DuFour, DuFour, Eaker, Many, & Mattos, 2016).

The Power of Intensive Tier 3 Remediation

Since Tier 3 remediation focuses on foundational skills and knowledge that students should have mastered in prior years of school, these efforts must be powerful in their effect. The term *intensive* is frequently used to describe Tier 3 remediation, but how is it defined? The following characteristics represent how to make remediation sufficiently intensive to help students who are years behind in the foundational skills (listed earlier) catch up with their peers.

▽ High in frequency

▽ Longer in duration

▽ Within a small-size class

▽ Targeted at deficiencies

▽ Administered by highly trained professionals

A preponderance of the research underlying RTI suggests that Tier 3 interventions should be daily. Students should receive this additional support for five days per week (O'Connor, Harty, & Fulmer, 2005). The duration of these supports should be longer than those received by students in Tier 2. Due to the complex nature of the problems faced by students at Tier 3, many researchers suggest a duration of approximately fifty minutes daily (Harlacher, Sanford, & Walker, n.d.). Of course, primary-aged students should not be subjected to fifty *continuous* minutes of remediation, but instead should have this time delivered in shorter segments.

Group or class size is one of the most daunting aspects of Tier 3 remediation. While many studies suggest a group size of 3:1 or less (Haager, Klingner, & Vaughn, 2007;

Simmons et al., 2007), we find this almost impossible for most schools to accomplish. For this reason, we recommend that schools focus intently on the remaining two characteristics—*targeted* and *administered by trained professionals*—as a way of mitigating the need for extremely small group size.

The more highly targeted the remediation, the more effective it will be over time. For example, we often ask educators which of the two following scenarios might be most effective.

1. Four students are deemed to be low readers. One needs help with phonemic awareness, one with decoding, one with fluency, and one with comprehension.

2. Eight students need help with decoding.

Most educators indicate that the second scenario is most likely to be effective, more effective than the first scenario, despite the fact that the group size in the second example is twice that of the first. This results from the ability to closely target the intervention on the cause of the problem, even with more students, rather than loosely grouping fewer students based on a vague and generalized cause (for example, a letter grade of F).

Finally, teachers can achieve the intensity of Tier 3 remediation by utilizing our most highly trained educators to work with these students rather than our least trained. Many schools have traditionally assigned poorly trained paraprofessionals or first-year teachers to work with the neediest students. If hospitals worked this way, the patients needing the most help would be assigned to nurses or interns rather than specialists.

Common Tier 3 Implementation Mistakes

While few debate the need for intensive Tier 3 remediation, Buffum et al. (2018) state, "We have found that many site educators, district administrators, and state policymakers misinterpret key concepts, skip critical steps, look for shortcuts, and fail to discontinue traditional practices that are counterproductive to the RTI process" (p. 5).

Following are some of the key implementation mistakes educators make relative to Tier 3 remediation.

1. **Assuming Tier 3 is only a special education process:** This thinking is a pernicious holdover from the past in which a student's failure in core instruction meant he or she must have a learning disability (Prasse, n.d.). This thinking was based on some forty years of waiting for kids to fail that were the unfortunate outcome of PL 94–142 (1975). This thinking has led to outrageous over-identification

and misidentification of students with learning disabilities. While approximately 4.5 percent of a general population may have some kind of specific learning disability (McFarland et al., 2018), many students without a specific disability have fallen behind and need intensive Tier 3 remediation. They should not need to be labeled *special education* to receive this help.

2. **Using Tier 3 as only a regular education process:** Too many schools and districts have built walls between their special education and regular education staff. If using our most highly trained staff is a key characteristic of intensive Tier 3 remediation, this would mean utilizing our highly trained speech and language pathologists, occupational therapists, school psychologists, and special education teachers to work with our neediest students, regardless of whether or not they have been identified with a specific learning disability. Not only is this desirable, it is legal under the Individuals With Disabilities Education Improvement Act (IDEIA). Melody Musgrove (2013, as cited in Pierce, 2015), director of the Office of Special Education Programs (OSEP) for the U.S. Department of Education, writes:

> Pursuant to 34 CFR §300.208(a), special education teachers fully funded by Part B (non-CEIS) funds may perform duties for children without disabilities if they would already be performing these same duties in order to provide special education and related services to children with disabilities. For example, a special education teacher is assigned to provide five hours of reading instruction per week to three students with disabilities consistent with those students' IEPs. The IEPs provide that the students need specialized reading instruction that is at grade level but handled at a slower pace because of auditory processing issues.

> The school decides that, although they are not children with disabilities, there are two general education children who would benefit from this instruction. The special education teacher must prepare lesson plans for each of these classes regardless of the number of children in the class. She may do so and conduct the class for all five children because she is only providing special education and related services for the three children with disabilities and the two children without disabilities are benefiting from that work.

3. **Applying the right medicine with the wrong intensity:** Under this scenario, a school or team selects a scientific, research-based intervention program, but then administers the program in a way that lessens its intensity. Many times, not only are the duration and frequency of the intervention insufficient, the program is not used in a highly targeted way nor administered by the most highly trained individuals in the school.

4. **Believing some students are incapable of learning at high levels:**
   In *Taking Action* (Buffum et al., 2018), the authors write, "Virtually all educators believe their students can learn, but many think that how much a student can learn varies depending on his or her innate abilities and demographic background" (p. 9).

In too many schools, faculty regard students who come from economically disadvantaged homes, many times minority and English learners, as "less academic" and thus less capable than peers who come from more advantaged homes. While we may acknowledge that a student's ethnicity, native language, and economic status do not reduce the student's innate ability to learn, minority students, English learners, and economically disadvantaged students are overrepresented in special education (Brantlinger, 2006; Ferri & Connor, 2006; Skiba, Poloni-Staudinger, Gallini, Simmons, & Feggins-Azziz, 2006). How can Tier 3 remediation be effective when educators begin with the assumption that some students can't learn at high levels because they lack some mysterious innate ability?

About This Book

As with all RTI at Work resources, this book is for practitioners by practitioners. It is part of a three-book series on best instructional practices for each tier of the RTI model. A vast majority of this book was written by two exceptional educators, Paula Rogers and W. Richard Smith. For them, the PLC at Work process and RTI model are not theories, for they have lived both and gained the type of firsthand, practical knowledge that can only be acquired through doing the work at a very high level. Local, state, and national public education agencies have recognized them as outstanding classroom teachers, site administrators, and district leaders. Both have led model PLC at Work schools and districts, advised state and national policymakers, and helped schools across the world. They were selected to connect their expertise and ideas to the overall RTI at Work process.

The interventions in this book focus on ongoing processes, not programs. These processes are grounded in proven instructional practices, and applicable at virtually all grades, in all subjects, and for all student demographics. Equally important, these interventions should not require the hiring of additional staff, buying additional resources, or extending the school day. Instead, it is about using your current time and resources in more targeted, effective ways. It is not about asking a school staff to work harder, but instead to work collectively smarter. Putting these ideas into practice will help more students learn and, in turn, transition your faculty from seeing RTI as a "Do we have to?" to "We want to!"

In this book, we also address the formation, role, and functions of the leadership team (sometimes called the guiding coalition), the school intervention team, the behavior intervention team, and collaborative teacher teams. The leadership team at a school consists of key staff members and works to ensure that there is focused staff commitment, collaborative team planning, schoolwide programmatic implementation, and consistent monitoring of the school's efforts toward the growth and development of all students. The leadership team works closely with the intervention teams and teacher teams. We will provide clear explanations and examples of how schools form intervention teams, as well as dictate their role and function as they address the learning and behavior needs of all students in Tier 3.

All chapters in this book include information on how the foundations at Tiers 1 and 2 support Tier 3, as well as helpful scenarios and a myriad of practical tools and strategies to support the implementation of the practices described.

Chapter 1 firmly establishes the prerequisite relationship and necessity for functioning of Tier 1 and Tier 2 as the foundation for effective Tier 3 implementation. It addresses the pitfalls and stumbling blocks to successful implementation as a cautionary warning to readers as schools plan Tier 3 implementation. This chapter discusses the relationship between effective collaboration in a PLC environment and Tier 3 as a foundational element to successful implementation. Chapter 2 addresses the need for a school's staff to be committed and share the responsibility to ensure the learning of *all* students. Staff commitment is foundational to ensuring that students with the greatest behavioral and learning needs are met by meaningful Tier 3 implementation. This chapter offers tools and strategies to assist in solidifying staff commitment and shared responsibility for the success of all students.

Chapter 3 outlines the organizational structures of the leadership and intervention teams as well as shared considerations regarding the relationship of Tier 3 to these critical teams. We devote an entire chapter to these two teams because of the essential role they play in the RTI at Work process at Tier 3. This chapter also examines the relationship between special education and Tier 3.

Chapter 4 focuses on best practices during Tier 3 design. It emphasizes the need for a school to be pragmatic and clear in purpose, the design, and the outcomes they seek for students in Tier 3. This chapter seeks to provide clarity through critical design questions that both the leadership and intervention teams must consider as they work for meaning and effective implementation of Tier 3.

Chapter 5 provides specific processes and practical examples for using multiple types of assessment to identify students' targeted needs. This chapter articulates the purpose for using ongoing assessment and the importance of general education teachers and intervention teachers working together to align the goals or learning targets being addressed in intervention to grade-level essential standards.

Chapter 6 offers a detailed explanation of the critical importance of explicitly teaching essential academic and social behaviors as well as specific examples of how to support students needing intensive behavior intervention at Tier 3. This chapter provides both research and practical examples for the leadership team, intervention team, and teacher teams to use as they teach and intervene in the area of behavior.

Chapter 7 details examples of practices that schools use when building a strong academic foundation at Tiers 1 and 2 as well as strategies for students needing intense support at Tier 3. This chapter emphasizes the importance of genuine collaboration and proactive team planning with the needs of all learners in mind. It offers practical examples supporting the goal of high levels of learning for all.

Chapter 8 provides activities and tools educators can use as they learn and apply the principles of RTI at Work. Each activity is accompanied with an explanation of how it supports Tier 3. This chapter is intended to help all teams as they learn and grow together.

The strategies and tools provided in this book are designed to accelerate and provide critical considerations for implementation of meaningful and effective Tier 3 interventions. Effective implementation of Tier 3 at the elementary level will provide opportunities for many students who are desperately in need of behavioral and learning support. Effective and targeted Tier 3 support for these students is the critical element to ensure their success during the school years and beyond.

The Power and Purpose of Tier 3 Intensive Interventions

W e can all relate to hearing a teacher say, "I don't know what to do—he is so far behind the other students." Unfortunately, for many teachers and students, Tier 3 focuses solely on students with learning disabilities, which eliminates intense support for many students who need it or provides no opportunity for teacher teams to work collaboratively across tiers, leaving teachers working in isolation. Both situations leave teachers frustrated and students lacking the interventions needed to be successful.

The power of the RTI at Work model is that it creates a systematic process for identifying and targeting student needs at Tiers 1, 2, and 3. This system provides opportunities for teachers to work collaboratively and give the support necessary for *all* students to learn at high levels. This means educators can realize their ultimate goal: to make a difference in the lives of all students.

This chapter provides further clarification, presents critical elements, and focuses on the nuts-and-bolts of how to intensify instruction within RTI at Tier 3 as a part of a cohesive system in elementary schools.

Within every school, there are some students who do not progress as expected, even though they receive high-quality instruction directed at mastery of the essential standards and skills for their grade level. These students quickly fall behind their peers. They may be receiving small- and large-group support from their teachers and school yet continue to struggle to learn the critical standards and skills. In some schools, these students may even receive interventions targeted at their specific learning needs beginning at Tier 1 and moving to Tier 2, but they still lack sufficient academic and behavior progress. A teacher's approach to each student must focus on his or her specific learning needs to accelerate learning of the essential skills and knowledge.

As educators, we must acknowledge that mastering essential grade-level academic and behavior standards is necessary for success. These standards represent skills that are critical for school as well as life beyond school. Students must master these skills to attain high levels of learning. Working collaboratively to create a system that supports teachers and students in achieving the goal of all students mastering essential learning is everyone's responsibility.

The Foundation at Tiers 1 and 2

By laying the foundation with the implementation of explicit instruction and assessment of essential standards at Tier 1, matched with supplemental time and support at Tier 2, schools create a strong base for a systematic process that meets the needs of all students. Achieving the goal of high levels of learning for every student requires that schools have processes at Tiers 1, 2, and 3 that are aligned, systematic, and targeted to the needs of each student.

Within the RTI at Work model, all students receive core instruction in the identified essential standards with their peers as the foundation for learning. This core instruction occurs in the classroom with teachers working to check for understanding (CFU) and adjust instructional strategies to meet student needs. Should a student demonstrate a need for additional support to master the identified essential standards and skills, he or she receives supplemental Tier 2 support. Tier 3 is more intensive and focuses on filling gaps in learning the foundational skills necessary to master essential learning. In *Taking Action*, Buffum et al. (2018) explain the relationship between the tiers of intervention:

> If a school provides students access to essential grade-level curriculum and effective initial teaching during Tier 1 core instruction, and targeted supplemental academic and behavioral help in meeting these standards at Tier 2, then most students should be succeeding. But there inevitably will be a number of students who still struggle because they lack the critical foundational skills needed to learn—skills that span all subject areas and grade levels. (p. 226)

Having alignment of the instruction in Tiers 1, 2, and 3 ensures focused and targeted support for each student. The clear definition of these tiers provides school staff an effective, systematic approach to increasing the time and intensity of instruction necessary to ensure learning. Schools with well-thought-out tiers of intervention are better able to proactively intervene to meet the targeted academic and behavior needs of students.

Pitfalls, Confusions, and Stumbling Blocks

For many schools, a major impediment to meaningful implementation of RTI has been the varying goals and recommended procedures of traditional RTI models found in the literature. A quick review of literature shows models that are strictly problem-solving approaches; others are protocol based and focus on specific programs and procedures. Most traditional models primarily focus on identifying and monitoring students at Tiers 2 and 3 without providing processes or systems for alignment with Tier 1. The lack of clarity surrounding RTI has caused confusion and created stumbling blocks for many schools when they attempt to implement a schoolwide approach to RTI.

Unfortunately, it is not unusual to find schools with 60–70 percent of their students placed in Tier 2 and Tier 3 intervention. In these cases, there is little responsibility for the classroom teacher to monitor and adjust core instruction to meet students' needs. In these schools, there is little reteaching at the classroom level and no driving force to improve classroom instruction if a student doesn't learn the first time he or she received intervention. Mike Mattos (2016) is fond of saying about these schools, "They don't have an intervention problem; they have a core instruction problem."

The reverse situation occurs in schools that have defined intervention tiers with small numbers of students at each tier due to the criteria they have established for placement. In most of these cases, the schools have set an arbitrary level of performance to receive support. We have found that many schools take their state test results, count from the lowest achieving students, and select a limited number of students for Tier 2 and Tier 3 intervention based on the space available.

This practice is more about an arbitrary quota of students to be served rather than the specific learning needs of individual students. The intervention tiers are stripped of the ability to provide meaningful learning support to students at risk with the greatest needs. In this type of quota system, the tiers' primary focus is based on arbitrary numbers of students to be served rather than valid, meaningful learning assessment data for tier placement. *Intervention tiers lose the ability to provide support to students at risk when the tiers' primary focus is on artificial or invalid assessment data.*

A compounding factor for both schools with large intervention numbers and those with too few students being served by the intervention system is the lack of comprehensible criteria or method measuring if a student is making progress and when a student's needs have been met by the intervention. The lack of progress monitoring and review of progress for future intervention support often leads to teachers placing students in a tier for long periods of time—in some cases, years. These students become *intervention students* with little to no opportunity to escape their label. Intervention becomes a prison sentence rather than a process to accelerate learning through targeted and focused support. There is no systematic agility or flexibility to meet the real needs of those students being served.

The RTI at Work model is a proactive model that focuses on implementing timely and targeted interventions. The focus is not on creating labels or having rigid timelines for students to qualify for help. At the core of RTI at Work is a belief system grounded with systems and processes that address the academic and behavior needs of all students.

RTI Is About *All* Students

The following RTI scenario is real but unfortunately, all too common.

Paul (fictional name), principal of a high-achieving elementary preK–5 campus, fidgeted in his chair as he shared his school's story of implementing an RTI system of interventions.

"My school is the highest-performing campus in our county. Ninety-one percent of our students are performing at or above grade level on our state's assessment. We have won multiple national and state awards for our efforts. Our program of interventions is saving most students, but we are struggling to make a difference with *all* students."

Paul shares that his staff refer to students who are not making progress as *those students,* and that the program is not moving forward.

Paul and his staff have worked to build a system of interventions that is meeting the needs of most students, but not *all*. *Those students* who are not finding success have moved through a system of interventions with little or no improvement. In a school like Paul's, with collective responsibility to all students, this is not acceptable. However, he and his staff have done all that they know how to do.

The frustration that Paul's staff are feeling is common among schools that have worked to build a system of interventions by providing for most students. However, when confronted with *those students* who are not showing the academic or behavioral successes, they begin to question the students' academic potential. Often, staff blame the student directly without consideration of instructional or programmatic modifications. The frustration for the lack of academic and social development can lead to consequences for these students for the remainder of their academic schooling and beyond into their adult lives. The impact of the label and categorization of *those students* can lead to even more detrimental labels such as: *slow, unmotivated, bad, illiterate,* or *behavior problem.*

If our fundamental purpose as educators is to ensure that *all* students learn a guaranteed, viable curriculum, we must seek solutions that meet the learning needs of every student. It is our responsibility to seek these solutions rather than assign labels and blame the student. The choice is very straightforward: we can either admire the problem, or we can seek solutions. The choice is clear; we must solve the issues and ensure learning for all students.

As stated in *Revisiting Professional Learning Communities at Work* (DuFour, DuFour, & Eaker, 2008), "It is impossible for a school or district to develop the capacity to function as a professional learning community without undergoing profound cultural shifts" (p. 91). This culture will never be more tested than when a school embraces the challenge and responsibility of reaching high levels of achievement with those students who have the greatest academic and behavioral challenges.

As previously noted, students who exhibit the greatest need are too often labeled and placed into categories that reinforce the belief that they are too far behind or that they are beyond the best efforts of a school. In the most extreme cases, these students are written off early in their academic career as *special education*, and schools do little or nothing to intervene until they meet the criteria for placement into a special education program. In these schools, the belief that these students' needs are beyond the capacity of the school extinguishes any sense of urgency to seek solutions, and it destroys and removes consideration of what they can do other than wait for placement in special education. Unfortunately, years of opportunities that could make a difference for these students just slip by, and the achievement gap continues to grow. Far too often, *all* does not mean that all students receive the time, intensity, and focus so desperately needed. Schools must examine their beliefs, their culture, and their practices and align those with a commitment to success for every student.

In the book *Simplifying Response to Intervention: Four Essential Guiding Principles*, Austin Buffum, Mike Mattos, and Chris Weber (2012) define *certain access* as "a systematic process that guarantees every student will receive the time and support needed to learn at high levels" (p. 10). This definition does not exclude students with disabilities, *nor does it imply that students must be referred to special education*. The focus is meeting the learning needs of all students in a systematic way without using the pyramid as a road to placing students in special education.

The tiers of the RTI pyramid represent the increase in time and intensity of effort to meet the needs of students, not a countdown to special education placement. The RTI pyramid is also not exclusive to students who are in special education. The benefits of a systemic pyramid of interventions must focus on meeting students' learning needs and not as a check-off list toward placement in special education, which has become a common practice across the nation. We address this in later chapters more deeply, but it is a foundational core tenet that educators must use the RTI pyramid to focus on student learning and behavioral needs rather than to label students.

RTI at Work and PLCs

The RTI at Work model is rooted in the three big ideas that drive the work of a PLC (DuFour et al., 2016):

1. A focus on learning

2. A collaborative culture and collective responsibility

3. A results orientation

Implied, but not stated in these three big ideas are some critical components that deepen and enrich them.

1. A focus on learning *for students and the adults who are working to meet their learning needs*

2. A collaborative culture and collective responsibility *that provide a relentless focus on learning for all students*

3. A results orientation *focused on improving practice and fueling continuous improvement and learning for all*

The heart of a PLC is the systematic commitment and devotion to collaboration by the staff of a school focused on ensuring every student is learning at high levels. Collectively, teams of educators work together to answer the four critical questions of a PLC (DuFour et al., 2016):

1. What do students need to know and be able to do?

2. How will we know when they have learned it?

3. What will we do when they haven't learned it?

4. What will we do when they already know it? (p. 251)

These same big ideas and critical questions are integral to the functioning of RTI. The collective commitment and collaborative efforts of educators working together to answer these questions fuel the focus and urgency of each tier of the RTI pyramid.

> "Alone we can do so little; together we can do so much."
>
> —Helen Keller

We find that many schools have collaborative planning and data review processes at Tiers 1 and 2 but do not replicate those same effective processes for teachers serving students with the greatest challenges. Schools should ensure that the teachers and interventionists who provide services at Tier 3 have the same opportunity for meaningful collaboration and planning for the individual student goals as they do for the general curriculum.

In 2016, *Education Week* named Steve Sandoval the Executive Director of Special Services at the Adams County School District in Colorado, and its Leader to Learn From for his work in creating an interventionist framework that integrates supports for all students in his district. Sandoval states, "No one teacher has truth in a bottle; no one teacher can do it all, regardless of how great he or she is as a teacher and how well they differentiate in the classroom" (as cited in Sparks, 2016). He recommends that schools consider identifying students for interventions based on skills, not labels, and designing professional development that allows teachers specializing in working with gifted learners, special education students, and English learners to find common strategies and blend funding streams between programs.

Schools must draw from the talents and knowledge of all staff members. Collaboratively, teams must review trends in student learning data to determine if interventions are working without rigid checklists and documentation. The success of all students takes all staff—regardless of role or responsibility. To make this transformation, schools must be willing to change traditional practices if they are not working for the best interests of all students (see figure 1.1).

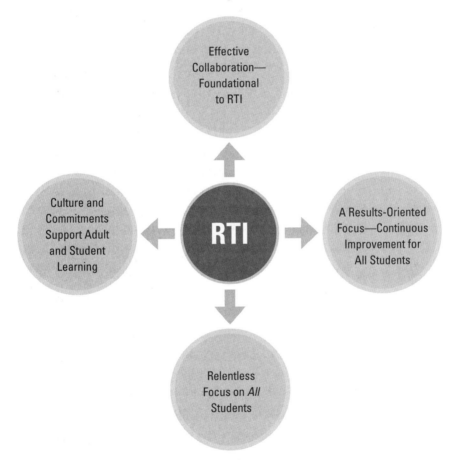

Figure 1.1: Foundational considerations for implementation of effective RTI.

As educators, we must challenge ourselves regarding our expectations and beliefs about students with significant academic and behavioral challenges. To meet the challenges that face us, schools must embrace the belief that every student is special and unique and deserves the type of education that provides him or her with endless possibilities for a successful life. There must be a sense of urgency to close the achievement gaps that exist between students. We must eliminate the traditional walls between special education and general education. We must embrace the fact that there are students in every classroom who may be gifted, English language learners, or have learning disabilities who will benefit from the combined talents of teachers with various educational specialties.

Teams should ask themselves:

▽ "Do we believe that all students are capable of high levels of learning?"

▽ "Are we committed to ensuring that *all* students learn at high levels, and are we willing to take collective responsibility for achieving it? What will that look like? What changes must be made?"

▽ "Are we holding students with disabilities to the same expectations as other students? Are we offering the timely and prescriptive support necessary for them to reach this goal?"

▽ "Do teachers offer all students access to high-quality, research-based Tier 1 instruction? Are we differentiating instruction so we can address the needs of all students in the classroom?"

As a vision for what a school must become, Mike Mattos often presents at his workshops the following commitment that his staff made to parents of the students he served:

▽ "It does not matter which teacher your student has at our school, all students in every class will learn a guaranteed curriculum at high levels."

▽ "If your student needs extra time and support to learn at high levels, we guarantee he or she will receive it."

In working with schools, Mike Mattos asks the staff:

▽ "Do you believe that this is possible at our school?"

▽ "How close are we to this vision or commitment?"

▽ "What must we change or improve to be able to make this commitment?"

As an evaluation of the school's culture and beliefs, these questions are fundamental to implementing effective classroom instruction, ensuring *all* students learn, and developing effective RTI interventions. Willingness by a school staff to strive for this commitment or vision ensures that we build a successful Tier 3 program and ensure all students, including those receiving Tier 3 interventions, are successful.

The four Cs of RTI, as presented by Buffum et al. (2012), provide a framework that teams of educators use to ensure that PLC implementation and RTI implementation are not separate initiatives. And they use this foundation to develop critical questions that guide the development of Tier 3 interventions.

1. **Collective responsibility:** A shared belief that the primary responsibility of each school staff member is to ensure high levels of learning for all students (Why are we here?)

2. **Concentrated instruction:** A systematic process of identifying essential knowledge and skills that all students must learn and master by determining the specific learning needs of each student to ensure learning (Where do we need to go?)

3. **Convergent assessment:** An ongoing process of collectively analyzing evidence to determine the specific learning needs of each student and the effectiveness of instruction the student receives in meeting these needs (Where are we now?)

4. **Certain access:** The systematic process that guarantees every student will receive the necessary time and support needed to learn at high levels (How do we get every student there?)

Buffum et al. (2012) consistently stress that for schools to answer these questions effectively, the staff must work collaboratively as they review student learning data, seek best instructional practices, and target an agreed-on curriculum of standards and skills. They stress that the DuFour et al. (2016) PLC approach to collaboration is foundational to the development of RTI.

Working as a PLC provides schools with the philosophy, foundation, and framework so RTI implementation is seamless and systematic. Collaborative teams lead the intervention process at Tiers 1 and 2 to ensure that they provide supplemental support in learning essential core standards and English language during the school day (Buffum et al., 2012). Schools must have collaborative teacher teams in place to plan common instruction aligned to the standards, design common assessments that provide the short-cycle data critical to monitoring progress, and determine how to reteach and intervene to ensure the success of students before they fail. Teams should explicitly design a system of planning instruction and assessments and reviewing data to prevent, rather than react to, school failure at Tier 1.

This system also includes a proactive or preventative behavior system or positive behavior intervention and support (PBIS) for all students. Leadership teams collaboratively work to ensure that the necessary structures, such as schedules, are in place as well as lead Tier 2 interventions for students with motivation, attendance, and behavior issues.

Tier 3 development requires consistent and focused collaboration across the school site. To effectively meet the learning needs of Tier 3 students, a team of educators must work collectively and collaboratively to define, monitor, and seek best practices to ensure student success. The learning outcomes for students being served by collaborative teams are often based on the team's ability to communicate and openly share data and best practices. We provide Carson's Story as an example of the approach taken by two different teams and schools.

Carson's Story

Carson is an energetic eight-year-old who is looking forward to third grade in a new school. He is bright and eager to learn. His second-grade teacher indicates that he will be on track for third grade in numeracy but will have gaps in reading. His reading fluency is at kindergarten level. He has great difficulty in memorizing sight words and with phonetic analysis. He is currently receiving Tier 2 reading intervention in addition to small-group work in his class. He has made very little progress. His teachers had referred him for more diagnostic testing.

Imagine the difference in the outcome for Carson as you read about two teams in different schools and their approach to working with students with learning gaps.

Team 1

Team 1 works in a small suburban school. Most students in this school are successful.

This team is made up of four tenured teachers who have worked together for a number of years. The community views them as the experts in third grade, and they have many parental requests for their classes.

When a visiting consultant asks team members what their process is for working with students with large learning gaps, team members respond that they have done this for years and have worked with all types of students. They have a system that they believe works. If students can't learn with them, then typically those students are special education.

Team 2

Team 2 works in a school that has embraced working with collective commitment for overall school improvement.

This team is made up of four teachers with varying levels of experience. Two of the teachers are new to the campus. One of the new teachers has experience as a reading interventionist.

When a visiting consultant asks team members what their process is for working with students with large learning gaps, team members respond that they would work with interventionists and use diagnostic reading assessments to target their needs. They would also meet with interventionists regularly to align Tier 2 interventions and monitor progress. If they don't make any progress, they would contact the campus RTI team. If the students needed intensive intervention at Tier 3, all team members would work together to ensure students' success.

Team 2 is an example of a team whose team members not only take action on the team's beliefs, but also work collaboratively to align interventions. They have a commitment to all students and a systematic process for using data to target interventions and monitor progress.

RTI Alignment at Tiers 1, 2, and 3

It is not uncommon to find schools that place their sole focus on Tier 3 when they are facing the challenge of school improvement. While this is understandable and may result in the improvement of some Tier 3 practices, it most likely won't result in sustained high levels of achievement for all students. Tier 3 is most successful when teachers work in a cohesive system of support beginning at Tier 1. Tier 3 is designed to provide intensive support in the universal or foundational learning skills. Students needing this help may or may not have learning disabilities. Tier 3 is not solely for students with learning disabilities, and receiving Tier 3 support should not prevent students from getting access to grade-level essential learning.

Consider figure 1.2 (page 26) and the actions at each tier. These actions are just examples and are not an exhaustive list. As you analyze the actions that take place at Tier 3, consider their relationship to Tiers 1 and 2. How do the processes at each tier work together to support all students? How do the outcomes for students change by having an aligned system?

Conclusion

When schools commit to the RTI at Work process at every tier of instruction, then *all* really does mean *all*, and we see students needing intensive intervention move from accessing instruction to achieving the level of achievement necessary for them to fulfill their hopes and dreams. The work of all teachers at a school must be collaborative and focused on using formative learning data to monitor mastery of the guaranteed curriculum while promoting the development of best practices to ensure success for *all* students.

In subsequent chapters, as we detail the elements of a successful Tier 3 program, we will seek to provide clarity by sharing best practices, success stories, and common implementation mistakes and challenges learned through experience. As practitioners, we know that this work is hard, but we also know that it is doable and necessary for all students to achieve success in the classroom and in life.

"Traveler, there is no path. The path is made by walking."

—Antonio Machado

Process	What This Looks Like at Tier 1	What This Looks Like at Tier 2	What This Looks Like at Tier 3
Develop a Common Team Mission and Vision and Values and Goals	District and campus leaders and teachers work to develop a common vision and team commitments. Teams share collective responsibility to achieve goals that result in high levels of learning for all students.	Teacher teams (including interventionists) work collaboratively to reteach and intervene with students by the student, by the standard, and by the learning target. Teams work with a sense of urgency and collective responsibility.	Interventionists, special education teachers, and core teachers work together to monitor learning, share best practices, and demonstrate a commitment to each student.
Identify Essential Standards	Grade-level teacher teams work to teach essential standards (a common, guaranteed curriculum) to ensure grade-level mastery for all students. These essential standards receive more time and focus than nonessential standards that may be taught. Teachers use essential standards as the basis for unit maps and common assessments.	Tier 2 supplemental interventions support student success on grade-level essential standards.	Grade-level teacher teams use learning progressions to monitor student performance. They develop learning progressions by: (1) identifying the essential skills necessary to master essential standards and (2) vertically aligning the essential skills so they can determine where student capabilities are now and set goals based on the precise skills students have not yet learned.
Give Common End-of-Unit Assessments	Grade-level teacher teams give common, end-of-unit assessments so they can monitor student progress and determine support or preventions at Tier 1. Teams should consider giving mid-cycle common formative assessments in order to respond more promptly.	Grade-level teacher teams give common assessments, which are the critical part of the data used to identify students for Tier 2 intervention as well as monitor student progress.	Grade-level teacher teams, including interventionists, monitor student progress on individual goals that target specific foundational skills leading to the mastery of grade-level essential standards. Common assessment results are used to track progress on essential standards.
Ensure Access to Grade-Level Standards	Grade-level teacher teams provide students with core instruction in essential standards but do not pull students from instruction during this time.	Grade-level teacher teams do not pull students from essential standards instruction. Tiers 1 and 2 teachers work collaboratively to ensure interventions are aligned.	Grade-level teacher teams do not pull students from essential standards instruction. Tier 3 interventionists work collaboratively with Tiers 1 and 2 to monitor students' progress toward mastery.

Identify and Teach Academic and Social Behaviors	The school leadership team ensures that essential academic and social behaviors are identified, and a plan for them to be explicitly taught is in place.	Grade-level teacher teams provide additional time and support to those students who need re-teaching, or specific strategies to be successful mastering essential behaviors.	An interventionist or assigned staff member provides intensive support to those students who need re-teaching, or specific strategies to be successful mastering essential behaviors.
Provide the Time for Teachers to Work in Collaborative Teams	Grade-level teacher teams analyze standards, design instruction, develop unit plans, write common assessments, review data for the purpose of regrouping and re-teaching, and study best practices. Teams may be same subject, same grade, vertical, or electronic or virtual.	Grade-level teacher teams take the lead in Tier 2 interventions. They may provide the intervention or work with interventionists. They use data to ensure they assign students interventions by the student, by the standard, and by the learning target. Teams monitor progress and adjust interventions as necessary.	Grade-level teacher teams work collaboratively to problem solve, review progress, and share best practices. Collaborative teams may include regular classroom teachers and other interventionists, including special education teachers. Special education teachers should have opportunities for meaningful collaboration.
Provide Collaborative Teams and Teachers the Structures and Support Necessary to Be Effective	The school establishes the following structures for collaborative teams: • Time • Protocols • Norms Support: Professional development is job embedded, and there is direct training that is specific to the identified needs of individuals, teams, and groups of teachers. All professional development provides teachers with research-based best practice strategies and processes that support high levels of learning for all students. Coaching: Individual and team coaching regarding the implementation of collaborative structures such as common planning and using data to reteach and intervene	Teachers working at Tier 2 receive the structures and support that they need to: • Collaborate with core teachers and interventionists • Use data to target interventions to the needs of individual students • Understand and utilize best practice strategies	Teachers working at Tier 3 receive the structures and support that they need to: • Monitor the progress of students and brainstorm next steps • Meet with other interventionists to problem solve • Provide support to Tiers 1, 2, and 3 teachers

Figure 1.2: RTI alignment at Tiers 1, 2, and 3.

continued →

Process	What This Looks Like at Tier 1	What This Looks Like at Tier 2	What This Looks Like at Tier 3
Establish a Process for Schoolwide Intervention Identification	The school establishes a process using screeners, diagnostic assessments, and common formative assessments as well as other measures to determine the targeted needs of individual students. This process allows all students to begin receiving interventions within one to two weeks after school begins. Grade-level teacher teams can monitor students at least every four weeks thereafter.	Teachers use all assessment data when designing targeted interventions at Tier 2. They measure student progress and use these data to continually adjust interventions as needed. A site intervention team is in place to problem solve and make recommendations for those students not making progress.	The intervention makes recommendations for students to receive Tier 3 interventions in addition to Tier 1 and perhaps Tier 2, depending on need. The team uses these data to target interventions and monitor progress. This process does not create rigid rules or timelines before providing more intensive intervention or additional assessment.
Create a Dynamic Site Intervention Team	The schoolwide leadership team creates a dynamic team consisting of team members with varied experience and expertise to serve on the site intervention team.	The school establishes a process all staff understand to refer students to the site intervention team if they are not making progress at Tier 2. The intervention team may meet to brainstorm problems and determine additional support or new ideas to implement at Tier 2.	The intervention team identifies and monitors progress for all students at Tier 3.
Extend Student Learning	Teachers use pre-assessments and formative assessments to determine students who need to have learning extended beyond mastery of the essential standard. Teachers should plan for learning extensions in the same way they plan for reteaching at Tier 1.	Students receive additional time and support to extend learning just like those who receive support to reach mastery.	Students with large gaps in foundational skills should receive Tier 3 interventions. However, teachers should not assume that a student receiving Tier 3 support will not have a skill or an area in which their learning needs extending.

Visit go.SolutionTree.com/RTIatWork for a free reproducible version of this figure.

Chapter 1 Action Steps

With your team, engage in the following action steps to review and implement the learning from this chapter.

1. Examine the assumptions and beliefs of the staff at your school. Do you really believe that all students are capable of learning at high levels? If so, do you accept responsibility when students don't learn, or do you assign blame to others?

2. Examine the percentage of students currently receiving Tier 2 and Tier 3 support. If the percentage exceeds 30–40 percent of the school population, perhaps you have a Tier 1 problem that also needs your attention.

3. Use figure 1.2, RTI Alignment at Tiers 1, 2, and 3 (page 26) to identify your school's strengths and weaknesses.

    a. Ask individuals (without discussion) to rank each indicator on a scale of one to five, with five being the highest.

    b. Have collaborative teams compare and contrast their individual rankings.

    c. Have a schoolwide discussion to identify your three greatest needs and discuss specific actions to address them.

The Need for Collective Commitment and Responsibility

As Buffum et al. (2012) note, *collective responsibility* is "a shared belief that the primary responsibility of each member of the organization is to ensure high levels of learning for every child" (p. 9). Once staff have established a collective commitment, they must follow that by establishing collective responsibility for the necessary steps and efforts to meet that commitment. The collective commitment of ensuring high levels of learning for every student must be matched by the collective responsibility of a staff to ensure processes and procedures focus directly on the commitment they have established. In this chapter, we stress the need and the critical importance of teacher efficacy and share practical steps for building shared commitment and responsibility in teams.

Most of us have had the experience of visiting a school and, within a few minutes, thought that this is a school you would want your child to attend. These schools have a pervasive belief system that permeates every conversation with every employee—they embrace all students and are excited about learning. You hear references to *our school* and *our students*, not *my school* or *my class*. You see teachers working together as they review data and consider best practices. You hear teachers asking for help and see teams collaborating to design instruction. You see boys and girls with and without disabilities working and learning together. There is an atmosphere of teamwork, trust, and collaboration between all staff and all programs. All staff members understand the reasons why various structures and processes are in place and can explain how they benefit students.

All too often, the efforts of schools and teachers to collaborate and focus on student learning concentrate on the mechanics of collaboration and exchanging information rather than on fundamental changes to school culture. RTI implementation often becomes focused on logistics without a shift in educators' fundamental beliefs, collective commitments, and collective responsibility.

In many cases, schools forsake Tier 3 improvement because it requires too much change in the school's status quo. Improving learning outcomes for all students requires that schools ask themselves if they believe that all students can learn, and if the students at the school are the collective responsibility of all teachers and staff. Excellence at all tiers of instruction, especially with those learners with significant challenges, will be isolated to individual staff members if this belief and commitment do not guide the collaborative practices of the school.

In his book *Transforming School Culture*, Anthony Muhammad (2009, 2018) describes two types of school reform efforts: (1) technical change and (2) cultural change. *Technical change* focuses on structural and operational issues, such as the school's master schedule, instructional materials, and policies. Obviously, creating a multitiered system of supports requires technical changes. But structural and operational changes alone will have little impact on the overall increase in student achievement. The school must implement the cultural changes necessary to have collective beliefs, ownership, and responsibility for student learning before student learning outcomes improve.

> "When confronted with a challenge, the committed heart will search for a solution. The undecided heart searches for an escape."
>
> —Andy Andrews

There is a significant body of research that supports the premise that when there is a group of teachers who are committed to and believe it is their responsibility to ensure that *all* students learn, and hold one another responsible for teaching all students regardless of background, students reach higher levels of achievement in all subjects.

Valerie Lee and Julia Smith (1996) find that teachers with minimal collective responsibility tend to blame external factors beyond their control, while those with high collective responsibility all share in the commitment to student achievement. Additionally, Lee and Smith (1996) found that teachers with high levels of collective responsibility also adapted their lessons to meet the needs of students' successes and failures. Schools with staff that have clearly established collective commitments and responsibilities continually work to improve their efficacy to ensure learning for all students. These schools are constantly working to improve with a focus on learning outcomes.

Substantial cultural change must precede technical change. Muhammad (2009) argues that technical changes "are definitely necessary to effect an improvement in student performance, but they produce very few positive results when used by people who do not believe in the intended outcome of the change" (p. 15). The structural and operational changes we make as we implement RTI and build Tier 3 interventions run the risk of having little to no impact on learning without a schoolwide, shared belief that all students can learn and that collectively it is our responsibility to ensure that this occurs.

Minjong Youn (2016), researcher at the National Institute for Early Education Research (NIEER) at Rutgers University, notes in his research that academically disadvantaged students in schools with a high level of teacher responsibility are more likely to show improvement in learning at the end of first grade. These findings demonstrate that teachers' attitudes within the classroom may play a role in reducing the stratified learning outcomes gained at an early age.

Furthermore, he notes, teachers' sense of responsibility moderates the association between school readiness and mathematics learning growth over the course of elementary school years, which contributes to reducing the learning-growth gap engendered by low school readiness.

Throughout the K–12 continuum, teachers' beliefs about the ability of students to learn and the need for collective responsibility for learning become essential to ensure learning by all students. This cannot be truer for students who are being served in Tier 3.

Lee and Smith's (1996) research points to a shift in ownership and responsibility for all student learning due to an acceptance of collective responsibility by a school staff. Lee and Smith (1996) state:

> Results were very consistent: achievement gains are significantly higher in schools where teachers take collective responsibility for students' academic success or failure rather than blaming students for their own failure. Achievement gains were also higher in schools with more cooperation among staff. Moreover, the distribution of achievement gains is more socially equitable in schools with high levels of collective responsibility for learning. (p. 103)

As schools consider their beliefs regarding *all* students, teachers should recognize that a very small percentage of students have severe intellectual disabilities, such as very low IQ, health factors, or other challenges that are so severe that they significantly reduce the expectation that students will become independent adults. This discussion should include a clear message that recognizing students' challenges does not provide an excuse or alleviate the teachers' responsibility for their learning. It only recognizes the significance of the challenge and that a very small percentage of students have different goals and learning targets. We are not suggesting that these students cannot learn or that schools do not have a responsibility for their education. Schools with a collective responsibility for all students work each and every day to challenge themselves to maximize the achievement of every student. We must start the journey by accepting the primary responsibility for what we can control—student mastery of essential academic and behavior skills, knowledge, and dispositions—and assume that each student can achieve these outcomes, regardless of his or her demographic background or label.

Consider the alternative. If a school is unwilling to commit to the word *all*, then the educators are, by default, accepting a mission that *most* students will learn at high levels. In reality, most students are currently making it at most schools. So the school does not have to change anything, or commit to RTI, to achieve this outcome. The school has already acknowledged that some students will fail—it is a given. These schools usually keep their public mission statement claiming they are committed to every student's success but privately agree that there will always be academic collateral damage. If a critical mass of the staff is not willing to commit to a mission that embraces the words *ensure* and *all*, it is unlikely they will fully commit to the RTI model.

Our mission to educate all students and provide the most comprehensive program of supports to meet their learning needs takes on a new urgency when we consider that as students exit school, they will live and work in a world that requires them to possess the academic and behavioral skills necessary for success. We must make a collective commitment to ensuring a system with a comprehensive approach to meeting the needs of all students. We must own the challenges to educate each student so that as a preK–12 system, we are working together to prepare students for the future. This requires a sense of urgency and commitment by all staff.

Genuine schoolwide collective responsibility for the success of all students can emerge as a distinct alternative to business as usual. There must be clear vision and desire to move to a deeper trust that leads teachers to take risks and work together to achieve goals.

Teams can use the survey in figure 2.1 to improve collective responsibility for all students.

The reliance on district and state assessments as a means of accountability has led to a frontal assault on the idea that *all* means all students must learn the essential standards. The idea of collective responsibility by the staff to ensure all students learn is in direct conflict with the perceived need to raise test scores by strategizing who should receive additional supports and time versus those who should not. Some of those who need additional support and time include the bubble students.

Bubble Students

The *bubble student* is a concept that has taken root as teachers and administrators attempt to improve scores. *Bubble students* are those students who have missed state or district proficiency status by only one or two points. These students are within striking distance of crossing the proficiency line by answering one or two more questions correctly on the state test. These students are *on the bubble*, and educators think that with a bit more help, they will move to proficiency, thus raising the status of the teacher or school with a higher percentage of students who have achieved.

Staff Collective Responsibility

When filling out this survey, please be ready to give examples of why you scored each area positive (1 to 5), neutral (0), or negative (−1 to −5). Any area marked in the negative range is a target area for staff discussion and follow-up.

Low Degree of Collective Responsibility (nonexistent or inconsistent)	Score	High Degree of Collective Responsibility (consistent and strong)
Teachers blame lack of student learning on external forces.	−5 −4 −3 −2 −1 0 1 2 3 4 5	Teachers share responsibility for seeking solutions to student learning needs.
The school has an unstated or unshared mission. Each teacher may have developed individual mission, goals, and objectives.	−5 −4 −3 −2 −1 0 1 2 3 4 5	The school shares explicit and intentionally stated goals, mission, and objectives.
Teachers believe that it is the students' responsibility to learn what they teach them.	−5 −4 −3 −2 −1 0 1 2 3 4 5	Teachers believe that they are responsible for ensuring students learn the essential content.
The school has an environment of isolationism.	−5 −4 −3 −2 −1 0 1 2 3 4 5	Staff share best practices, planning, and learning data.
Teachers do not use learning data to adapt lessons to students' learning needs.	−5 −4 −3 −2 −1 0 1 2 3 4 5	Teachers use learning data to adapt lessons to meet students' learning needs.
Teachers feel a sense of helplessness and lack of control over educational issues and learning outcomes.	−5 −4 −3 −2 −1 0 1 2 3 4 5	Teachers have a clear understanding of the areas where staff have control of educational issues to ensure positive learning outcomes.
Teachers use the word *my* to describe ownership at the school.	−5 −4 −3 −2 −1 0 1 2 3 4 5	Teachers use the word *our* to describe ownership at the school.
Staff members feel they need to compete with one another.	−5 −4 −3 −2 −1 0 1 2 3 4 5	Staff members collaborate well together.
Teachers plan for student learning in the short term only with no monitoring.	−5 −4 −3 −2 −1 0 1 2 3 4 5	Teachers collectively plan and monitor student learning beyond one year at a time.
Staff believe *all students* means *most students*.	−5 −4 −3 −2 −1 0 1 2 3 4 5	Staff believe that *all students* means *all students*.

Figure 2.1: Team collective responsibility survey.

*Visit **go.SolutionTree.com/RTIatWork** for a free reproducible version of this figure.*

To ensure this happens, schools and staffs identify the bubble students, divide them into groups, and tutor them relentlessly for several months prior to the state or district exam. At first glance, this seems like an appropriate use of data and a reasonable approach to ensure learning for these students by a committed staff. Unfortunately, this is seldom the case.

What happens to students who miss proficiency by five, six, or maybe ten points or more? Schools might reason that these students are unable to raise scores enough to help the school's rating, so they ignore them. Schools might think that time and effort put into these students are a waste of valuable energy when the students can't help them. In other words, work with the students who can make you look good and allow the others to continue to fail.

Focusing on bubble students helps school ratings; it is not meant to help all students who need it. It is a morally reprehensible thing to do and sends a message to both adults and students that some students are worthy of helping, while others are not. Schools that support this concept dole out valuable time and support as if there is a limited supply of learning. There is no collective commitment to all students. These schools may have an RTI system only in name and only when it is convenient. Students in Tier 3 quickly lose their support as testing time draws near, as teachers redistribute resources to the bubble students.

Schools that practice the bubble strategy would be hard pressed to explain to their students the logic that goes into targeting one set of students over others. At best, it is wrong; at its worst, it breaks down the belief that all students have worth and that, as a staff, we have a collective responsibility to ensure that all students learn. The impact of this negative belief system has a lasting, negative impact on the staff's view of one another, their students, and the need to provide time and support to those who have the greatest learning needs.

Lessons Learned

Through our research and work in schools, we have learned to consider several critical points while staff work to establish collective commitment for the implementation of an RTI tiered system of interventions. When considering the comprehensive support required to meet the learning, behavior, and social needs of students needing intensive intervention, these points become even more essential.

1. **Schools must state their collective commitment objectives explicitly and intentionally:** Schools that state, "Well, everyone knows that our staff believe all students matter," without intentionally working to create explicit statements of their commitments, have created a mirage of a belief. It is not enough to think that everyone understands and is

committed to all students without taking the time to create, collectively define, and put those commitment statements in writing.

2. **Schools must take the time to ensure collective commitment and conduct intentional reviews and renewal:** Lee and Smith (1996) point out in their research that collective commitment takes time to develop and ensure. Our practical experience bears this out. Collective commitment cannot be a one-time event if all staff are to embrace it. It is a rarity to find deep, collective commitment by all staff members at the onset of this work. Too often, staff members accept the initial commitments but internally add provisos to those commitments. "We believe all students can learn . . . if they have supportive parents." "We believe that students must learn the essential skills and knowledge, but it is their responsibility to motivate themselves to do so." "We believe students must be taught socially acceptable behaviors and skills, but they should come to school knowing these things." If we are to truly have explicitly and intentionally understood collective commitments, we must revisit them and remove stipulations.

   Staff members who continually add conditions to the collective commitments chip away at the resolve and assurance that all students' learning, behavior, and social needs are addressed. The vocal "naysayer" clearly is problematic when moving commitments to action, but even more problematic is the staff member who conditionally agrees with the collective commitments yet ignores students with the greatest need, believing that someone else should or will meet their learning needs.

   It is essential that the school give staff the time for discussing, intentionally and explicitly, the needs of students and their commitment to provide time and support. Without taking the time for these discussions, the naysayers and those staff members with provisos will continue to slow the progress and impact of efforts to build a comprehensive RTI system. At worst, they will intentionally or unintentionally damage the opportunities needed by students in Tier 3.

3. **All staff must have an understood commitment that they will not accept deviations from collective commitments:** This is hard for most teams, but it is critical for these teams to stay on course. Teams should discuss how they will handle colleagues who make statements in direct conflict of the established collective commitments. Failure to acknowledge deviations from the collective commitments by a colleague sends the subtle message that you are accepting of the deviation. Quiet acquiescence allows colleagues or fellow staff members

to create their own version of commitments. Your silence signals that you may agree with them and their version of the commitments. Worst yet is the staff member who nods in agreement with a deviation from the collective commitments to avoid conflict or to gain acceptance. The affirmation sends the message that it is okay to have your own beliefs, even when it is in direct conflict with the collective commitments and is damaging to the growth and opportunities for students to learn. These instances become opportunities to reaffirm a school's collective commitments or to tear them down. They provide opportunities to come together to work for students or slam the door on students who have the greatest needs. They become the true test of collective commitments and the turning point as to when, or if, a staff will rally around the explicit and intentionally stated collective commitments they created.

Consider the following scenario.

A second-grade team adopted the belief statement *Every student, every day*. Teachers discussed and agreed to the meaning of this statement as well as how they represent it in their daily work. They agreed that this belief requires that they proactively plan and intervene with each student. Using formative data to target individual needs would also be necessary to fulfill this mission. They agreed that they would rely on the strengths and talents of the team and collectively ensure that every student achieved grade-level mastery on the essential standards.

At the beginning of the year, they agreed that they would hold each other accountable for actions that matched their beliefs. They discussed that one way they would do this was by having norms for all meetings. They agreed that if a team member violated meeting norms, they would all hold their hand in the air and say, "Norm!" They also agreed that they would immediately hold a respectful discussion with the team member who had violated a collective commitment or norm.

In a team data review meeting, all teachers were sharing their most recent common assessment data. One of the meeting norms was "We review data to help students; it is not about you." They displayed the data electronically, student by student and teacher by teacher. The team discussed each student, his or her performance, and his or her targeted needs for intervention or extension. As the meeting progressed from one teacher to the next, Mrs. Taylor offered the explanation that students A, B, and C were "special education" as the reason for their low scores. Immediately, the air was full of hands and team members saying, "Norm!" Think of the message this sent. Without confrontation, the team immediately sent the message that this was unacceptable. The team had a discussion as to why this thinking violated their beliefs. They had agreed that they would be responsible for *all* learners. This action solidified the commitment of this team to every student.

Over the years of work with schools, three activities and tools stand out as effective steps to establish, reinforce depth of understanding, and solidify a school's collective commitment.

Tools and Strategies to Establish and Reinforce Collective Commitments and Responsibilities

This resource includes tools and strategies that may be used to establish and reinforce a school's collective commitments and responsibilities. They are designed to open a dialogue so staff members can work to hear one another, clarify their beliefs, and confirm their willingness to establish collective commitments and responsibilities that form the foundation of their efforts.

Establish What You Believe by Reviewing Others' Beliefs

In working with a variety of schools over the years, we have discovered that when we ask staff to list their beliefs about educating students, they provide statements such as "We make a difference" or "Every student, every day." But when pressed, they can't explain in their own words what those phrases mean to them personally. These phrases are great when they have meaning to a team, but unfortunately, they are typically printed on posters with little meaning or impact on practice.

We have found that to promote a deep discussion, it is often easier to discuss another school's beliefs initially. Educators are willing to examine and discuss someone else's beliefs and commitments in deep terms. These discussions begin to uncover educators' true feelings, beliefs, and willingness to collectively commit. The goal is to work back toward putting into words your own beliefs and commitments. Consider the following as a means of spurring forward the conversation and truly examining the staff's beliefs as you move toward collective commitment.

Ask your staff to follow these steps.

1. Have the staff sit in groups or in teams. Write the following belief system on the board or display it on chart paper.

    a. Hope is not a strategy to ensure learning for students.

    b. Don't blame the students for how they come to us.

    c. Our work is about student learning.

2. Ask teams to answer the following questions while using chart paper to record responses.

    a. What do you believe each statement means?

        ▸ Individually write the meaning of each statement displayed.

> ‣ As a team, discuss and write your team's version of each statement's meaning.

> ‣ Record your consensus on the chart paper.

b. Do you personally agree or disagree?

> ‣ Individually write why you agree or disagree with the statement.

> ‣ As a team, come to agreement and record your consensus responses on the board or chart paper.

3. Having discussed the meaning of the three statements and recorded your teams' consensus, what would be the three statements of belief that your team can come to consensus around? List those three statements on chart paper.

4. The facilitator of the meeting then compares the responses of all groups and records on a single chart paper each statement that is not repeated by the groups to produce a list of shared beliefs.

5. When necessary, the facilitator asks groups to clarify their statements to find commonality between the different groups.

6. Once the list has been compiled, the facilitator asks all groups to review and discuss the list in consideration for adoption by the entire staff as a set of collective beliefs and commitments.

7. After their discussion, the facilitator asks teams to come to consensus using a strategy such as fist to five, in which participants raise their hands and show five fingers for enthusiastic agreement, one finger for marginal agreement, and make a fist if in disagreement. (It has been our experience that teams who disagree can begin to resolve these issues in smaller group discussions.)

8. Once resolution occurs, the entire staff must be brought back together to repeat the final activity.

Make It Personal When Establishing Team Beliefs

It is important that we remind ourselves that all parents have similar goals for their children. With very few exceptions, children and their parents enter elementary school with the same hopes and dreams for a bright future.

Teams can use the activity in figure 2.2 to consider the goals they have for students and the actions necessary to make those goals a reality, and determine the commitments teams must make to take those actions and achieve those goals.

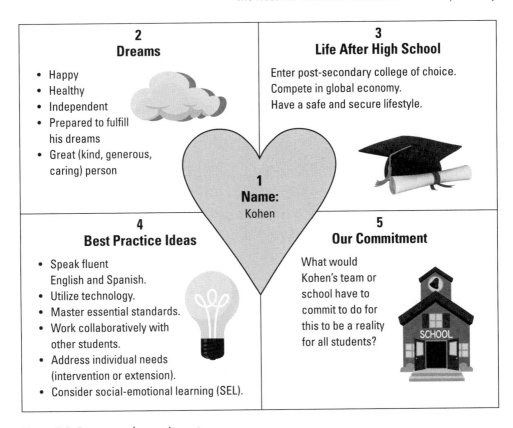

Figure 2.2: Dreams and commitments.

*Visit **go.SolutionTree.com/RTIatWork** for a free reproducible version of this figure.*

Teams can complete the activity by projecting the image and asking teams to work from chart paper or by providing each person with a personal paper copy. Then have participants follow these instructions.

1. Name the child or children that you love the most in the world. Write the name on the heart. It can be your own child, children, grandchildren, family members, or friends. Take a moment to picture this child and tell a team member near you the child's name.

2. List your hopes and dreams for the child you identified. If the image is projected, you can do this on chart paper. If a team is working together, each team member can list the hopes and dreams he or she has for his or her child.

3. The group leaders ask participants to list what the child would need to be prepared to do when leaving high school in order for these dreams to come true.

4. List the strategies, or best practices, the child's school would have to implement in order for him or her to be prepared to fulfill those

goals when leaving high school. For example, in figure 2.2 (page 41), a goal for Kohen's life beyond high school is to be able to compete in a global economy. To do this, he would have to be bilingual, master the essential standards, and be able to work with others. His school would have to utilize the strategies listed to prepare him with these skills.

5. After outlining the best practice strategies you would want a school to use with your own child, you are ready to outline your commitment to *all* children. Look at the list of goals and strategies and consider that all parents have similar goals for their children. In box 5, write a commitment statement reflecting the actions you and your teammates commit to do to make the hopes and dreams of all students a reality.

   For example:

   ▸ All staff will have high expectations for all students.

   ▸ All staff commit to working as a collaborative team and using best practice strategies that include:

   - Identifying essential standards

   - Measuring progress with formative assessment and common summative assessment

   - Using regular data analysis

   - Providing timely and targeted interventions to ensure high levels of learning for every student

6. Reconsider your commitments and any changes you would make if the child you named, the child you love most in the world, had a significant academic or behavioral issue. Team members should consider if their actions and commitments reflect what the students with the greatest challenges need from you.

This process provides a positive foundation for beginning the conversation about beliefs and commitments to every student. It reminds us that we should be prepared to commit to the same actions we expect others to do for our own children.

Establish Beliefs and Commitments by Evaluating the Meaning of Common Mantras

We have experienced teams using their district and campus goals as a starting place to begin a conversation about the collective responsibility of staff to all students. This process is simple and effective, as long as we drive the conversation with responsibility to students rather than test scores. We should see test scores as a reflection of how well the school is doing in fulfilling the mission of learning. However, if our words and actions are only for the purpose of achieving recognition for high test scores without a deeper conversation about what the scores represent, then our work to develop deep commitment will be in vain.

In this activity, the facilitator begins by asking teams to review the school's current goals for achievement. The facilitator asks teams to acknowledge the reality of the specific areas that need to change or improve. This provides teams the *why* for their actions. Very specific discussions regarding those students who are not successful, why essential standards are important in their life, as well as a discussion and consensus on the meaning of *all* students would precede the creation of a team mantra.

For team members to create a team mantra, they should follow these four steps.

1. The facilitator asks team members to answer these simple questions about their beliefs and how they will work to achieve the goals of their district or campus.

    ▶ *What we believe*—What do we believe in regard to all students achieving high levels of learning?

    ▶ *Our non-negotiables*—For what do you accept collective responsibility?

    ▶ *Our commitment*—What must we do to fulfill our purpose? What actions will make our beliefs a reality?

2. The facilitator shares sample team mantras and asks teams to discuss what beliefs they reflect. For example:

    ▶ No excuses

    ▶ All kids are our kids

    ▶ Prevent school failure—every day

    ▶ Whatever it takes

3. The facilitator provides chart paper or sentence strips and gives the groups directions to create a statement that says who they are, sort of like a bumper-sticker slogan. Teams should be ready to explain why this slogan captures their beliefs and collective commitments. All teams will share and provide clarifications if needed.

4. Teams then create a T-chart that outlines what their classrooms, meetings, and interactions with both students and adults will look like and sound like to be in keeping with their slogan. Schools may elect to create a campus slogan and looks-like-and-sounds-like chart

for actions by coming to consensus around one of the slogans or using them as a springboard to create one for the campus.

Figure 2.3 shows team actions for creating a school mantra.

Example Mantra: Prevent School Failure	
Looks Like: **What will we see in our school if the staff are committed to the mantra becoming a reality?**	**Sounds Like:** **What actions or conversations will demonstrate this commitment?**
The school has a laser focus on every student mastering essential standards.	Teacher teams: • Analyze standards in planning meetings • Plan in advance for every learner • Use common formative assessments to target interventions
The school has a systematic process for intervening in academics and behavior.	Teacher teams plan, teach, and support essential academic and behavior standards. Intervention teams respond in a timely and targeted manner for academics and behavior. The school measures student progress in all interventions for both academics and behavior.

Teacher teams use student data.	Teacher teams:
	• Set student goals for achieving essential standards
	• Plan and utilize differentiated instruction
	• Use learning targets and goal setting with all essential standards to enable students to answer the following questions:
	  - Where am I going?
	  - Where am I now?
	  - How will I get there?

All staff and programs work collaboratively to achieve campus goals.	The leadership team, intervention team, and teacher teams work together to achieve goals. The leadership team ensures time is scheduled for collaborative planning and data review. The leadership team ensures that collaborative planning time exists for intervention teachers and special education teachers to (1) plan instruction and (2) monitor progress, brainstorm, and (3) problem solve. All teachers work with a collective commitment for the success of all students. The routine practice of all teachers includes communicating with colleagues about student goals, sharing and improving instructional practices, and using student data to drive interventions.

The school has a focus on learning that is demonstrated by promoting learning as the priority.	The leadership team and teacher teams look at all times of day as opportunities for learning. For example, they plan learning-related activities when elementary students are waiting in hallways for buses or during parent pick-up time (such as providing book bins in halls to promote reading while waiting for the bus, reviewing essential vocabulary charts while students wait in line, or using wait time to model schoolwide behavior expectations).
The school leadership team and teacher teams enlist parents as partners in the focus on learning.	The leadership team and teacher teams work together and make every effort for personal contact between school staff and every parent the first week of school, using methods such as the following: • Phone calls • Home visits • Audio, video, and text messages • Bus rides and parent greetings at bus stops • Back-to-school events in local parks • Ongoing communication in various formats that respect parents' work schedules during the year

Figure 2.3: Sample mantra and team actions.

*Visit **go.SolutionTree.com/RTIatWork** for a free reproducible version of this figure.*

The Leadership Teams' Work for *All* Students

The leadership team or guiding coalition is responsible for leading the implementation of RTI at Work at a school. This team must not only lead the efforts in creating collective commitments, they must reinforce adherence to those commitments through their work, actions, and words. They must ensure that all staff explicitly and intentionally hold one another accountable to the collective commitments in a respectful and professional manner. Doing this in a way that builds teams rather than causes fractures is essential.

One successful strategy is the explicit and intentional statement to all staff that it is everyone's responsibility and obligation to hold one another accountable to the collective commitments. And when someone deviates from those commitments through words or actions, all staff members are expected to challenge the deviation. This is not easy, but it must be the expectation. No staff member has the right to run down students, take away students' opportunities to learn, or use student "categories" to describe their potential without the team challenging him or her based on the agreed-on collective commitments.

Having made this statement, it is incumbent on the leadership team to provide staff with a means to do this that does not fracture interschool relationships, create animosity, or build in a system of negativity or staff bullying. Educational speaker and author William M. Ferriter shared a quote from David Jakes that best sums up a pathway that has proven extremely successful in assuring adherence to a school's collective commitments: "Driving change in challenging circumstances depends on leaders with a willingness to ask 'What if?' when faced with the never-ending stream of 'Yeah, buts . . .'" (Ferriter, 2012). The premise of this quote is simple: when faced with actions or words that deviate from their collective commitments, staff have the right and responsibility to pose the question, "What if?"

This simple question changes the trajectory of negative words and actions back toward solutions to ensure student learning. The "What if?" question opens the realm of possibilities. At a grade-level collaborative team meeting, our group was confronted with a partner who was frustrated with one of her Tier 3 student's lack of progress. A fellow teacher turned to her and asked, "What if you and I worked together with this student for the next week?" The conversation immediately turned to seeking solutions and working together to meeting all students' learning needs. The impact of asking, "What if?" is powerful.

At Sanger Unified School District in California, the leadership team explicitly and intentionally stated that all staff have the right and responsibility to use the following phrase when confronted with a deviation from the collective commitments, "I hear your frustrations; what can we do as a solution?" (Ferriter, 2017). The simple acknowledgment that the business of educating students can often be frustrating opens the door for seeking solutions by asking for the suggestion of a solution. Again, the statement changes the trajectory of the conversation toward solutions framed in the school's collective commitments.

The leadership team reminded staff that when they do not confront and challenge negative statements and actions, they have acquiesced and sent a subtle message that it is okay to deviate. Some staff typify these types of deviations from the collective commitments as *gripe sessions*, *shared misery*, and *time to blow off steam* and send the message that it is okay to deviate. It is not, and the leadership team must meet these types of discussions with statements that promote the search for solutions that support the success of all students. The leadership team must remind staff that it is their right and responsibility to confront and to promote the search for positive solutions to students' learning needs by giving them the phrases and tools to do this in a collegial, professional manner. Negativity chips away at our collective commitments and inhibits the search for solutions that are meant to drive our RTI tiers.

Conclusion

The creation of collective commitments is essential to the success of a school's implementation of RTI. These commitments ensure that all students receive the time and support necessary to learn the essential skills and knowledge to be successful beyond their time in school. *All* must mean *all students*, and we must be committed to this position.

Determining collective commitments cannot be an event, presented as an administrative document of requirements, or as something pulled from a book. The commitments must be driven by staff through the process of open discussion and staff consensus. These commitments may prove to be a challenge for staff members who wish to add conditions. The leadership team must bring these staff members so their beliefs may be shared and vetted. They cannot sit on the sidelines or be allowed to deviate from the adopted commitments.

For the collective commitments to take hold and lead to substantive change, there must be accountability, monitoring, guidance, and follow-through. Forming a guiding coalition whose role is to provide leadership to the process and assure adherence to the collective commitments is essential to the success of RTI implementation. The guiding coalition must support and acknowledge that all staff members are responsible for explicitly and intentionally seeking solutions based on the staff's collective commitments. All staff members are obligated to confront deviations from the collective commitments.

> "There is no power for change greater than a community discovering what it cares about."
> —Margaret J. Wheatley

Students deserve every opportunity to learn the essential skills and knowledge in every grade level and course through additional time and support. Staff commitment is the difference between a system of supports in which actions match beliefs and one that provides only lip service to beliefs.

Chapter 2 Action Steps

With your team, engage in the following action steps to review and implement the learning from this chapter.

1. In order to reinforce the importance of collaboration and collective responsibility, ask that before every meeting, the team:

    ▸ Clarifies the exact purpose of the meeting

    ▸ Clarifies what it seeks to accomplish through collaboration and collective responsibility

2. This allows the meeting to focus on "how we will need to work together to accomplish our goals" rather than focusing only on "how we will need to behave."

3. After conducting the activity outlined in the section Establish What You Believe by Reviewing Others' Beliefs (pages 39–40), be certain to clarify that the fist-to-five activity is intended to identify when the group has reached consensus. DuFour et al. (2016) claims that a group has come to consensus when it meets two criteria: (1) "all points of view have not merely been heard, but have been actively solicited," and (2) "the will of the group *to those who most oppose it*" (p. 32). Schools need not wait for 100 percent agreement, but instead should recognize that one or two persons should not be allowed to hold an entire school back from moving ahead.

4. The T-chart in figure 2.3 (page 44) provides an excellent opportunity for staff to hold one another accountable by catching each other doing something that looks and sounds like actions that help prevent school failure. In other words, staff should not only use this chart to generate discussion when staff are not living out the school's mantra; it can also provide opportunities to encourage individuals and teams *living* the mission of the school.

Collaborative Team Structures at Tier 3

In this chapter, we address the organizational structure of the leadership and intervention teams as well as share important considerations regarding the relationship of Tier 3 to these two critical teams and special education services. We also address the use of split funding for materials and personnel as food for thought for both the leadership and intervention team as they plan to ensure the maximization of Tier 3 interventions. We have included foundational, basic practices that ensure team effectiveness as well as helpful tools. We have devoted an entire chapter to these two teams because of the essential role they play in the RTI at Work process at Tier 3.

The Leadership Team and the Intervention Team

"Can you help us? We have been to a lot of training, and we think we know what needs to be done to implement RTI, but we are teachers. We can't change master schedules, ask people to attend meetings, or address schoolwide behavior. Our principal supports us, but she is too busy to come to our meetings, and we don't know what to do next."

We hear this common plea often as we work in schools across the United States. It represents what happens when principals and teachers don't fully understand the roles and responsibilities of a schoolwide leadership team. This guiding coalition of leaders from across a campus is responsible for leading the implementation of all the systems and processes for implementing RTI at all three tiers.

The Role of the Leadership Team at Tier 3

The school principal should lead the leadership team, and members should represent a wide variety of expertise. Many of this team's duties require principal approval and instilling a culture of collective responsibility for all learners. The team may have other facilitators, but the principal is a key member of this coalition.

Buffum et al. (2018) outline the critical importance of the leadership team and the actions it takes in implementing RTI the correct way:

> We recommend that the school's leadership team serve as the site's guiding coalition. Because of this recommendation, we use two terms— (1) *leadership team* and (2) *guiding coalition*—which are interchangeable throughout this book. To achieve this goal, many schools need to redesign or repurpose their existing leadership team, as we find that most site leadership teams rarely function as a guiding coalition dedicated to ensuring high levels of learning for all students. (p. 36)

Buffum et al. (2018) continue with explaining the reason for this change in the role of the leadership team: "Unless the right team leads the RTI process—a team that focuses its efforts on the right work—the anxiety and inevitable obstacles inherent in this level of change will overwhelm the best organization's intentions" (p. 36).

> "Major change is often said to be impossible unless the head of the organization is an active supporter."
> —John P. Kotter

As we visit schools across the United States, we have found that most have formed a variety of leadership structures for a variety of purposes, including compliance, inclusion, input, or decision-making purposes. The labels schools use to name these structures vary. As previously noted, the term schools use most often is *leadership team*. For the purposes of this book, we will use the term *leadership team* synonymously with *guiding coalition*.

Regardless of the label used to describe this group, it is essential that we are explicit and intentional about understanding the goals and function of the leadership team, as well as the membership criteria for those who serve on this coalition. This team must be capable and focused on leading change, and building a culture that believes the school, staff, and all students must and can achieve and learn at high levels.

The leadership team must state its goals and tasks explicitly and intentionally so all guiding coalition members and school staff have clarity about the purpose of this group. The guiding coalition must take explicit schoolwide actions and work collaboratively to build consensus for the school's mission of collective responsibility.

▽ Create a master schedule that provides sufficient time for team collaboration, core instruction, supplemental interventions, and intensive interventions.

▽ Coordinate and seek schoolwide human resources to best support core instruction and interventions.

▽ Allocate the school's fiscal resources to best support core instruction and interventions, including school categorical funding.

▽ Assist with articulating essential learning outcomes across grade levels and subjects.

▽ Ensure all students have access to grade-level core instruction.

▽ Lead the school's universal screening efforts.

▽ Lead the school's efforts for schoolwide behavior expectations, including attendance policies and awards and recognitions.

▽ Ensure that sufficient, effective resources are available to provide Tier 2 interventions for students in need of supplemental support in motivation, attendance, and behavior.

▽ Identify students who need intensive support at Tier 3.

▽ Create a dynamic problem-solving or site intervention team.

▽ Prioritize all available resources to meet students' needs with the greatest challenges in the areas of the universal skills of reading, writing, number sense, English language, motivation, attendance, and behavior.

▽ Continually monitor schoolwide evidence of student learning.

▽ Create a systematic process for referring students to the site intervention team.

▽ Assess intervention effectiveness.

The structures and processes established by the leadership team are critical to the success of the intervention team in meeting the needs of students at Tier 3. These two teams have interrelated responsibilities for the implementation and success of Tier 3 intensive intervention.

The Role of the Intervention Team at Tier 3

The primary role of this team is diagnosing and prioritizing Tier 3 interventions. Team members will utilize the structures put in place by the leadership team, such as meeting times, the talents of varied team members, as well as the various assessments utilized at Tiers 1 and 2 to diagnose and treat student needs at Tier 3. Actions that this team must undertake include:

▽ Utilize all pertinent assessment information to determine the reason a student is not progressing in mastering foundational learning (reading, writing, comprehending and speaking the English language or the primary language of the school, essential academic and social behavior, and health and home)

▽ Determine the targeted interventions needed to accelerate learning for students in the targeted areas of need

▽ Ensure the proper intervention intensity

▽ Monitor student progress and adjust interventions as needed

▽ Utilize a problem-solving, solution-oriented approach to addressing student needs

▽ Determine if students require special education

In order to perform these duties, given the wide variety of issues that students with significant gaps in learning present, team members should have varied expertise and the passion to work with persistence and serve those students with the greatest academic and behavioral challenges. Team members must understand that they will face many obstacles in finding solutions for students who have been unsuccessful with current instructional methods. The students needing their support are frequently multiple years behind their peers in foundational academic or essential behavior skills. This team must be comprised of problem solvers who work with determination to succeed. They must not be afraid to reach out for additional expertise or learn new strategies. Their job is to find the reason a student is not progressing and then determine the targeted interventions to accelerate their learning. They must be open to the reality that they will need to frequently change and adjust the time, intensity, or type of intervention.

The intervention team is the vehicle that ensures Tier 3 functions and meets the learning and behavioral needs of students with the greatest deficits, while ensuring the highest level of communication, collaboration, and sharing with all other stakeholders at the school. The task and responsibility of these team members require an understanding of RTI principles, assessment, progress monitoring, and the goal of ensuring that Tier 3 students' deficits are closed at an accelerated rate.

The Relationship Between the Leadership Team and Intervention Team

The leadership team and intervention team work hand-in-hand to implement the structures and processes necessary for a high-functioning system of interventions at Tier 3. They have a common goal, but their roles and responsibilities are different. The leadership team is responsible for ensuring that all the organizational structures are in place so the intervention team can be effective. The intervention team is the problem-solving team. Table 3.1 addresses two primary areas of consideration: (1) identifying and determining targeted needs and (2) prioritizing and ensuring intervention intensity. This table helps clarify the roles of each team and how team

Table 3.1: Leadership Team and Intervention Team Tier 3 Responsibilities

Tier 3 Action	Leadership Team	Intervention Team
Identify students for Tier 3 interventions and determine targeted needs.	Ensure a systematic and timely process is in place to identify students to refer to the site intervention team. Ensure the intervention team membership has the expertise needed to address both academic and behavioral concerns.	Analyze pertinent data, solve problems, and determine the cause of the gaps in learning essential skills for students referred to their team. Ensure principal participation, implement efficient and timely communication with the leadership team, and prioritize necessary resources.
Prioritize resources and ensure proper intervention intensity.	Consider schoolwide needs and prioritize resources to ensure it can meet the needs of students with the greatest learning challenges. Ensure the best resources available for Tier 3 interventions.	Analyze data, solve problems, and determine students' targeted needs. Target interventions to the causes of students' challenges, and ensure these interventions are implemented with the time and intensity necessary to close learning gaps.

Visit **go.SolutionTree.com/RTIatWork** *for a free reproducible version of this table.*

members support each other to meet students' needs. As you review this table, consider the planning, communication, and coordination necessary for these two teams to function seamlessly.

The leadership and intervention teams must believe that all staff are responsible for all students. It is the role of the leadership team to ensure that RTI is effective at all tiers, while the intervention team assumes the essential role of diagnosing and problem solving at Tier 3. The interrelated relationship of these two teams and the type of work they do make their team members an essential element of their success.

Considerations for Team Membership

Following are some suggestions for forming dynamic and effective leadership and intervention teams.

Leadership Team Membership

Choosing the right members for the leadership team is critical. A leadership team that is intentionally formed with a focus on the clearly stated goals and tasks will take action to achieve school goals and RTI implementation. They will seek best practices, consider resources more thoughtfully, and build consensus for the collective commitments adopted by the staff.

Dennis Goin (2012) of Kotter International published a blog post on Forbes.com describing the importance of the guiding coalition and its membership:

> That coalition—a powerful, enthusiastic team of volunteers from across an organization—is a crucial tool for leaders looking to put new strategies into effect and transform their organizations. And deciding who should take part in the guiding coalition is essential.

Seeking team members with the following characteristics will assist leaders in creating a highly committed and energetic coalition.

▽ Credibility

▽ Expertise

▽ Influence

▽ Position power, or what someone has when he or she has responsibility for key resources, control, or responsibilities at the school

▽ Sufficient time to participate

▽ True interest and commitment to participating in a coalition that ensures all students are learning the essential standards and skills

In addition to these characteristics, the following steps will help in creating an effective leadership team.

▽ Invite members who are committed to attaining the goal of high levels of learning for all students and have the necessary organizational and communication skills to work with others to achieve this goal.

▽ Invite members who listen well, give frank and honest observations, and have all students' best interests at heart. Forming a leadership team that provides honest guidance and feedback is paramount, and carefully selecting members is key to finding the best solutions. Encourage coalition members to openly share and consider all points of view without judgment or fear of ridicule to promote divergent thinking and internal coherence.

▽ Ensure that prospective members clearly understand the coalition's purpose. No one should be on the leadership team who cannot clearly articulate the purpose and goals of the team.

▽ The coalition must also have representation from different groups and collaborative teams that have a vested interest in the work of the coalition. In addition to administrative representation, the leadership team should have teacher representatives from each collaborative teacher team. At the elementary level, this will most likely be grade-level leaders. Additionally, representation from support staff, the special education staff, speech and language teachers, psychologists, and counselors will help build a team with a comprehensive view of resources and possible solutions to best allocate schoolwide resources to support students and the school's system of interventions.

A thoughtfully constructed, well-balanced leadership team provides a comprehensive picture of implementation through multiple perspectives. It focuses on offering multiple solutions and ideas that are essential to successful RTI implementation. One of the critical duties of this team is creating and determining members of the intervention team.

Intervention Team Membership

The leadership team should carefully consider the membership of the site intervention team. We recommend that the principal serve on the intervention team as well as the leadership team because of his or her ability to provide organizational management, determine resources, and approve scheduling. We recognize the many requirements on a principal's time. However, we do not know of a commitment worthier than the intervention team, which is responsible for determining the needs and targeting the interventions of students with the greatest challenge on a campus. The principal's membership on this team communicates its importance in achieving the mission of the campus. Other leadership team members are likely candidates for the intervention team, but the backgrounds, talent, and skills needed may dictate a need for a more varied group of team members. The school should place special emphasis on selecting staff that have a passion and belief that all students can and must learn. It should consider key staff members such as the school psychologist, nurse, interventionist, teachers with specialized skills or training, or the reading specialist.

Determining the membership of the intervention team becomes an issue for many small schools due to the limited number of staff. There are often not enough staff members to have a leadership team and an intervention team with separate team members. There are two possible solutions that we have seen as pragmatic, successful answers to this common problem.

1. **The intervention team is a committee or taskforce of the leadership team:** In this case, a limited number of the leadership team members (principal and three to five staff members) meets as a subcommittee of the overall leadership team. This group serves as the intervention problem-solving team and reports back to the leadership team as a regular component of the leadership team meetings. The overall leadership team provides the support

and structure to ensure that the work of the intervention team is understood and successful.

2. **The leadership team does double duty:** In this scenario, the leadership team meetings have a two-part agenda. During the first part, the leadership team meets to review progress on team goals and set follow-up actions on the schoolwide implementation of RTI for academics and behavior, as well as identify students needing intensive support. During the second part, the team moves into a problem-solving and progress-monitoring approach with students identified as needing Tier 3 interventions. This approach utilizes the same people for both teams but requires two-part meetings and a commitment to address all the requirements of the leadership and intervention teams.

As the school determines the intervention team structure and membership, it is critical for staff to recognize the wide variety of needs for those students in intense Tier 3 intervention. In order to problem solve and determine these students' needs, the intervention team will need members who represent the varied expertise necessary to address the critical foundational skills indispensable to success in school and life. Consider for a moment the following universal skills that schools must address at Tier 3 and the type of expertise needed to address them.

▽ Decoding and comprehending text

▽ Understanding numbers, sequencing, and basic mathematics functions

▽ Writing

▽ Comprehending and speaking English or the primary language of the school

▽ Understanding essential academic and social behaviors

Figure 3.1 is very helpful when determining the site intervention team membership.

Leadership and Intervention Team Effectiveness

The effectiveness of the leadership and intervention teams depends on many variables, including building capacity to increase the skills of each team member and structuring meetings so members know what to expect and how to behave.

Capacity Building

In order to build the capacity of all team members to increase their skills while building capacity for the future, we recommend rotating the responsibilities among

Building a Site Intervention Team

Team members: _____

Use the following to build a site intervention team. Remember, when you don't have access to someone with the exact title or role in the first column, ask yourself, "Which staff member is best trained to meet this need?"

Essential Role	Recommended	Staff Members Best Trained to Meet This Need
Administration	Principal	
Reading	Reading specialist	
Writing	English language arts specialist	
Mathematics	Mathematics specialist	
English language	English learner specialist	
Language	Speech and language pathologist	
Teaching differentiation	Special education teacher	
Behavior	Psychologist	
Social-family	Counselor	
Instructional resources	Librarian	
Community resources	Community resource officer, social worker, counselor	

When will this team meet? (Determine a weekly meeting time and location.)

- Time: _____

- Location: _____

What are the team norms?

_____

_____

_____

_____

_____

_____

_____

Source: Buffum et al., 2018, p. 237.

Figure 3.1: Building a site intervention team.

*Visit **go.SolutionTree.com/RTIatWork** for a free reproducible version of this figure.*

team members during the school year. By asking team members to rotate their roles and responsibilities, the team will be stronger and better prepared when a team member leaves. Consider the following roles.

▽ **Facilitator:** Keeps track of the agenda, ensures the team addresses all agenda items, and ensures meetings stay focused on the stated outcomes

▽ **Time keeper:** Closely watches the time during meetings and reminds the group when it is time to move forward in order to address each agenda item

▽ **Note taker:** Records the minutes and agreed-on actions of all meetings

▽ **Follow-up person:** Shares follow-up actions and timelines with the team

▽ **Data manager:** Ensures that data necessary for the meeting are available in advance

Meeting Structure

Establish the following components of effective meetings to ensure meetings are organized and there is an effective agenda in which members can accomplish set goals.

▽ **Meeting agenda:** All coalition members should receive the agenda twenty-four hours in advance of the meeting so they can come prepared. When specific students are being considered for intense academic or behavior support, a designated team member should make students' information available to all team members or the member in charge of data, with the expectation for respect and confidentiality. Some teams review data prior to meetings to be prepared for discussion at the meeting; others review and discuss data at the meeting.

▽ **Norms:** The team must establish a set of norms to guide their meetings. Members can write the group norms at the top of each agenda or read as a reminder of the guidelines and rules for the function and relationships of the team.

▽ **Minutes with outcomes:** The team should select a meeting secretary or recorder who works with team members to establish the agendas for each meeting and keeps minutes. The meeting agenda should have a clearly stated purpose for the meeting and the outcomes to be achieved by the conclusion of the meeting. The meeting minutes should correspond with the agenda and explicitly state the meeting outcomes.

▽ **Hard start and end times:** Teams work much better when there are hard start and end times for the meeting. Members are much more likely to stay on task and focused on outcomes. We have found that if coalition members have the agenda twenty-four hours in advance and they know that there is a hard start and end time, they come prepared for discussions and move more efficiently and effectively to decision making and outcomes.

▽ **Regularly scheduled meeting dates and times:** Team members must know, in advance, when and where their meetings are on a consistent basis. Teams should record these dates and times on a master calendar to ensure other activities and functions do not prevent members from attending. If at all possible, leadership and intervention meetings should be scheduled consistently on the calendar at minimum twice a month but at most once every week.

Schools that hold meetings "when they need them" learn that their coalition meeting's importance will be preempted by every emergency, school function, and, at worst, simply forgotten. The subtle message in these schools is that "this RTI stuff is not that important, and the coalition is a nice thought but not really practiced." The movement will die due to neglect and lack of follow-through.

The Purpose of Teams in Supporting Tier 3 Interventions

In utilizing collaborative structures to ensure the most impactful Tier 3 plan, we must always consider our purpose versus the structures we are creating. Our efforts to support students with the greatest needs require us to work and collaborate closely with one another to examine, plan, implement, and monitor our programmatic efforts. The implementation of effective leadership, intervention, and teacher teams requires us to move from ego- and power-driven decision making to one with a focus on student needs.

All district and school members share the accountability and follow-through for student growth, but we can never assume that it just happens. The structures and logistical plans we construct must be explicit, intentional, and transparent to all stakeholders. The purpose and structure of our work must go hand-in-hand. Our purpose is to ensure high levels of learning for all students. A major measure of our efforts and outcomes is the progress of students who require Tier 3 intervention. Meeting our intended goal or the purpose of our work requires the intentional and explicit use of data for brainstorming, problem solving, student identification, and progress monitoring.

In our work, we have seen schools use data in amazing ways to determine the cause of problems, intervene, and help teams solve issues with learners who have tremendous challenges. We have also seen schools use data in a manner that creates negative situations for both students and teachers. We provide more detailed information about using convergent assessment information in chapter 5 (page 91). However, a discussion about team effectiveness and the purpose of the team's work should include recommendations for baseline considerations for how and why we use data. We encourage leadership and intervention teams to consider the following as they set the norms and goals for their work.

The following considerations allow teams to develop norms for how they will respectfully and professionally utilize student data to serve students.

▽ **Set an intention:** Give the data review focus and purpose. Different meeting outcomes might cause members to review different types of data. Setting the intention for data review helps teams focus on the goal and not become sidetracked from the purpose of the review. They might do this by having a brief discussion in which the facilitator asks each member to state his or her intention for the data review. For example: "I will be looking for a pattern in the student's data that helps determine the root cause of the problem," or "I will be looking at trends in the data to help me determine how well subgroups are performing in relation to other students."

▽ **Give a face to the data:** All team members may not personally know each student. In order to help everyone get to know the students behind the numbers, some teams have photos of the identified students; others might offer a one-minute introduction in which someone shares the student's background information, such as how long the student has attended the school and his or her interests. Teams must always remember that there is a student behind the numbers.

▽ **Dig below the surface:** Teams should prepare electronic spreadsheets in advance showing the data they will analyze. For example, if they are reviewing data for the purpose of looking for successful interventions, it needs to be strategically sorted to consider the success for all students. The analysis should consider the overall success rate as well as the success of student subgroups. Teams can do this by looking at data by race, gender, individualized education program (IEP), or home language. If the whole group has a 90 percent success rate, that may seem positive until team members realize that a small number of students with disabilities is within that group, and 100 percent of them are not making progress.

▽ **See the whole picture:** Teams should consider all available data that are pertinent to the purpose of the data review. If the team identifies students needing intense intervention or problem-solving support, they need a broad range of data that gives a comprehensive picture of the student. This may include academic data, behavior data, home data, and data identifying areas of success as well as areas in need of improvement. If the team is reviewing progress in one subject, such as writing, they may look at common assessment scores, writing samples, exit tickets, and scoring rubrics to see the whole picture of progress in writing.

▽ **Use data to find solutions:** Students needing intense intervention often have multiple issues, and the information from team members may contain statements such as:

  ▶ "Refuses to work"

  ▶ "Can't work with others"

  ▶ "Angry and aggressive"

  ▶ "Can't perform at grade level"

Teams must understand that these statements are clues to problems, not judgments. We must shift our perspective of how we see students if we are to find solutions to problems. Behind each of these statements is a reason. A student who refuses to work may have suffered trauma. A student who does not work well with others may have communication or self-regulatory issues that the team needs to address. Teams must constantly ask themselves why the problem exists and then determine the solutions.

> "See a child differently and you'll see a different child."
> —Stuart Shanker

▽ **Above all else, use data *correctly*:** Teams can use data powerfully right or powerfully wrong. Teams must not be afraid to use data as their greatest resource to solve students' complex problems. But, above all else, consider each individual student as the unique person that he or she is. Treat the student, teacher, and process with respect by using data to help reach the goal of high levels of learning.

The Relationship Between Tier 3 Interventions and Special Education

Tier 3 is intended to provide intensive interventions based on targeted needs, not labels. Special education should be considered as a critical partner as you work to implement Tier 3, but it must not be designated as the sole owner and provider of Tier 3 interventions. An aligned system of interventions from Tiers 1, 2, and 3 requires ongoing collaboration among educators at all tiers. It is important for general education and special education teachers to analyze essential standards and have a common understanding of what students must know and do to demonstrate mastery. All teachers who serve individual students must participate in monitoring progress and contributing data to the intervention team. All interventionists must stay in constant communication in order to know if students are making progress and filling gaps necessary for success on grade-level standards.

Unfortunately, many schools have not put the necessary structures in place that allow teachers the time or opportunity for this level of communication. As we work in schools and share information about the importance of collaborative practices, special education teachers frequently approach us and ask, "Special education teachers do not participate in common planning or data meetings. What should we be doing?"

If a school is committed to high levels of learning for all students, it requires a belief system and practices that access the expertise of all staff. It is the responsibility of the leadership team to ensure this level of communication. We find schools that do this through traditional face-to-face conferencing as well as electronic data walls that all teachers and interventionists can access to see a student's current performance in essential standards and assessments. Electronic data walls are efficient and provide immediate information to all stakeholders, but collaboration between the interventionist and teachers is still critical for aligning interventions, monitoring progress, and sharing best practices.

Buffum et al. (2018) explain the rationale for teachers working together for the benefit of all students:

> The premise of RTI is that schools should not delay providing help for struggling students until they fall far enough behind to qualify for special education. Instead we should provide timely, targeted, systematic interventions to all students in need. Because RTI is a multitiered system of supports, students who are years behind in foundational skills can receive intensive remediation while still learning essential grade-level curriculum. Regardless if a student qualifies for special education, the RTI process should collaboratively build on the collective training and skills of all site educators to meet that student's unique needs. (p. 270)

By putting purposeful structures in place that promote collaboration between general education and special education, all learners benefit.

Hanover Research (2014) examined best practices for improving student achievement for certain student subgroups, including students with disabilities. As you read the eleven characteristics of schools effective in educating students with disabilities, consider how collaborative practices between the leadership team, intervention team, and collaborative teacher teams, including special education and general education, are necessary:

- A pervasive emphasis on curriculum alignment with the state framework.

- Systems to support curriculum alignment. There were "people present in the school whose job it was to support fidelity of implementation; to help teachers who had never done standards-based instruction."

- An emphasis on inclusion and access to the general education curriculum. The schools carefully planned how kids were included in the content. Students were included in meaningful ways in a community of students their own age, and special education teachers worked with general education teachers who knew the content.

- Culture and practices that support high standards and student achievement. Everyone at these schools, from bus drivers and cooks to teachers and superintendents, is on the same page. All adults were there to "help every child—and learn at high levels."

- Well-disciplined academic and social environments. These schools expected the students to behave and had systematic school-wide approaches for ensuring appropriate behavior. With proactive behavioral management techniques, students were not behaving in ways that interfered with their own learning—or other students' learning.

- The use of student assessment data to inform decision making. These schools "didn't rely on large-scale, state-wide assessments to get their data. They used formative assessments; their teachers talked about data and about student work."

- Unified practice supported by targeted professional development. These schools had mentoring systems in place to help teachers implement the programs, strategies, and approaches they had learned.

- Access to targeted resources to support key initiatives. These schools "used their data to figure out where things were working and where they were not. They developed their training and their support to coach people so that [their own] problem areas could be addressed."

- Effective staff recruitment, retention, and deployment.

- Flexible leaders and staff working effectively in a dynamic environment. The leaders in these schools "welcome change."

- The determination that effective leadership is essential to success. (Hanover Research, 2014, pp. 13–14)

If we are going to provide the greatest inclusive and comprehensive supports, it's necessary that special education, guided by the efforts of the leadership team and in partnership with the intervention team, and teacher teams work hand-in-hand in the school's intervention system. We must be willing to challenge the status quo and find a way for all staff to regularly communicate for the benefit of all students.

It is important to understand that RTI at Work is not intended to be a pre-referral process for special education or to block or deter schools from identifying students as having a disability. RTI at Work is intended to provide the targeted support students need at the earliest possible moment—being proactive rather than reactive to student needs. The goal is to provide timely, targeted, and systematic interventions to all students in need of additional time and support. If a student's need for special education is justifiable, then the school should utilize this intervention.

We do not see students as special education students, Tier 3 students, or general education students. We see all students as unique learners with their own gifts and challenges that may require support at one tier or all tiers of intervention at any given time.

Our only caution to educators is in determining whether we can justify a student's need for special education. Labels last a lifetime, and it is not a decision to take lightly. The site intervention team should reference Buffum et al.'s (2018) critical questions for special education identification from *Taking Action: A Handbook for RTI at Work* when considering special education placement (see figure 3.2, page 66).

Consider the example scenario of a conversation between the principal of a PLC model campus and a young mother she met at a social gathering. It emphasizes the importance of the leadership and intervention teams having a systematic process established with all stakeholders, including special education placement on the first day of school.

Jack is the perfect example of a student who will enter public school needing a proactive process to respond to his needs. There is no reason to wait for months to begin interventions. There will undoubtedly be records from his speech therapist and preK teacher that the school can pair with additional screeners to determine the level of support he needs the first week of school. As his teachers work with interventionists and the intervention team on his level of support, they may or may not need to intensify the interventions. However, if a school has the systematic processes in place, Jack can begin to receive help immediately.

The future will tell if Jack needs special education for academic support, and the school should not allow fear of state testing or a perceived label to dictate that support. Regardless of whether or not the school identifies Jack as needing special education services at Tier 3, the school should utilize the expertise of special education teachers and support staff as a part of the collaborative team to determine his targeted needs and interventions.

Parent: I am worried about what will happen to Jack when he enters public school. He is in preK at our church school now, but I know we have a lot of big decisions to make. He will go to our local public school for kindergarten.

As the principal watched Jack play and interact with other students, she noticed developmental delays in communication as well as his strengths and social skills. She asked the parent to tell her about Jack.

Parent: Jack has been in speech therapy for several years and is doing much better. He speaks in phrases, has improved social skills, plays with other children, and has become independent in dressing and toileting. Close friends told us that he has the characteristics of a child with autism. I know he can keep getting speech therapy, but what if he is slower to learn than other students? Does he have to be in special education to get the help he needs?

Principal: Jack may or may not need the support of special education for academics or behavior. It depends on Jack and his needs, not the fact that he has the signs of autism. I have many students in my school with autism. Most are successful with little or no academic support, and a small number need intensive support. Some receive the services of special education, but most do not. We look at each student and his or her individual needs. It is important for you to know that my school believes *all* students should have access to essential core instruction. If they need support, they get it.

Parent: I want him to get the help he needs. I just know that he is making progress and don't understand why people tell me that he has to be in special education because he has the signs of autism and someday will face state testing. His speech therapist tells me to be ready because his school will put him in special education.

Principal: I encourage you to stay positive and keep working to help Jack with his academic, social, and speech skills. When he enters school, talk to his team about how they can support Jack, and be sure to point out all his strengths and the growth he has made to date. Be sure and take them all his records and progress reports. Let's focus on his needs and not a perceived label.

Once a school determines a student's needs, the challenge for the leadership and intervention teams is finding a way to utilize the expertise and talent of the staff while complying with the rules governing the funding that pays their salaries and Title I, special education, and state categorical funding sources. Split funding might be a solution.

Critical Questions for Special Education Identification

The site intervention team must ask the following questions when considering a student for special education placement.

Tier 1

- Did the student have ready access to essential grade-level curriculum as part of his or her core instruction?

- Did the student receive effective supports, accommodations, or differentiation to support his or her success in learning essential grade-level standards? What were these supports?

- Is there evidence that the school's core instructional practices are working for a large majority of students, including similar students?

Tier 2

- Did the school identify the student for supplemental support in a timely manner?

- What were the student's specific learning needs at Tier 2? (The team should be able to list exact standards, learning targets, and behaviors.)

- What caused the student to not learn these essential learning outcomes?

- What research or evidence-based interventions did teachers use to address the student's specific learning needs?

- Did the school provide these interventions in addition to Tier 1?

- Is there evidence that these interventions were effective for similar students?

Tier 3

- Did the school identify the student for Tier 3 interventions in a timely, proactive manner?

- What quality problem-solving process did the school use to better identify the student's specific learning needs and the cause of the student's struggles?

- What were the student's specific learning needs at Tier 3? (The team should be able to list exact standards, learning targets, and behaviors.)

- What research- and evidence-based interventions did the school use to address the student's specific learning needs?

- Did highly trained professionals in the student's areas of need provide these interventions?

- Did the school provide these interventions in addition to Tier 1 and Tier 2?

- How often did the school monitor the student's progress for each intervention? What revisions or modifications did the school make based on this information?

- Is there evidence that these interventions were effective for similar students?

- Are there any other interventions or supports the school should try before considering special education placement?

- Does the site intervention team unanimously feel that special education identification is necessary and appropriate for this student? What benefits will the student receive due to this recommendation that could not be provided without it?

- Would team members make the same recommendation if the student in question were their child?

Source: Buffum et al., 2018, p. 274.

Figure 3.2: Critical questions for special education identification.

Visit go.SolutionTree.com/RTIatWork for a free reproducible version of this figure.

Split Funding to Support Interventions

A major obstacle for both the leadership and intervention teams in planning to meet the learning needs of all students is the constraints of funding streams schools use to provide staff and materials. In many cases, the school is unable to utilize skilled staff who could prove to be a resource to Tier 3 student support due to the constraints of targeted funding sources' specific rules for use.

Personnel resources, who are already on the campus and who could have an immediate impact on student success, are often barred by district, state, or federal directives due to concerns related to compliance with funding regulations. The funding streams that provide for personnel and materials on campuses do have specific provisions for use. The U.S. Department of Education and state legislation enacted these provisions with the best of intentions, ensuring that funding reached targeted students and programs. In some cases, they enacted these provisions in response to real abuses in the use of funding.

A major consideration for the leadership and intervention teams in seeking to bridge this impediment is the use of split funding for key staff members. In this case, a school can fund a single staff member through multiple funding streams, including Title I, special education, and district funding. Depending on state and federal regulations, the school would adjust funding by percentages to allow for a specific teacher to provide services in Tier 3. By matching funding sources to the percentage of time a teacher provides services, the leadership and intervention teams can achieve tremendous flexibility in designing Tier 3 resources.

Taking advantage of the split-funding approach requires the leadership and intervention teams to understand available funding sources, specific personnel funding, and the compliance requirements of each funding source. This strategy requires deep and ongoing collaboration and flexibility between various departments at the school and in the district with the goal of strategically using available funding to best meet students' needs. The understanding and efforts of the leadership and intervention teams to investigate the possibilities of split funding provide these teams with resources that may have not been apparent as they work to design Tier 3.

> "Putting together the right coalition of people to lead a change initiative is critical to its success."
> —John P. Kotter

Tools to Support Teamwork

It is important that the leadership and intervention teams have a process for setting goals and monitoring the progress of their work. If a team does not document their action steps and determine timelines and a method for monitoring progress, it becomes very difficult to maintain focus on the established goals. The following tools can help teams in these endeavors.

1-2-3 Action Planning

The form in figure 3.3 can help teams with a big-picture view of the actions they have agreed to take as a team and provides each team member with a method for documenting the steps they will take for the duties assigned to them. In addition to documenting actions, teams can outline the professional development or coaching needed and specify how they will monitor progress. Column 1 outlines the district-level goals, column 2 indicates the campus goals that align with the district goal, and column 3 allows each team member to note his or her next steps to fulfill assigned duties. A team may choose to modify the tool and omit column 1 if they are only addressing campus or department goals. It can also include as many actions as needed.

District Goal	Campus or Department Implementation	My Next Steps
Action 1 Example: All campuses have collaborative planning and data meetings during the school day. Special education and intervention teachers participate in collaborative planning to support all students.	**Action 1** Example: Campuses build time into the master schedule. Curriculum and special programs provide coaching and support to teacher teams at all tiers.	**Action 1** Example: Meet with principals regarding scheduling. Meet with curriculum and special education department teams to develop and establish a support plan. Ensure roles and responsibilities for special education and intervention teachers in planning.
Professional Development or Coaching Needed Example: Teams receive professional development on outcome-based common planning— why, how, setting norms, analyzing standards, and the four essential questions for learning. Teams need ongoing coaching. Teams need to understand the importance of why we must meet all students' learning needs, and how to plan for all learners in advance of instruction.	**Professional Development or Coaching Needed** Example: Campus and department teams participate in professional development to provide support to teacher teams at all tiers.	**Professional Development or Coaching Needed** Example: Department members participate in professional development or coaching regarding their roles and responsibilities.

Monitoring: When and How Example: Monitor PD calendar August and January to ensure training is provided. Attend team meetings to determine the type of support needed.	**Monitoring: When and How** Example: Monthly leadership meetings will include agenda items to discuss the planning process, needs, and support provided.	**Monitoring: When and How** Example: Maintain action plan and timeline to ensure goals are met. Share timeline and progress in monthly leadership team meetings.
Action 2	**Action 2**	**Action 2**
Professional Development or Coaching Needed	**Professional Development or Coaching Needed**	**Professional Development or Coaching Needed**
Monitoring: When and How	**Monitoring: When and How**	**Monitoring: When and How**

Figure 3.3: 1-2-3 action planning.

Visit ***go.SolutionTree.com/RTIatWork*** *for a free reproducible version of this figure.*

Monitoring Our Progress

Having a system in place to monitor the progress on goals is a very important element of team success. It establishes organization, focus, and accountability for the actions necessary for success. Any team may use this tool to document agreed-on actions, timelines, and methods for monitoring progress as well as planning its next steps (see figure 3.4).

Action and How to Measure Progress	Timeline for Monitoring	Results or Progress	Next Steps
Name the action that you will monitor and how you will measure it. What data will you use, and what is the target goal?	In advance, determine a timeline for monitoring progress.	Review progress and share with team members.	Determine the next steps for continuing improvement. Add as new actions, and determine timelines for monitoring progress.

Figure 3.4: Monitoring our progress.

Visit ***go.SolutionTree.com/RTIatWork*** *for a free reproducible version of this figure.*

Roles and Responsibilities of Teams at Tier 3

The chart in figure 3.5 is a tool designed to assist the principal and the informal school leadership team as they work to establish formal team structures, such as roles and responsibilities, meeting dates, required data, as well as other tools and protocols.

Topics for Consideration	Leadership Team	Intervention Team
Responsibilities	**Responsible for Tier 3**	**Responsible for Tier 3**
Who are team members, and what are their roles and responsibilities? Example: • Recorder: Records minutes and decisions during meetings • Facilitator: Runs meetings, sets agendas • Time keeper: Keeps track of timing for agenda items during meetings	• Identifies students needing Tier 3 interventions • Creates problem-solving intervention team • Prioritizes resources • Monitors intervention effectiveness	• Diagnoses cause of gaps in learning • Determines targeted interventions • Monitors progress • Ensures proper intervention intensity • Determines if special education is needed and justifiable
When are meeting dates? Schedule, create, and share calendar in advance.		
What assessment data will the team use?		
What tools or protocols are needed? Examples: • Problem-solving tools • Data spreadsheets • Action plans		

Figure 3.5: Roles and responsibilities for teams at Tier 3.

*Visit **go.SolutionTree.com/RTIatWork** for a free reproducible version of this figure.*

Conclusion

In this chapter, we discussed the roles and responsibilities of the two teams essential for successful implementation of Tier 3—the leadership team and the intervention team. In chapter 4 (page 73), we discuss in greater detail the actions these two teams must take as they set goals, design, and plan the systematic processes at

Tier 3. It is our hope that the tools and next steps provided in this chapter will assist you with this work. As you move forward, we urge you to hold fast to the goal of all students learning at high levels. Make your actions match your beliefs, and move forward in changing the lives of students who depend on you.

Chapter 3 Action Steps

With your team, engage in the following action steps to review and implement the learning from this chapter.

1. When using figure 3.1, Building a Site Intervention Team (page 57), note that the third column is titled Staff Members Best Trained to Meet This Need. Few schools are so blessed to have full-time staff in each essential role listed in the first column. So, ask yourself who is the best person on your campus, readily available, to take on each of these roles? For example, perhaps your school does not have a full-time reading specialist. Do you have a teacher at your school who was formerly a special education teacher, has a master's degree in reading, or has a reading specialist certificate?

2. Prioritize your next steps. After reading this chapter, you will probably have identified numerous next steps for both the leadership team and intervention team. Revisit the 1-2-3 action planning activity (see page 68). Make a list of goals for each team, and then prioritize your lists. What tasks must teams do immediately? What tasks can teams do over the course of the current school year? What things will probably need to wait until next school year? Don't spend too much time on tasks that are more than a semester away. Instead, intensely plan for those tasks teams can accomplish immediately.

Tier 3 Design to Ensure High Levels of Learning

4

I n October of 2018, we visited a large preK–5 elementary campus led by an energetic and focused principal and leadership team that were eager to share the work that they had done in creating a comprehensive pyramid of interventions. Team members had led their campus out of a school improvement required by their state and were justifiably proud of their accomplishments.

When we visited a grade-level team collaborative planning meeting, we observed teachers analyzing essential standards, considering what students must know and do to master the unit of instruction, and collaboratively designing assessments and instruction. When we visited classrooms, we observed teachers using student learning data to improve their practice by sharing with their peers what worked. In every classroom, we saw examples of teachers continuously checking for understanding and adjusting instruction by using best practices and differentiation strategies.

It was clear that the school had come to a common commitment that it would make every effort in each classroom to ensure that *all* students would master the essential standards. Teachers proactively utilized a team approach for regrouping and reteaching. During collaborative time on Tuesday of each week, teams looked at common exit tickets from Monday and divided the students between team members for reteaching for a twenty-minute time period they commonly agreed to on Wednesdays and Thursdays of each week. They divided students into groups based on skills, and teachers taught groups in which their students performed well. They called this *shared learning time*. The school had clearly established Tier 1 as first-best instruction with differentiation strategies commonly understood and utilized.

We shared our deep appreciation for their work at Tier 1 and asked to see what they did with students who had not mastered the taught essentials. The principal and his leadership team were equally proud of their Tier 2 work. The school had allocated thirty minutes per day for focused instruction on essentials that students had yet to master. A member from each grade-level collaborative team conducted this reteaching; he or she fully understood the essential standard and behavior and had data from the common assessment that focused reteaching in Tier 2 to exactly what each student in the tutorial needed to reach mastery.

When a student was able to prove consistent mastery of the essentials, he or she was immediately dismissed from Tier 2 support. The number of students being served in Tier 2 was small due to the work of the staff in Tier 1. The focus in Tier 2 was laser-like, and the impact on student learning in these small groups was nothing less than amazing. Tier 2 at this school was resting on the firm foundation of Tier 1 and together, Tiers 1 and 2 ensured that 95 percent or more students were learning the essentials to mastery.

The efforts of the principal and staff had created a system in which it was harder to fail than it was to be successful. The collective and collaborative efforts of the staff raised student achievement to high levels and had significantly cut the achievement gap between all students. We were eager to see what the school had done to develop their Tier 3 system. We stated how impressed we were and asked to learn more about their efforts in Tier 3. They met our request with an awkward silence. Sensing the awkwardness, the principal explained for the group, "We have not been successful in our efforts in Tier 3 to make a difference for our students."

They led us to a classroom where ten students were receiving interventions in the school's Tier 3 program. The classroom was dismal and dark. They had removed the teacher from Tier 1 due to poor performance and moved her assignment to providing Tier 3 instruction. She was working with the students using various workbooks and textbooks with no explicit instruction. The students were completing worksheets or copying from the textbook. Students were disengaged, and the classroom was chaotic with students meandering around the classroom, talking, and sitting on the floor amusing themselves with items they had in their backpacks. The teacher and teaching assistant were sitting behind a desk talking. The principal and the leadership team explained that this group of students included those with disabilities as well as some who did not qualify for special education.

For all that was effective and impactful in Tiers 1 and 2 at this school, the Tier 3 program was opposite in its effectiveness and impact on student learning. This situation called the belief system of the campus into question and demanded that the school ask itself if its purpose was to serve *all* students or just *some* students.

In this chapter, we focus on the design of schoolwide systems and processes at Tier 1 as well as processes unique to Tier 3 that support high levels of learning by all students. These systems and structures are grounded by the belief that all students can and must learn at high levels. As stated earlier, we do not see students as Tier 1, 2, or 3 students; we see all students as unique learners who may need targeted support at different times. We approach this chapter with the following understandings.

▽ The students receiving Tier 3 intense interventions are also learning current grade-level essentials at Tier 1 and may or may not need support with grade-level essentials at Tier 2.

▽ Tier 2 provides supplemental support in grade-level essential learning in academics and behavior.

▽ Tier 3 provides intensive support for students who are multiple years behind grade level in the universal or foundational skills of reading, writing, mathematics (number sense), English language, social and academic behaviors, and health and home.

▽ Although students may receive instruction in all three tiers simultaneously, each tier has its own distinct purpose and role in meeting students' needs.

Chapters 5, 6, and 7 provide focused information regarding assessment, behavior interventions, and academic interventions supported by the systems, structures, processes, and beliefs discussed in this chapter.

The Foundation at Tiers 1 and 2

The work done by teacher teams in Tiers 1 and 2 is critical as schools work to build a comprehensive system of interventions. Increased teacher efficacy, the effective use of learning data, and open collaboration focused on meeting *all* students' learning needs provide the foundation for Tier 3 implementation. There needs to be a constant quest for and utilization of high-level practices that positively impact student learning.

High-Leverage Practices

There is no substitute for high-quality Tier 1 instruction. It is the foundation. Every classroom teacher is the first interventionist for every student. Ensuring that Tier 1 is effective provides a firm foundation of learning that enables success at Tiers 2 and 3.

Ensuring high levels of learning for all begins with teachers utilizing best practices in every classroom. TeachingWorks (n.d.) at the University of Michigan identified nineteen high-leverage practices (HLPs) that are key to helping students learn important content and developing social and emotional competencies. These practices provide a foundation for success for all learners. It is critical that leadership teams work with both new teachers and veteran teachers to provide the level of support needed for these practices to be well understood and regularly used schoolwide.

> "We can, whenever and wherever we choose, successfully teach all children whose schooling is of interest to us. We already know more than we need to do this. Whether we do it or not must finally depend on how we feel about the fact that we have not done it so far."
>
> —Ron Edmonds

The practices identified by TeachingWorks (n.d.) for Tier 1 align with the *High-Leverage Practices in Special Education* (McLeskey, Barringer, Billingsley, Brownell, Jackson, Kennedy, et al., 2017) that we recommend as foundational for all Tier 3 instruction described in detail in chapter 7 (page 167). By analyzing the alignment between the Tier 1 high-leverage practices and the recommended Tier 3 practices, you can quickly see how utilizing HLP at Tier 1 supports students who may also receive intensive intervention at Tier 3. The Tier 1 practices support all learners, and the alignment shows that students needing the support of intensive interventions benefit when their Tier 1 classroom utilizes these practices as a part of their instructional strategies.

Figure 4.1 outlines each Tier 1 practice and provides a brief description as well as alignment to a high-leverage practice recommended for Tier 3.

As you review the high-leverage practices in the left column, consider the following:

▽ How many teachers or classrooms at your school regularly use these practices?

▽ Out of the nineteen practices, which ones do teachers in your team or building need to better understand?

▽ Do you consider these practices to be foundational practices that all teachers should utilize on your campus?

▽ How do teachers or teams support each other in implementing these practices?

▽ When students are having difficulty, do teachers seek and utilize high-level practices?

The Design of Tier 3

Let's begin with the reason or purpose for having a Tier 3 program. Answering this question provides insight into the focus and direction of a school's efforts and expectations for students in Tier 3. Whether we call this support *intensive intervention* or *remediation*, the intent is clear—to provide intensive support that accelerates mastery of prior skills and knowledge from previous school years. Teams should clarify the goal of Tier 3 and what systems, processes, and practices they will establish to ensure they meet that goal.

High-Leverage Practice at Tier 1	Tier 1 and Alignment to High-Leverage Practice at Tier 3
Leading a group discussion	Tier 1: Teachers and students work on specific content together. *Active participation and active listening* are key. Teachers develop a technique to monitor participation, so all students are included. Active listening includes strategies such as giving students listening tasks and reducing the time teachers talk while increasing student collaboration. Alignment of HLPs for Tier 3: • Teach social behaviors. • Teach cognitive and metacognitive strategies to support learning. • Promote active engagement.
Explaining and modeling content, practices, and strategies	Tier 1: Teachers use verbal explanations or modeling, demonstrating metacognitive strategies such as problem solving or self-assessment. Alignment of HLPs for Tier 3: • Teach cognitive and metacognitive strategies. • Use explicit instruction. • Teach students to maintain and generalize learning across time and settings.
Eliciting and interpreting individual student thinking	Tier 1: Teachers determine a student's thinking through carefully chosen questions and tasks. By interpreting student thinking, teachers can correct misconceptions or errors. Alignment of HLPs for Tier 3: • Use strategies to promote active engagement. • Provide positive and constructive feedback to guide students' learning and behavior.
Diagnosing common patterns of student thinking and development in subject matter domain	Tier 1: Teachers who are familiar with common patterns of student thinking and development and who are fluent in anticipating or identifying them can work more effectively and efficiently as they plan and implement instruction and evaluate student learning. Common strategies include analyzing student work for error patterns and asking students to explain their thinking. Alignment of HLPs for Tier 3: • Systematically design instruction toward a specific learning goal. • Adapt curriculum materials and tasks for a specific learning goal.

Source: Adapted from CEEDAR Center, n.d.; TeachingWorks, n.d.

Figure 4.1: High-leverage Tier 1 practices.   continued →

High-Leverage Practice at Tier 1	Tier 1 and Alignment to High-Leverage Practice at Tier 3
Implementing norms and routines for classroom discourse and work	Tier 1: Norms, processes, and routines vary across teachers and subjects. Examples include establishing a hypothesis, providing evidence for claims, and showing one's thinking in detail. Teachers must teach students about these processes, why they are important, and how to use them, as they are crucial to building understanding and capability in a given subject. Alignment of HLPs for Tier 3: • Establish a consistent, organized, and respectful learning environment. • Teach social behaviors.
Coordinating and adjusting instruction during a lesson	Tier 1: Teachers take care to coordinate and adjust instruction during a lesson to maintain coherence, ensure that the lesson is responsive to students' needs, and use time efficiently. Learning to scaffold instruction for groups and individual students is key. Alignment of HLPs for Tier 3: • Provide scaffolded supports.
Specifying and reinforcing productive student behavior	Tier 1: Teachers establish clear expectations for student behavior and explicitly teach positive behavior to students, reward it, and strategically redirect off-task behavior. This helps create classrooms that are productive learning environments for all. Alignment of HLPs for Tier 3: • Provide positive and constructive feedback to guide student learning and behavior. • Conduct functional behavior assessments to develop individual student behavior support plans.
Implementing organizational routines	Tier 1: Teachers organize time, space, and materials and strategically and deliberately teach students how to complete tasks such as lining up at the door, passing out papers, and asking to participate in class discussion. Alignment of HLPs for Tier 3: • Establish a consistent, organized, and respectful learning environment.
Setting up and managing small-group work	Tier 1: Teachers use small-group work when instructional goals call for in-depth interaction among students and collaboration. Teachers choose tasks that require and foster collaborative work. Teachers also use small groups for reteaching critical skills. Alignment of HLPs for Tier 3: • Use flexible grouping. • Promote active engagement.

High-Leverage Practice at Tier 1	Tier 1 and Alignment to High-Leverage Practice at Tier 3
Building respectful relationships with students	Tier 1: Teachers increase the likelihood that students will engage and persist in school when they establish positive, individual relationships with them. Techniques include greeting students positively every day; having frequent, brief check-in conversations with students to demonstrate care and interest; and following up with students who are experiencing difficulties. Alignment of HLPs for Tier 3: • Establish a consistent, organized, and respectful learning environment. • Teach social behaviors.
Talking about a student with parents or other caregivers	Tier 1: Regular communication between teachers and parents or guardians supports student learning. Teachers communicate with parents to provide information about students' academic progress, behavior, or development; seek information and help; and request parental involvement in school. All communication should be respectful of language and cultural norms. Alignment of HLPs for Tier 3: • Collaborate with families to support student learning and secure needed services. • Organize and facilitate effective meetings with professionals and families.
Learning about students' cultural, religious, family, intellectual, and personal experiences and resources for use in instruction	Tier 1: Teachers actively learn about particular students to design instruction that meets their needs. Teachers should deliberately seek to understand: • Cultural norms for communicating • How cultural and religious views affect what is considered appropriate in school • Topics and issues that interest individual students and groups of students Alignment of HLPs for Tier 3: • Collaborate with families to support student learning and secure needed services. • Use multiple sources of information to develop a comprehensive understanding of students' strengths and needs.
Setting long- and short-term learning goals for students	Tier 1: Teachers establish clear goals referenced to external standards to ensure all students learn expected content. Explicit goals help teachers maintain coherent, purposeful, and equitable instruction over time. Alignment of HLPs for Tier 3: • Identify and prioritize long- and short-term goals. • Use assistive and instructional technologies.

continued →

High-Leverage Practice at Tier 1	Tier 1 and Alignment to High-Leverage Practice at Tier 3
Designing single lessons and sequence of lessons	Tier 1: Teachers carefully sequence lessons to help students develop deep understanding of content and sophisticated skills and practices. Teachers design and sequence lessons with an eye toward providing opportunities for student inquiry and discovery and include opportunities for students to practice and master foundational concepts and skills before moving on to more advanced ones. Alignment of HLPs for Tier 3: • Systematically design instruction toward a specific learning goal.
Checking student understanding during and at the conclusion of lessons	Tier 1: Teachers use a variety of informal methods to assess what students are learning during and between lessons. Frequent checks provide information about students' current level of competence and help teachers adjust instruction during a single lesson or from one lesson to the next. Alignment of HLPs for Tier 3: • Use student assessment data, analyze instructional practices, and make necessary adjustments that improve student outcomes.
Selecting and designing formal assessments of student learning	Tier 1: Teachers use effective summative assessments to obtain information about what students have learned and where they are struggling in relation to specific learning goals. Effective summative assessments provide both students and teachers with useful information and help teachers evaluate and design further instruction. Alignment of HLPs for Tier 3: • Use student assessment data, analyze instructional practices, and make necessary adjustments that improve student outcomes.
Interpreting the results of student work, including routine assignments, quizzes, tests, projects, and standardized assessments	Tier 1: Teachers analyze student work, including all kinds of assessments, looking for patterns that will guide their efforts to assist specific students and the class as a whole and inform future instruction. Student work is the most important source of information about the instructional effectiveness. Alignment of HLPs for Tier 3: • Collaborate with professionals to increase student success.
Providing oral and written feedback to students	Tier 1: Teachers provide effective feedback that is specific, not overwhelming in scope, focused on the academic task, and supports students' perceptions of their own capabilities. Alignment of HLPs for Tier 3: • Provide positive and constructive feedback to guide student learning and behavior.
Analyzing instruction for the purpose of improving it	Tier 1: Teachers study their own as well as their colleagues' teaching to improve their understanding of the complex interactions between teachers, students, and content and the impact of specific instructional approaches. Alignment of HLPs for Tier 3: • Use student assessment data, analyze instructional practices, and make necessary adjustments that improve student outcomes.

Visit **go.SolutionTree.com/RTIatWork** *for a free reproducible version of this figure.*

If we are truly to design best practices at Tier 3, then we must be much more pragmatic and clear in our purpose so there is no confusion as to our direction. Tier 3 systems that are the most effective are focused on accelerating the learning of critical prerequisite or foundational skills so students can be successful in mastering grade-level essential standards and behaviors. The key term is *focused acceleration*. If we are remediating without a sense of urgency, then the learning curve for these students will continue to leave them significantly behind their peers. Remediation without a sense of urgency will not provide accelerated learning.

The school administration, leadership team, teaching staff, and even the students must have a clear understanding that the Tier 3 program provides targeted remediation that accelerates learning the foundational skills students need to master grade-level essential standards.

As previously stated in chapter 3 (page 49), the leadership team must ensure that all teams embrace the school's mission and vision and work with collective responsibility for high levels of achievement for all students. The systems and processes that the leadership team put in place for identification and referral of students to the intervention team are central to the success of Tier 3.

The school charges the intervention team with diagnosing, treating, prioritizing, and monitoring Tier 3 interventions. As stated in chapter 3, the leadership and intervention teams are two teams working hand in hand to achieve a common goal.

Critical Questions for Designing Tier 3

The intervention team must meet clarity of purpose with clarity of action if it is to produce the best possible support students need. To effectively meet students' needs, we strongly recommend the leadership team utilizes a protocol when designing Tier 3 that provides a comprehensive view of student needs and guides their thinking on critical structural elements such as collaborative time for teachers. The leadership team must consider the following questions when designing Tier 3 protocol. The intervention team can also use these questions as they do their work to inform the leadership team of ongoing needs, changes in scheduling, or the types of interventions provided. Questions such as these help guide design, logistics, and outcomes. The team must consider these questions with due haste and urgency to ensure students have certain access to the remediation they so desperately need.

We initially discussed the roles and responsibilities of the leadership and intervention teams in chapter 3. We provide the following additional clarification of their roles related to design and implementation of Tier 3. As you read each question and the responsibilities of each team, consider the difference in outcomes for students when they use this level of focus in implementing or improving Tier 3.

For these students, what specific skills or behavior deficits do the data indicate?

Leadership team considerations: The leadership team must analyze student data from a wide variety of sources to give them a picture of the needs of student groups and individual students at Tier 3. Team members should use this information to prioritize resources for identified students.

Intervention team considerations: The intervention team must utilize all available assessment information (convergent data) to determine students' targeted needs. As the year progresses, it will inform the leadership team of changes to scheduling or types of interventions needed.

What are the intervention strategies or programs to address these specific skill or behavior deficits? (When possible, teams should use research-based strategies and programs.)

Leadership team considerations: Determining student needs must dictate the selection of remediation strategies or programmatic approach. The leadership team must be flexible, creative, and prepared to respond to students' changing needs. The thought that Tier 3 is a set program or uses only one strategy is akin to the one-size-fits-all mindset.

In order to accelerate learning at Tier 3, we must match student learning and behavioral needs with targeted and tailored approaches, strategies, and programs. We recommend that schools work to create a menu of resources available to them by grade level and by need. This includes a list of staff and the certifications and expertise they possess as well as a menu of differentiated instructional strategies that fall within the five major areas of differentiation: (1) content, (2) process, (3) product, (4) affect, and (5) learning environment (Tomlinson, 2003).

Many schools have been trained to use only research-based interventions. We agree with this priority for designing remedial programs with one major caveat: *if one is available.* Too often, schools come to a total stop in their Tier 3 implementation because they have not found a research-based program or cannot afford one. We must remember that teachers are experts, and with a thorough understanding of standards and the unique and targeted needs of an individual student or groups of students, they can design highly successful intervention plans and instruction. Teachers need the support and partnership of the intervention team and other teachers when doing this level of work. It is a team effort!

Intervention team considerations: The intervention team must take the lead in determining the types of interventions for individual students. The intervention team by design has members with a wide variety of skills and expertise that allows them to problem solve with efficiency. The leadership team accepts the responsibility of ensuring needed resources are available. We recommend that the campus principal be part of the intervention team to maintain this key communication of need.

What are the intervention delivery grouping and scheduling to ensure the necessary time and intensity to accelerate learning?

Leadership team considerations: The leadership team must prioritize resources to ensure that they are available. This is an ongoing responsibility the team must consider in planning. Team members should consider how and when they will look at student data and input from the intervention teams and adjust interventions to meet targeted student needs. At times, this means adjusting the number of available periods or time frames due to student needs, and at other times it might mean researching and implementing interventions not previously needed. Schools must ensure that students receive interventions based on their needs rather than on the number and type of interventions available.

Intervention team considerations: The intervention team has the responsibility of ensuring proper intervention intensity. The logistics of delivery and scheduling must be the domain of the intervention team. They must be able to review all school, grade-level, and department schedules. Only by having access to these schedules can they ensure that Tier 3 delivery does not conflict with core instruction. They must also know the availability and schedule of those on the educational team who may be able to provide instruction in Tier 3. Once they have this information, they must consider the students who have behavioral and learning needs that are similar or the same. The goal is to provide the frequency and intensity necessary to accelerate learning of targeted fundamental skills and behaviors through effective grouping and scheduling.

In 2005, Sanger Unified School District in California was one of the first school districts to fully implement RTI with all three tiers. In establishing the schedules for interventions, teachers provided a minimum of thirty to sixty minutes of targeted instruction per day for students in Tier 3 at each elementary school across the district. In observing the most effective Tier 3 approaches across all twelve Sanger elementary schools, we found that, at a minimum, forty-five to sixty minutes were a better guideline and produced better learning results when coupled with a systematic approach and focused instruction (W. R. Smith, Deputy Superintendent, Sanger Unified School District, personal communication, February 27, 2020).

Student grouping is of utmost importance when providing focused instruction. Teams must group students by similar learning needs and behavior deficits, making every effort to limit group size. Experience has taught us that academic groups of no more than six to eight students with the same targeted need at the elementary level are ideal and very effective. In forming groups, teams must consider the impact of students' skill and will needs.

It is important to target the needs of students with behavioral deficits in the same manner as academic needs. They should give careful attention to those students who have skill issues versus those who have will issues. Mixing these two groups with differing targeted needs compromises the achievement of the entire group. The logistics of schedules and groups should be a major focus of the intervention team.

Who will provide remediation during Tier 3 intervention time?

Leadership team considerations: We advocate putting the most qualified staff member with those students with the greatest need. The leadership team must consider this as they plan Tier 3 interventions. Realizing that schools have finite staffing resources, the leadership team should work to create a staffing document detailing the collegiate majors, specific specialized trainings, and areas of academic strength of each staff member at the school. In doing this at several schools, we came to realize that each staff member had tremendous expertise and knowledge. If the most qualified teachers were unavailable due to job-specific requirements, they could lend their expertise as an advisory resource to those available to provide Tier 3 support. This was especially true with special education teachers, whose schedules and rosters often prevent them from providing Tier 3 services, but whose expertise in differentiation, assessment, and progress monitoring made them invaluable.

The use of Title I educators, counselors, and auxiliary credentialed or licensed staff provided a tremendous resource for not only direct instruction of Tier 3 groups but also for advisory resources. The flexibility of scheduling these staff members provided opportunities to form groups so students did not miss core instruction, and group size and makeup could be manipulated for greatest impact.

With each subsequent year of Tier 3 implementation, the leadership team develops a deeper ability to plan more effectively to ensure that they create the availability of the most qualified staff through targeted scheduling efforts. Year after year, the leadership team should strive to build expert staff resources.

Intervention team considerations: The intervention team is responsible for ensuring targeted interventions, ensuring proper intensity, and monitoring interventions. In response to the dilemma of who will serve a specific student or group of students, it is critically important for the intervention team to continually communicate requirements for the type and frequency of resources necessary to meet the needs of identified students.

What are the data reviewed, the method for collecting the data, and duration between data points for progress monitoring?

Leadership team considerations: The leadership team must assess the overall effectiveness of interventions, while the intervention team monitors the progress of individual students. These two teams should communicate regarding the types of learning and behavior data used for monitoring progress, the frequency of data collection, and how to manage data to have a seamless system for addressing these interrelated responsibilities.

Intervention team considerations: The intervention team and teachers providing Tier 3 support must answer the basic question, "How do we know each student is learning and accelerating?" The question revolves around the systematic implementation of progress monitoring. We can only answer this question by using data targeted and generated by the assessments and work being done in both the student's grade-level classroom and in Tier 3 interventions. Classroom and Tier 3 teachers work together to collaboratively design progress monitoring. The design, consistency, frequency, and recording of data from this monitoring help to inform the intervention team, teachers, and students themselves.

The Center on Response to Intervention (www.rti4success.org) is an excellent resource for progress monitoring tools. Additional resources for the intervention team include available commercial assessments, consults with special education staff onsite, and the district curriculum writing team or curriculum department who may be in a position to develop local tools for this purpose. Once again, the issue becomes determining the best progress monitoring tool for the grade level and the academic content or behavioral issues being addressed.

Alignment of progress monitoring to the addressed learning needs of Tier 3 students is by far the most important factor in guiding instruction to ensure learning. In many schools, we have seen teacher teams and interventionists do amazing jobs in writing assessment and monitoring tools they can use to monitor progress on district essential standards as well as individual student learning targets. Grade-level and Tier 3 teachers should collaboratively monitor behavioral growth and development by recording positive and negative actions based on the student's performance.

The recording of these data may be much more frequent. We recommend that teams work with interventionists to develop a targeted behavior rubric to use for monitoring progress. Tools may be as simple as time-on-task monitoring tools that provide the percentage of time a student is engaged or a student self-monitoring checklist.

The intervention team should consider monitoring instruments that they can review as frequently as every two weeks. This allows teams to work with a sense of urgency and change interventions quickly if a student is not making progress. The implication of frequent monitoring is that it must be quick, focused, and produce useful data without cutting into valuable instructional time. The intervention team must understand the balance between efficiency and effectiveness. Above all, the team must ask, "Does our monitoring tell us what we need to know and as frequently as we need to know it to adjust our focus and instruction?"

What are the expected outcomes of Tier 3 interventions and the specific goals that these students should strive to meet?

Leadership team considerations: As stated earlier, the leadership team must establish a schoolwide belief system and goal for the intervention purpose and outcome. When the team aligns the tiers of interventions and establishes a belief system in high levels of learning for all, all staff will understand that the outcome for interventions must be mastering grade-level essential learning.

Intervention team considerations: The intervention team and the teachers working with students in Tier 3 must create clear goals for each student that address his or her specific, fundamental academic and behavioral deficits. Team members must explicitly and intentionally state and record these goals. They must also share these goals with students. All students, even very young students, learn and respond better when they understand their targeted goals, where they are currently performing in relation to those goals, and the plan for them to reach their targets. When teachers have a growth mindset and explain to students that "you are on your way" and "this is how we will get there," rather than "you are currently failing," intervention becomes a positive and rewarding experience.

Teachers can partner with students in setting goals by helping them maintain their own progress logs and data notebooks as early as kindergarten. The combination of clear goals, short and long range, and monitoring data maintained by both the teacher and the student provides a focused environment of collaboration. The clarity of having goals and a way to monitor progress toward those goals illuminates the pathway and provides fuel for growth and development.

What are the intervention schedule and process, and who are the core teachers who will collaborate regarding these students' progress?

Leadership team considerations: As the leadership team undertakes the plan for designing Tier 3, it is essential to develop a schedule that allows intervention teachers and core teachers to collaborate with each other. If the goal is for teachers to work with a sense of urgency to accelerate learning and close learning gaps, then teachers must have regularly scheduled time to align their instruction and discuss what is working and what is not working. They need to compare progress notes and work as a team to ensure the student is progressing as planned.

Intervention team considerations: As intervention teams monitor student progress, they will consider the progress a student is making in intervention and whether or not that progress is translating to closing the gap in learning with grade-level peers. If a student is progressing on an intervention goal but not showing progress in core instruction, the team must consider the alignment of goals to essential standards and the alignment of strategies between the intervention and core class. Collaboration between teachers is essential to these determinations.

These seven questions give coherence and provide the leadership and intervention teams with a comprehensible pathway to building their school's Tier 3 interventions that focus on meeting all students' learning and behavioral needs.

Conclusion

Schools working to implement Tier 3 should seek to address the key points raised in this chapter. Initially, the development of Tier 3 is heavy lifting; but in doing the heavy lifting, the process begins to become more fluid and with greater purpose. The lack of implementation and action does not give us the opportunity to learn and improve. We must be better tomorrow than we are today for the benefit of our students. Lean forward and take the first step toward implementing Tier 3. The subsequent chapters are aimed to help teams do just that—learn by doing.

> "Learning by doing is the only way I know how to learn."
>
> —Tony Fadell

Chapter 4 Action Steps

With your team, engage in the following action steps to review and implement the learning from this chapter.

1. **Secure effective resources:** Tier 3 interventions often lack the necessary resources to be effective. To address this issue, write down the name and job description (for example, *grade 4 teacher*, *instructional aide*, *psychologist*) of *every* full-time or part-time employee on your campus on a 3 × 5-inch index card. Without regard to which of these employees may serve more than one campus, begin to arrange the index cards in a way that would represent the ideal structure to serve the neediest students on your

campus at Tier 3. Next, compare this plan to your current staff utilization. Are you serving your neediest students with your most qualified staff? If not, how could you move in that direction? Do the same with any programs on your campus, your categorical (restricted) funds, and noncategorical funds. How could you better utilize all the resources on your campus?

2. **Measuring student response to intervention at Tier 3:** Many schools do not truly have RTI—they have I (intervention). These schools intervene at Tier 3 yet have no degree of certainty that students are actually responding to the interventions. In order to ensure your interventions are actually resulting in the desired outcomes that meet students' needs, ask the following questions regarding your Tier 3 interventions.

   ▸ "What tools will we use to monitor the progress of students receiving Tier 3 interventions?"

   ▸ "How will we define what determines an adequate response to our Tier 3 interventions?"

   ▸ "How does our determination of an adequate response reflect acceleration of learning?"

   ▸ "How have other students receiving these same interventions responded?"

   ▸ "How will we utilize student responses to consider testing for specific learning disabilities?"

Convergent Assessment for Targeting at Tier 3

All educators can recall discussing the needs of a student with large gaps in learning and hearing a teacher say something like, "This student has so many gaps, I don't know where to start." This lack of direction is frustrating for teachers and, even worse, prevents students with the most intense needs from receiving the help they so desperately need.

Utilizing convergent assessment allows the intervention team to use the targeted information gained from an ongoing and systematic process to determine targeted interventions, monitor progress, and make changes to interventions as needed. Convergent assessment enables teams to understand why students are not achieving and provides certain access to Tier 3 intensive remediation in the universal skills necessary to close learning gaps. Analyzing and problem solving with multiple types of data allow teams to see the *why* behind students' challenges.

In this chapter, we examine the importance of using multiple types of assessment data to identify students' targeted needs as well as monitor student progress. The practical examples we offer allow you to consider how intervention teams work collaboratively with stakeholders to ensure high levels of learning for all students. Student success requires that teams have a systematic process for using student assessment information and work with a solution-oriented mindset, such as in the examples we share. We also include various tools to assist you in taking action.

The Foundation at Tiers 1 and 2

The goal of convergent assessment at Tier 1 and Tier 2 is to establish a proactive process for using student data to identify why students are having difficulties and intervening in a targeted manner as soon as possible to prevent failure. However, some students require the intense level of intervention provided at Tier 3. The leadership team is responsible for implementing a systematic process to refer students needing remediation at Tier 3 to the intervention team. It is critical that the intervention team receives timely information that provides the details necessary to understand a student's strengths, weaknesses, and current level of performance in order to identify the underlying causes of problems. This team relies on having a complete picture of a student's needs in order to be prescriptive in determining interventions.

In the book *Taking Action: A Handbook for RTI at Work* (Buffum et al., 2018), the authors refer to assessment as the "'life blood' of an effective system of interventions" (p. 13). They describe *convergent assessment* as "an ongoing process of collectively analyzing targeted evidence to determine the specific learning needs of each child and the effectiveness of the instruction the child receives in meeting these needs" (Buffum et al., 2018, p. 13).

If schools believe that assessments provide the critical information needed to improve outcomes for students, their assessment process at Tiers 1 and 2 will reflect this belief in the following manner.

▽ They will have a systematic process for using various types of assessments to improve instruction.

▽ They will use formative and summative assessment information to create action plans for improving student outcomes on essential standards.

▽ They will see common formative assessments designed and analyzed by teams as the lynchpin for improving achievement.

▽ They will have teams that utilize information from multiple assessments to identify gaps in student learning, determine the reason for those gaps, and plan targeted interventions.

▽ They will use ongoing assessments to monitor intervention progress.

▽ They will have teachers continually use data to determine where students are currently performing in relation to the target.

▽ Their process for reviewing student data to determine targeted interventions and make changes based on student progress will be systematic beginning at Tier 1 and well understood by all.

▽ They will make a common practice of using student data to proactively intervene before students fail.

As you read the following two scenarios about Chloe, consider:

∇ The beliefs of the school

∇ How the school uses assessment information

∇ The process at Tiers 1 and 2

∇ How the Tiers 1 and 2 processes impact Tier 3

∇ Whether the process is proactive and preventative or reactive in nature

---

Team 1: Traditions

Day 1: Chloe moves to her new school at the beginning of the year; she is in sixth grade. Chloe's parents ask the counselor if they can schedule a conference with the teachers so they can meet and discuss Chloe's background. The counselor explains that there will be a "meet the teacher" event, in which scheduled dates for parent conferences will be shared.

Day 3: Chloe and her parents attend the "meet the teacher" conference. All parents receive calendars, assignments, and the projects due during the first grading period. The teacher shares the school's behavior, attendance, and grading policy. During the informal question-and-answer session, Chloe's parents ask to schedule a conference. The teacher explains that parent conferences happen on scheduled dates, and those dates are on the calendar. She encourages Chloe's parents to send notes if they have questions before then.

End of week 2: Chloe brings home her assignments and grades. There are many zeros. Chloe explains that she is having difficulty reading the worksheets, and she doesn't understand her work.

Week 3: Chloe's parents send a note and call the school to schedule a conference with all her teachers in advance of the date given at registration. The reading teacher responds with a time to meet. At the meeting, she explains that she will represent the team. She reassures the parents that Chloe is adjusting to a new school, and that this is common because they have higher standards than many surrounding schools. Chloe's parents explained that at her old school, Chloe was included in a small group pulled for reading by the classroom teacher in addition to grade-level reading instruction, and that three times a week, she saw a reading specialist.

Week 6: Chloe receives all failing grades on her report card.

Week 7: Chloe's parents call the school and again request a conference with all her teachers. The reading teacher calls back Chloe's parents and explains that she is calling on behalf of the team. She states that Chloe's teachers are trying to help her. She shares that the team feels that Chloe needs to develop more independence and explains that Chloe is immature and lacks prerequisite reading skills.

continued →

Week 12: Chloe is still failing. The teacher team meets with the school counselor, and they agree to refer Chloe to a reading specialist for testing. Her teachers state that they have tried everything. The counselor contacts Chloe's parents, who agree to testing by the reading specialist.

Week 18: Six weeks after Chloe is referred for testing, the school counselor contacts Chloe's parents and tells them Chloe has been diagnosed with dyslexia. Chloe begins to attend a Tier 3 intervention for dyslexia. The reading teacher tells Chloe's parents that Chloe won't be in a small group for additional support in her class because she is in Tier 3.

Team 2: Whatever It Takes

Day 1: Chloe registers at her new school. During registration, Chloe and all other students are asked to complete a very short reading and mathematics screener that the sixth-grade teachers developed based on their essential standards. The campus counselor explains to students and parents that this screener is used by teachers to identify students who need additional support to master the campus reading and mathematics essential standards. During registration, Chloe's parents meet with the campus counselor and explain that Chloe has a history of struggling in reading.

Day 5: All students take a universal screener in reading and mathematics. This screener assesses broad reading and mathematics skills. The leadership team uses the information from the universal screener to identify students who have learning gaps requiring intensive Tier 3 interventions.

Day 6: Chloe's classroom reading teacher begins to work with her in a small group in addition to her reading instruction. The small group targets the skills needed to master the essential standard being addressed.

End of week 2: The reading teacher calls Chloe's parents and explains that a campus intervention team has met to review Chloe's progress. After looking at the two screeners and small-group progress notes, which include her error patterns, the team recommends that Chloe immediately begin to receive additional support in a pull-out reading group with a reading specialist. She will meet with the reading specialist three times a week during a thirty-minute period in which the whole school participates in some type of intervention or learning extension.

Week 3: Chloe's teacher team and the reading specialist meet and discuss Chloe's reading data and progress. The reading specialist explains that he has conducted informal assessments, and Chloe is displaying several of the characteristics of dyslexia. He recommends several classroom strategies and more diagnostic assessment by the dyslexia specialist. He also shares this information with intervention team members who agree to contact the dyslexia specialist. The reading teacher volunteers to contact Chloe's parents regarding the additional assessment. Chloe's parents are appreciative and agree.

Week 4: After the dyslexia specialist completes her assessment, she meets with the intervention team. Team members agree that based on the data reviewed, Chloe will spend her thirty-minute intervention time with the dyslexia specialist a minimum of four days per week and continue in small groups in her classroom. Her classroom teacher will use the recommended strategies. The classroom teacher and dyslexia specialist will discuss her progress every two weeks. The campus intervention team will review Chloe's progress in interventions as well as essential standards every four weeks. All information is shared with Chloe's parents.

Week 6: Chloe's parents receive her grades and are pleased to see Chloe's improvement. Her teachers meet and review all the data and determine that she is making progress. They agree that they will continue to assess Chloe every three weeks with her peers on common assessments to determine progress on essential standards, and they will monitor her reading progress weekly. The intervention team will continue to monitor her progress to ensure that her intervention is indeed working. The dyslexia specialist will consult with her teacher team weekly.

Team Traditions is an example of a team with a regimented process that does not reflect a sense of urgency or flexibility in addressing the unique needs of individual students. These kinds of teams will say, "This is what we have always done." Unfortunately, this results in a situation that causes continued student failure.

Team Whatever It Takes is an example of a team with a solution-oriented process. Its goal is to be timely, targeted, and focused on student success. The teacher team and intervention team used the information from the screenings to target Chloe's needs and provide timely intervention. They worked collaboratively, and it is apparent that a well-understood process for screening, reviewing data, and determining student needs is in place.

Identifying and Targeting Needs at Tier 3

The most critical role of the leadership team is to establish a process for timely and targeted identification of students needing intensive support. Most students needing intensive interventions attend the same campus or district as they did the previous year. Schools can easily schedule these students to begin receiving support on the first day of school. We find many schools that hold end-of-year case management meetings for students with the greatest challenges. This allows students to have a seamless system of support from one campus to the next.

Campuses should be equally prepared for new enrollees. Students who are new to a campus should not have to wait for weeks or months for the team to identify them as needing support. Utilizing universal screeners, combined with other informal and diagnostic assessments, gives the intervention team the information necessary to quickly determine needs for Tier 3 intervention. Students do not have time to wait for a process that requires volumes of documentation and weeks or months before receiving needed interventions.

The leadership and intervention teams must carefully design the process for determining targeted needs, similar to triage in the medical field. If a patient comes to the emergency room with symptoms of a critical illness, the hospital immediately puts together a team who reviews all available information and responds with the exact prescription or procedure the patient needs. Campuses should respond in the same manner with new students. They should establish a process to quickly review all available student information, determine if more diagnostic assessment is needed, and formulate a targeted plan of action.

> "The odds of hitting your target go up dramatically when you aim at it."
> —Mal Pancoast

To be most effective, the intervention team should consist of team members with varied expertise and may include some of the same members as the leadership team. Very few schools have staff members with licensure in all the areas in which students present challenges and need in Tier 3. However, most schools have people within their reach that they can utilize, even if it's not an exact match for the need. For example, if a school does not have a licensed behavior specialist but instead has a teacher who is particularly good in dealing with challenging behaviors, that teacher may be able to provide great insight and offer suggestions for strategies to teach essential behavior skills to students needing support in this area.

The leadership team should ensure that a process is in place to provide information to the intervention team. This information may include formal and informal student assessments, as well as anecdotal records such as error patterns, behavior logs, teacher observations, and small-group progress notes. Providing all information related to academics, behavior, and health and home is helpful to the intervention team in determining the cause of students' difficulties.

In order for the intervention team to process the information provided, they should establish a problem-solving and action-planning process. The process shown in figure 5.1 provides an effective and efficient manner for the team to determine targeted interventions.

White Oak Primary is a model PLC campus (www.allthingsplc.com) located in White Oak, Texas. The following example of that campus's system to determine new students' needs is an illustration of a comprehensive, yet practical approach that any school can replicate. White Oak Primary is a small campus with limited staff, but the staff's collective commitment to the success of every student drives them to maximize their resources to meet the needs of all students (AllThingsPLC, n.d.b).

RTI Problem-Solving Process

Date: _____ Student name: _____	Team members:
Five minutes	**What is the problem? Why is it happening?**
	• What is the specific concern? • What do we think is causing the problem?
Ten minutes	**Brainstorm Solutions**
	• What have we already tried? • What strategies have worked well? • What will we do next?
Five minutes	**Determine Interventions**
	• What intervention will we try and for how long?
Five minutes	**Follow Up and Monitor Progress**
	• How will we monitor progress? **Follow-up date:** **Time:**

Figure 5.1: Intervention team problem-solving process.

*Visit **go.SolutionTree.com/RTIatWork** for a free reproducible version of this figure.*

At this small campus, some leadership team members also serve on the intervention team. They take responsibility for the duties of each team. The principal assumes the responsibilities of coordination and resource management that the leadership team holds.

Because White Oak Primary has a process for using convergent assessment to identify specific skill gaps early in the school year, staff are able to quickly determine students' needs and begin targeted interventions. Following is an overview of the process they used with a student new to their school—Sasha (her name has been changed to protect her privacy).

Sasha's Story

Sasha is a six-year-old first grader. This is her first year in the school district. She attended kindergarten in her prior district, which is in another state. Due to stress, violence, and neglect, the mother and children relocated to a family crisis center that provides shelter and crisis support such as counseling in our district. Initially, Sasha was often tired and hungry. Although she was safe and being cared for, she had difficulty sleeping due to insecurity. She experienced trauma and has very poor coping skills when corrected or when facing consequences for behavior. She displayed frequent outbursts of crying and refusing to try to attempt work. Sasha worked for praise, positive reinforcement, and personal interaction on most days. She read to the principal, got a reward from the assistant principal, came to the office to see the secretary, and was a very good classroom helper. They knew very quickly that she had issues with her speech and that her academic skills were not on level.

Reading

White Oak Primary administers a universal screener in reading to all students three times per year. It administers the beginning-of-year screener the first week of school. The campus uses the information from this screener to identify students who warrant additional observation and assessment. A typical first-time first-grade student in this school scores at level 6 (text level) with average fluency on the reading universal screener. Sasha scored level 3 with low fluency. Due to having a low text level combined with poor speech and limited sound and word knowledge, the school determined that more assessment was needed.

A reading teacher conducted an individual reading assessment to gain additional information. This assessment provided the school with the knowledge that Sasha's academic areas of weakness were:

- Word recognition, in which she scored a 0 in comparison to an average score of 20 for her grade-level peers

- Hearing and recording sounds, in which she had difficulty in writing any sounds she heard after the first letter of a word

Mathematics

In mathematics, Sasha's universal screening results (administered the first week of school) indicated that she could count to twenty but did not have the concept of numbers. She could not join or separate numbers. She had poor number sense. The typical first-time first grader has a solid foundation and concepts of 1–20. He or she has number sense, understands place value, and can join and separate the numbers with ease.

Speech and Behavior

In Sasha's case, speech and behavior were also of great concern. When she enrolled, her teacher saw that speech was an obvious issue. She was assessed for speech therapy in her prior district but had never received services. The speech therapist conducted updated speech assessments. In order to determine patterns of behavior, all Sasha's teachers recorded and maintained anecdotal notes regarding Sasha's behavior. The notes included the times of day, types of outbursts, reinforcements that worked, and those that did not.

The intervention team meets and reviews the reading and mathematics universal screening results on all students at the beginning of the second week of school.

However, for Sasha, in addition to universal screeners and reading, mathematics, and speech assessment data, Sasha's teachers had concerns regarding her social and behavioral skills. The intervention team considered all available formal and informal information.

The anecdotal notes that teachers made during Sasha's assessment are indicative of the type of valuable information gained from informal diagnostic assessments. These observations provide great insights that allow teachers to determine students' specific needs.

Sasha's teacher made the following notes about her reading skills and behaviors.

- She can read simple patterned books with fluency.
- She gains meaning from the text.
- She ignores errors and neglects visual information.
- She seems to hear beginning sounds first and then strings together the letters to make a word.
- She does not have control of her writing. Some letters only resemble letters.

The strengths noted, such as *hears beginning sounds*, as well as areas of concern, such as *strings together letters to make a word*, provide critical information needed for teachers to know the student's current proficiency level and next steps to take.

The teacher's behavior log provided the information necessary to determine a pattern of behaviors that provided the team with information to determine strategies as well as the student's need for small-group social skills instruction to deal with anger management.

continued →

Sasha received the following interventions during the second week of school.

- Speech therapy three times per week

- Counseling, scheduled in small groups three times per week

- Tier 3 individualized reading four to five days per week

- Tier 2 mathematics, small group for mathematics (number sense) every day for thirty minutes

Students enter first grade with a wide range of skills. In most cases, students respond to grade-level instruction and do not need intervention. However, by using convergent assessment, teachers quickly recognized that Sasha had multiple issues warranting further assessment. They understood that they had to learn the reasons behind her learning gaps in order to meet her needs.

Sasha's case is an example of the power of convergent assessment. Finding and using the information enable teams to quickly intervene and be prescriptive in determining targeted interventions. Reviewing multiple types of assessments, as well as anecdotal information, provides the information needed to pinpoint exactly where a student is related to grade-level standards and why he or she is having difficulty.

Buffum et al. (2018) state:

> While these students often need intensive interventions in the same foundational skills, they do not all struggle for the same reasons. Some students could be below grade level in reading because they can't decode text, while others have decoding skills but poor fluency and comprehension. So targeting each student's specific needs is critical to responding effectively. (p. 260)

The process for using convergent assessment does not have to be complicated or difficult. There is no need for teachers to lose instructional days by having a strict process with predetermined forms and waiting periods for a student to prove that he or she needs help. They can quickly determine this by using the formal and informal assessment information that is readily accessible. If a school is committed to high levels of achievement for *all*, it will not wait for gaps in learning to increase while a student continues to fail. Closing gaps in learning requires that schools work with a sense of urgency to determine timely and targeted interventions.

Establishing Learning Progressions

Mastering the universal or foundational skills required to be successful meeting grade-level academic and behavior standards is the goal at Tier 3. In order to do this, it is necessary to align goals or intervention learning targets to grade-level essential standards. Teachers do this by outlining the progression of essential skills or learning progressions that lead to mastery of each standard. A *learning progression* can be thought of as stepping stones that students follow on the pathway toward mastery of a grade-level standard. A student may begin this path below grade level, but by taking one step at a time or mastering one subskill at a time, he or she moves toward grade-level success.

A vertically-aligned continuum or progression of skills provides the teacher a clear path from the student's current level of performance (where we are now) to grade-level mastery (where we are going). Mastery of essential standards is the goal and by identifying critical subskills of the standard, teachers can set precise targets that lead to mastery. All schools have the challenge of meeting the needs of students with significant learning gaps. A clear progression of skills aligned to essential standards provides teachers the needed direction for student goal setting.

Vertically-aligned learning progressions provide teachers at all tiers of instruction an order of commonly agreed-on essential skills that lead to mastery of grade-level standards. Teachers can use learning progressions for teaching, assessing, and intervening.

In *Learning Progressions: Supporting Instruction and Formative Assessment*, Margaret Heritage (2008) describes the importance of learning progressions:

> Explicit learning progressions can provide the clarity that teachers need. By describing a pathway of learning they can assist teachers to plan instruction. Formative assessment can be tied to learning goals and the evidence elicited can determine students' understanding and skill at a given point. When teachers understand the continuum of learning in a domain and have information about current status relative to learning goals (rather than to the activity they have designed to help students meet the goal), they are better able to make decisions about what the next steps in learning should be. (p. 2)

Learning progressions can help teachers determine learning targets, formatively assess students' current level of performance, and monitor student progress toward the final goal of grade-level mastery. The Pearson blog post "How Learning Progressions Can Help With Both Monitoring Progress and Progress Monitoring" states that "the key to monitoring progress is understanding what students know and don't know at any given time. Learning progressions use research on how students learn to clearly define the learning pathway and conceptual milestones along that pathway" (Kobrin, 2016).

Collaborative teams should work together to determine learning progressions related to essential grade-level standards. Essential standards and skills are essential for all learners, so teams should agree on the continuum of learning leading to mastery of the standard. Learning progressions should not be developed in a vacuum by special education or intervention teachers working in isolation.

Figure 5.2 offers a visual reminder that learning progressions are comprised of the essential subskills that lead to grade-level mastery of essential standards.

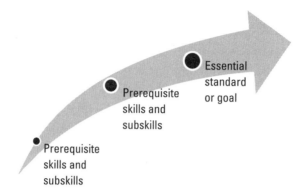

Figure 5.2: Progression of essential subskills leading to mastery of essential standard.

Learning progressions that have been vertically aligned from grade to grade are essential for teacher teams who work with students that have large gaps in learning. They provide these teams with a common pathway for setting goals and learning targets, and determining student progress.

Figure 5.3 shows an example of a vertically aligned learning progression and how a team might use it to determine and monitor progress on a targeted goal for an individual student. It's important that teams use progressions for identified essential standards in order to align intervention goals with the skills needed to master grade-level standards.

It should be noted that just as teams may have varying opinions of what the essential learning is when they unpack standards, there is no exact or one right learning progression. Teachers must use their experience and knowledge of instruction to develop what they believe is a logical progression of skills. Individual learners take different amounts of time, follow their own path, and need different types of instruction in skill mastery. Rather than seeing learning progressions as a rigid sequence, teachers should view them as stepping stones they can use to guide instruction and assessment. Learning progressions are a logical path for teachers to follow when determining goals and assessing progress for students with large gaps between current performance and grade-level standards. The key benefit to using a vertically aligned learning progression is that teachers have commonly agreed-on skills aligned to essential standards they can use to align core instruction and interventions.

	Grade 3 Standard: W.3.1
	Write opinion pieces on topics or texts, supporting a point of view with reasons.
	Grade 2 Standard: W.2.1
	Write opinion pieces in which they introduce the topic or book they are writing about, state an opinion, supply reasons that support the opinion, use linking words (e.g., *because, and, also*) to connect opinion and reasons, and provide a concluding statement or section.
	Grade 1 Standard: W.1.1
	Write opinion pieces in which they introduce the topic or name the book they are writing about, state an opinion, supply a reason for the opinion, and provide some sense of closure.

Student: Dominique

Current Grade: 3

Current Goal: Grade 1—Organize writing with beginning, middle, and end.

Legend:

✓ Mastered Skill:

→ Current Goal:

• Future Goal:

Grade 1	✓ State an opinion or preference about a book or topic provided.
	✓ Differentiate between important and unimportant reasons.
	✓ Identify and demonstrate effective introductions (one that includes the writer's opinion and hook).
	→ Organize writing with a logical beginning, middle, and end.
Grade 2	• Use simple transition or linking words that show order (for example, *first, next, finally*) or connect reasons.
	• Provide a concluding statement or section.
Grade 3	• Identify an issue in a topic or text.
	• Agree or disagree with the issue.
	• Choose an opening technique.
	• Create an introduction that hooks the reader using an opening technique.
	• Create a list of reasons that support the opinion.
	• Determine the best way to organize reasons that support the opinion.
	• Introduce the topic or text they are writing about, state an opinion, and create an organizational structure that lists reasons.

Source for standards: Delaware Department of Education, 2019.

Figure 5.3: Sample learning progression used for individual student goal setting.

Ideally, teacher teams would use a process such as the one in figure 5.4 (page 104) for determining goals for individual students.

Step 1	**Where are we headed?**
	The student's grade-level essential standard and corresponding vertically aligned learning progression
Step 2	**Where are we now?**
	The student's current level of performance on the learning progression
Step 3	**How will we close the gap?**
	The step-by-step progression of skills required for the student to advance from his or her current level of proficiency (where he or she is now) to grade-level mastery (where he or she is headed)

Figure 5.4: Determining goals for individual students.

*Visit **go.SolutionTree.com/RTIatWork** for a free reproducible version of this figure.*

This learning sequence allows teachers and interventionists to target instruction and monitor progress toward mastery of grade-level essential standards. As students progress in incremental steps toward mastery, teachers can see where misunderstandings occur and immediately provide corrective feedback.

Monitoring Student Progress

After collaborative teacher teams, including grade-level teachers and interventionists, identify students' needs and determine the targeted interventions necessary for students to achieve their goals, it is critical that they continue to use multiple points of data to monitor progress. Teams might use questions, such as the following, from the webinar *What Is Progress Monitoring?* by the National Center on Response to Intervention (n.d.; rti4success.org) as they discuss student progress.

1. Are students making progress at an acceptable rate? Is the progress occurring at a rate sufficient to close the gap between the student's progress and that of his or her peers?

2. Are students meeting short-term (intervention) goals, which will help them reach their long-term goals?

3. Does the intervention need to be adjusted (time and intensity) or changed (goals, strategies, or intervention)?

We can't overemphasize the importance of critical questions, such as those focused on progress monitoring at Tier 3. We must continually ask ourselves:

▽ "Where is the student currently performing in relation to the learning target or goal for his or her intervention?"

▽ "Where is the student's progress in relation to closing the gap with grade-level essential standards and skills?"

Intervention goal mastery can easily be assessed with quick oral or written checks for understanding that are appropriate for the content or skill being assessed. Teachers can determine progress on closing the gap in meeting grade-level standards by documenting progress on a learning progression or other type of comparison to grade-level achievement, such as assessing reading levels in comparison to grade-level peers and common assessments.

Determining mastery of isolated targets demonstrates whether the intervention or instruction is successful. However, if you do not measure progress against grade-level standards, you run the risk of thinking the student is doing better because he or she is making progress on an isolated skill, yet the student may not be closing gaps in grade-level mastery. Ascertaining if interventions are yielding progress on gaining the skills required for mastery of grade-level essential standards is the key element of progress monitoring.

In an interview published by Doing What Works ("Functions of Progress Monitoring"), Anne Foegen (2009) states:

> Progress monitoring is an important tool for teachers. We all know that there is no perfect intervention program or instructional strategy, and so progress monitoring gives teachers a way to know which students their instruction is working for and which students are not benefiting from that instruction. So by using this objective, efficient means of gathering data, teachers can adjust their instruction to best meet the needs of their students. (p. 3)

The primary purpose of all assessment is to inform the teacher about the student's current learning and misunderstandings as well as provide the information necessary to adjust instruction.

Tier 3 progress monitoring should include the following.

▽ Interventionists should monitor progress on learning targets addressed in Tier 3 interventions weekly.

▽ Teachers should monitor progress in grade-level curriculum for students in Tier 3 at the same frequency and with the same type of assessments as all other students. For example, we recommend that schools monitor progress on essential standards at least every three weeks with common formative assessments. Essential standards are essential for all students, so those students receiving Tier 3 interventions should have essential standards taught and assessed with their peers.

Schools construct a very tight safety net for students by assessing, reviewing, and acting on grade-level progress at three-week intervals and intervention progress at one-week intervals.

Consider how the school measured Sasha's progress in reading (see page 98). Sasha's intervention teacher measured Sasha's reading progress weekly. Her classroom teacher assessed her with the informal reading assessments and common assessments used with all students. Sasha's classroom teacher and intervention teacher met briefly each week to discuss her progress in intervention as well as her classroom performance.

Because the staff at Sasha's school worked collaboratively, established timely and targeted interventions at all tiers of instruction, and used ongoing assessments to continually monitor her progress, Sasha was meeting the minimum expectations for her grade level by the eleventh week of school. Figure 5.5 shows Sasha's progress in relation to the reading-level expectation for her grade.

All teachers and teams should have a plan in place to monitor student progress.

Tier 3 Teachers

The following questions will assist teachers at Tier 3 in thinking through their individual assessment and progress-monitoring plan.

1. **How will you monitor the learning target for the intervention?** How will you monitor the progress of each student on short-term goals? Will you use a skills-based assessment or a curriculum-based assessment? How will you organize instruction so you can build in time for weekly monitoring? Many teachers find that creating and utilizing a skills-based rubric or checklist as they work with students each week is an efficient way to monitor progress.

2. **How will you monitor progress toward grade-level curricula?** If the learning target is below grade level, what is the learning progression that will lead to grade-level mastery? Is this the same progression of skills used in general education? When will you meet with the general education teacher to see if intervention progress is transferring to the classroom?

3. **What is the process for determining formative assessments aligned to instruction?** Do you use formative assessment strategies to elicit data about a student's growth toward mastery of the learning target? Do you work with the grade-level teams to determine mastery levels for targeted skills?

4. **What is your system for tracking progress for each student?** How will you maintain classroom assessment information so you can monitor progress? Will you use portfolios? Will you maintain data electronically? Examples of tools you can use include tally sheets, data binders, spreadsheets, Google Forms, and so on.

Book Level	Week 1 9/16	Week 2 9/23	Week 3 9/30	Week 4 10/7	Week 5 10/14	Week 6 10/21	Week 7 10/28	Week 8 11/4	Week 9 11/11	Week 10 11/18	Week 11 12/2	Week 12 12/9	Week 13 12/16
Level 11												X	X
Level 10											X ★		
Level 9									X	X			
Level 8								X					
Level 7						X	X						
Level 6					X								
Level 5				X									
Level 4			X										
Level 3		X											
Level 2	X												

Level 10: Grade-Level Mid-Year Target

Figure 5.5: Sasha's progress in reading.

5. **How will you involve students in setting goals and tracking their own progress?** How and when will you provide feedback to students? Will students track their own progress? Will they be able to answer the questions, "Where am I going?" and "Where am I now?" Will they have a folder with bar graphs to chart progress, data binders, or journals to document their progress and questions?

6. **How and when will you determine which students to monitor for the day and week?** How will you ensure that you monitor progress and adjust instruction as needed for each student? Do you have a system for documenting the progress of each student at least one time per week?

7. **Do you have a simple way to collect data?** Will you use an electronic spreadsheet or other process that is easy to use and retrieve? What teachers or teams could you meet with to determine a common way to track data so you can collaborate?

8. **How will you collaborate and use data to make instructional decisions?** Do you have scheduled team meetings where you can share student data with your peers and get input about student progress and best practices? If you are the only teacher who intervenes with your grade or subject, consider the following options.

   ▸ Meet with Tier 1 teachers to gain insight on alignment with grade-level curriculum and how you might change or enhance instruction. Do they have ideas for strategies or academic vocabulary you should use?

   ▸ Meet with other interventionists. How can they help you increase student progress? A speech therapist may have great strategies for you to incorporate in reading and language, and a counselor may have ideas to assist with teaching social skills or working with families.

9. **How and when will you review formative student data and determine your next steps to ensure continual progress for each student?** How will you determine what is working and what is not? Will you make anecdotal notes as you work with students to document their progress and strategies that were successful? Will you consider student progress and successful strategies as you plan instruction each week?

Intervention Teams

Intervention teams can use the following questions to evaluate the assessment system for possible improvements.

1. **How do you communicate information between campuses and grades?** Based on the previous year's data, do you know which students may need to receive Tier 2 and Tier 3 interventions on the first day of school and the skills requiring intervention? Do you have information from prior grades or campuses within your district that tells you what interventions students were receiving and their current performance?

2. **How soon are universal screeners administered at the beginning of the year?** Do you have a universal screener that allows you to identify potential gaps in learning early in the school year (within the first week)? How do you use this assessment to help determine students' needs?

3. **What is your process for ensuring you are timely and targeted?** Do universal screeners and other available assessments provide the information you need to determine students' specific learning needs and provide timely intervention?

4. **What is your process for monitoring progress on essential standards?** Do you have a system for monitoring the progress of *all* students approximately every three weeks in their current curriculum with common formative assessments so interventions are timely and targeted?

5. **What is your process for monitoring the progress of students receiving intensive interventions?** Do you have a system for frequently monitoring the progress of individual students receiving Tier 3 interventions on their intervention goals as well as grade-level curricula?

6. **What is your process for guaranteeing certain access?** How and when do intervention teams review data, what data do they review, and how do they use the information to determine targeted interventions? How will you use this information to ensure you prioritize interventions for students with the greatest need?

Leadership Teams

The following questions can assist the leadership team in reviewing their roles, responsibilities, and the overall assessment process.

1. **Has the leadership team communicated and gained understanding with all staff regarding how data will be used and why?** Do all teacher teams and intervention teams understand the types of data they should review and know the timelines and process for intervention decisions?

2. **Has the leadership team ensured collaboration time exists for Tier 3 teachers and classroom teachers?** Is there a process in place for Tier 3 teachers and classroom teachers to regularly collaborate about student progress?

3. **Has the leadership team provided the structure (time) and support (training) for teacher teams to develop learning progressions for essential standards?** Have teacher teams worked to develop learning progressions for essential standards? Are interventionists and special education teachers included in this process?

4. **What is the process for progress monitoring at Tier 3?** Does the intervention team monitor progress for students receiving Tier 3 interventions in the same manner as all other students? Is there a schedule for meetings that ensures that the intervention team reviews student progress frequently?

5. **Has the leadership team worked with teacher teams and intervention teams to ensure that necessary protocols are in place?** Do all data teams have protocols, such as agendas, questions, and action plans, to support their work?

Revising and Extending Support at Tier 3

Teacher teams and intervention teams should rely on ongoing formative assessment to identify if students are progressing, what is working, and what is not working, and use that information to change instructional strategies or interventions as needed.

It is the responsibility of the leadership team to ensure that teacher teams have a comprehensive assessment process and receive the results of benchmarks and common formative assessments as soon as possible.

Teacher teams must actively review formative data for the purpose of discussing what is working and what is not, determining timely and targeted interventions, and extending learning opportunities for students who have mastered the content. The value of these teams is not restricted to Tiers 1 and 2. Teachers and interventionists supporting students at Tier 3 should be part of collaborative data review for the same reasons, but with a greater level of urgency than any other teacher. Unfortunately, teachers providing Tier 3 interventions often work and determine student progress in isolation.

Teachers at Tier 3 who are not part of a collaborative teacher team should identify peers who can best serve the role of partnering to review data, share best practices, and determine if students are making progress toward grade-level standards. The leadership team should ensure that all teachers serving students at Tier 3 have some-one who meets with them for this purpose. If necessary, the leadership team may determine leadership or intervention team members to serve in this critical role for the learners and teachers who need the most intense level of support.

In supporting students at Tier 3, we must not forget the unique and significant role of special education teachers. The Council for Exceptional Children (2008) explains its position on RTI in the paper "The Unique Role of Special Education and Special Educators":

> [RTI] must be viewed as a schoolwide initiative, with special education as an explicit part of the framework, spanning both general and special education in collaboration with families. The RTI process represents an inclusive partnership between all school personnel and families to iden-tify and address the academic and behavioral needs of learners begin-ning as early as the preschool years. (p. 1)

The council continues by explaining its position on RTI and team collaboration: "Team collaboration occurs in each tier and may involve educators, related service providers, administrators, and families. These new and expanded roles in team col-laboration will ensure that the needs of all learners are met" (Council for Exceptional Children, 2008, p. 2).

This manner of working is a significant shift in the traditional model of special education. Special educators possess tremendous expertise that is valuable across the school system. In order to meet the needs of all learners, we have to find ways to break down the barriers that sometimes exist between general education and special education so *all* educators are truly responsible for *all* students. Buffum et al. (2018) describe this as an "all hands on deck" philosophy. All staff members, including spe-cial educators, have specific duties related to their jobs that require a prioritization of time. However, the expertise of special educators in assessment and problem solving is essential to identifying and determining the targeted needs of students receiving intense support at Tier 3. We must work collaboratively and find a way to accom-plish this goal. Special educators should not be forgotten or considered as a separate program or separate part of the school. Their contributions are integral to the success of all students.

Using Tools to Support Your Work

The following examples and tools are provided to support the leadership team and teacher teams in taking action on formative data.

Data Team Template

Figure 5.6 is an example of an action plan completed by a grade-level team after a common assessment data review. The team determined targeted instructional responses by the level of proficiency. This example shows an action plan for students at varying levels of proficiency, including a student far below grade level yet still working toward mastery of grade-level standards.

Date:				
Teacher Name and Grade Level:		Subject and Unit, Section, and Topic:		
Grade 6 ELA Team		Standard: W.6.1.B Support claim(s) with clear reasons and relevant evidence, using credible sources and demonstrating an understanding of the topic or text.		
Assessment and Criterion for Proficiency (for example, 80 percent of questions correct—3 or higher in all areas)				
Unit Learning Targets: • I can organize and explain my ideas in writing. • I can organize a paragraph. • I can make a claim and use credible evidence to support it. • I can use correct spelling, punctuation, and grammar. • I can demonstrate that I understand a topic. *Students must score a 2 or 3 to demonstrate mastery.				
Collect and Chart Data				
Far Below	Below	Near Proficient	Proficient	Above
1	1	9	16	14
Analyze Students' Strengths and Obstacles (Error Patterns, Misconceptions)				
Strengths		Obstacles		
Grammar and punctuation strong across all groups		Students have difficulty understanding or differentiating between persuasive writing and making an argument with an evidence-based claim.		
Learning target identified for intervention based on the review of student data from the common assessment				
Target: I can make a claim and use credible evidence to support it.				
Action Plan and Timeline: What specific strategies will our team try, and what is the timeline?				

Far Below	Below	Near Proficient	Proficient	Above
Day 1 of intervention: Students watch video or read book such as *Otto Runs for President* by Rosemary Wells. They write, draw, or voice record one claim, one reason, and one piece of evidence to make an evidence-based claim.	Day 1 of intervention: Students use persuasion map or graphic organizer that provides sentence stems for the claim, reason, and evidence.	Day 1 of intervention: Using a real-life situation, students work in groups and provide an argument (claims, reasons, evidence) for their position.	Day 1 of intervention: Provide students with a topic with two stances— argument and persuasion. Students identify the stance and for each stance provided, students explain if it is persuasive writing or argumentative and justify their decision why.	Day 1 of intervention: Use text and have students read and identify a persuasive argument as well as an argument providing the claim, reason, and evidence. Students compare the two pieces of text they identify and outline their rationale for identifying one as persuasive and one as argumentative.
Reassessment Plan: How and when will we reassess to monitor progress? The progress of each student will be monitored on day 1 and any misconceptions corrected before moving to day 2. Day 1 and day 2 interventions may not be back to back.				
Far Below	Below	Near Proficient	Proficient	Above
Day 2 of intervention: Students listen to text or watch video and produce a graphic representation of the claim, reason, and evidence—by drawing, doodling, or using computer graphics, and then present their products orally.	Day 2 of intervention: Students use a persuasion map organizer without sentence stems.	Day 2 of intervention: Students write one to three paragraphs (topic provided) with argument, and include claim, reason, and evidence.	Day 2 of intervention: Students write three to five paragraphs and make an evidence-based claim using all criteria for an argument.	Day 2 of intervention: Students receive a text selection that includes the claim, reason, and evidence for an argument-based claim. They read this information and then present it orally to their class or working group as a persuasive claim.

Source for standard: National Governors Association Center for Best Practices & Council of Chief State School Officers [NGA & CCSSO], 2010.

Figure 5.6: Data team template example.

Visit **go.SolutionTree.com/RTIatWork** *for a free reproducible version of this figure.*

Tier 3 Team Data Analysis

The leadership and intervention teams can use the tool in figure 5.7 when they are reviewing and setting goals for improving their data review process.

All members of the team will analyze data for the purpose of the following.

▽ Determining if students are mastering individual targets

▽ Determining if students are closing the learning gaps in achieving grade-level standards at an acceptable rate

Review the follow criteria to determine steps to improve your process for reviewing Tier 3 data. Indicate the date the leadership and intervention teams reviewed this process. If the process is in place, enter the date under the *yes* column. If not, enter the date under the *no* column, and create an action plan for improvement.						
Enter Date:	**Yes**			**No**		
	Month	**Date**	**Year**	**Month**	**Date**	**Year**
The leadership team has created a process for teacher teams to collect and share common assessment data with the intervention team.						
The intervention team has multiple types of data to review: universal screeners, formative data, progress monitoring data, anecdotal notes, and so on.						
The intervention team has a proactive problem-solving process and protocols that can be used to formulate action plans for academics and behavior.						
A process is in place for intervention teachers to monitor the progress of students in Tier 3 interventions weekly.						
Data review includes identifying and documenting successful practices and instructional strategies.						
The intervention team regularly reviews the progress of students receiving Tier 3 interventions and changes interventions based on student data and student need.						
Tier 3 teachers and classroom teachers regularly discuss progress and review instruction based on data.						
Action Steps:						

Figure 5.7: Tier 3 team data analysis considerations.

*Visit **go.SolutionTree.com/RTIatWork** for a free reproducible version of this figure.*

Tier 3 Data Chat and Reflective Review Process

The data chat provides reflective questions that teams of teachers or individual teachers use when considering student data.

▽ **Teams:** Collaboration between the Tier 3 intervention teachers, classroom teachers, and other interventionists should include the following:

   ▸ Student progress on intervention goals

   ▸ Student progress on closing the gap in mastery of grade-level standards

   ▸ Instructional changes, new strategies, and action plans for their team and time to reassess

   ▸ Professional development on any subject needed

▽ **Individual teachers:** As each teacher reviews student assessments, they should analyze the most recent group and individual student data, use reflective questions, and determine progress. A reflective process for individual teachers should include:

   ▸ Seeking a team member to brainstorm

   ▸ Analyzing data to determine if they are meeting goals and if student learning gaps are closing at an acceptable rate

   ▸ Considering changes to instruction, initiating new strategies, and creating an action plan

   ▸ Determining any support needed

   ▸ Determining a time for reassessment

The following questions provide a systematic approach for examining any type of assessment performance. You should use any information attained from student data to establish action plans.

1. Did my students meet mastery in the skills assessed?

2. What are the specific skills my students were not successful with?

3. What does analysis of the assessment questions and student answers tell me?

4. Am I aligning my instruction to the rigor of the standard?

5. Have I collaborated with grade-level peers as well as other interventionists?

6. Do I need to use new strategies? Have I asked peers to give me their input?

7. Am I effectively progress monitoring each of my students using formative assessments?

8. Did I utilize preassessment and preteaching?

9. Do I require my students to track and take ownership of their data? How am I doing this, and did I actively assist my students in setting academic goals?

10. What will I do to improve my pedagogy to receive the desired outcome in student achievement?

11. Am I collaborating effectively with my colleagues to impact student achievement?

12. Have I developed an action plan with specific strategies (targeted to students' needs) and timelines for reassessment?

Conclusion

This work can be done and must be done. A convergent assessment process provides the information that we need to serve every child in a timely and targeted manner. We are only limited by our commitment, determination, and creativity in achieving the goal of high levels of learning for every student.

> "A very little key will open a very heavy door."
> —Charles Dickens

In closing, we urge all teams to move forward in using an ongoing assessment process in determining targeted interventions in academics and behavior. In the next two chapters, we focus on teaching essential behavior and academic skills at Tier 3. Using assessments to determine the *why* behind student challenges is essential to determining the targeted intervention necessary for students to close their significant learning gaps.

Chapter 5 Action Steps

With your team, engage in the following action steps to review and implement the learning from this chapter.

1. Teacher teams should remember that the first critical question of a PLC is "What do students need to know and be able to do?" (DuFour et al., 2016, p. 251). In other words, the microscopic detail included in this chapter cannot and should not be applied to every

standard in the curriculum—not to everything that a teacher team is going to teach. You should utilize this process for standards that teams have prioritized as essential for all students to learn.

2. Keep in mind that you should apply the process outlined in Sample Learning Progression Used for Individual Student Goal Setting (see figure 5.3, page 103) only to standards prioritized by teacher teams as essential. Have each teacher team complete this form for *one* student and *one* standard. Next, teams should use the form to provide additional time and support for the one student selected. Teacher teams should then reflect on what worked, what didn't work, and how the process could be improved moving forward.

3. Teacher teams should not undertake the identification and development of learning progressions for all grade-level essential standards simultaneously. Instead, working through them one at a time allows for more students to receive help more quickly.

Behavior Supports at Tier 3

|magine this scenario: a teacher has one student in her class who is absorbing most of her time and attention. In spite of her best efforts, the student's behavior continues to escalate. He is easily agitated, can't tolerate working in a group, and periodically loses control, tearing up papers and screaming. The teacher has no idea what to do next and is at her wits' end because of the chaos in her classroom.

Unfortunately, this scenario is not hard to imagine. Most educators have seen or experienced similar situations with students who need to be taught the essential academic and social behaviors necessary to be successful in school. However, a teacher cannot do this alone. It is a team effort.

In this chapter, we will consider the importance of teaching essential academic and social behaviors at Tiers 1 and 2, the role of teams, and proven strategies that support students needing intensive behavior intervention at Tier 3.

We must teach and intervene with behavior in the same manner as we do essential academic skills. We do this by providing strong Tier 1 instruction and support or preventions, Tier 2 interventions, and Tier 3 remediation. A comprehensive instructional program for behavior beginning at Tier 1 increases student success and reduces the number of students needing intense intervention. However, despite our best efforts, some students require this level of support.

Many students needing intense behavior interventions have complex issues that require the coordinated work of the schoolwide leadership and behavior intervention teams. Due to the unique skills needed to address behavior, some schools invite members of the faculty who are talented in this area to join the intervention team, and others create a unique team for behavior that fulfills the same role as the intervention team. These teams are often referred to as *behavior intervention teams*. In this chapter, we use the terms *intervention team* and *behavior intervention team* interchangeably. It is through collaboration, problem solving, and a commitment to finding the targeted intervention needed by individual students that we create safe and respectful campuses in which all learners achieve at high levels.

The Foundation at Tiers 1 and 2

Student achievement is directly related to the quality of Tier 1 instruction. Behavior is no different. Clearly identified behaviors that are explicitly taught at Tier 1 to students with targeted interventions for those who need them at Tier 2 lay the foundation for intensive intervention or remediation at Tier 3. Positive behavior intervention and support (PBIS) is a schoolwide framework for implementing the overall process of RTI at Work in the area of behavior. PBIS provides the system that supports teaching and responding to behavior beginning at Tier 1.

> "The behavior you're seeing is the behavior you've designed for (whether intentional or not)."
>
> —Joshua Porter

Buffum and Mattos (2015) explain the importance of Tier 1 schoolwide PBIS as follows:

> The most important role we have in any school is to ensure a safe environment. Well-implemented schoolwide PBIS does this. However, schools should take caution when trying to partially implement this type of system without all necessary levels of instruction and support at all tiers of the behavioral pyramid. Just as an academic pyramid of interventions will not be successful without strong Tier 1 instruction, implementing a behavior model at only Tier 3 will not either. Without a strong Tier 1 program, too many students will be referred for intervention, and those receiving Tiers 2 and 3 interventions will not be able to have services reduced and be successful at Tier 1. (p. 221)

According to the OSEP Technical Assistance Center on Positive Behavioral Interventions and Supports (n.d.a), schoolwide behavior instruction is based on the following core principles.

∇ We can effectively teach behavior to all children.

∇ Intervene early.

∇ Use a multitiered model, such as RTI.

∇ Use research-based interventions.

∇ Monitor student progress to inform interventions.

∇ Use data to make decisions.

∇ Use assessment for (1) screening for total number of discipline referrals; (2) analyzing diagnostic data to determine type of problem, time, and location; and (3) progress monitoring to determine if interventions are working.

Schoolwide Tier 1 behavior instruction includes determining the essential academic and social behaviors students must learn in order to be successful. Teams should identify and teach expected behaviors in the same manner as academic essential standards. These behaviors might include academic behaviors, such as being prepared for class, as well as social behaviors like keeping your hands and feet to yourself.

The leadership team should determine a process that includes all staff in determining schoolwide expectations or essential behaviors for all areas of the building, including common areas such as hallways, cafeterias, and libraries. This is typically done through a matrix or chart that is well communicated and used for explicit instruction. In developing this matrix, the leadership team might consider the behavior expectations for all areas of the school. For example, *respect others* is an essential behavior standard, and students can demonstrate that expectation by *being polite*, which is the learning target to explicitly teach and support.

Figure 6.1 shows a sample schoolwide behavior teaching matrix.

Behavior Expectations or Standards Consistent With School Mission	Behavior Targets for All Areas	Behavior Targets for the Hallways	Behavior Targets for the Cafeteria	Behavior Targets for the Bus
Respect Others	Be polite. Be helpful.	Walk. Keep hands and feet to yourself.	Keep your place in line. Speak in a quiet tone.	Sit in your assigned seat. Maintain space between you and others.
Respect Property	Pick up trash. Recycle.	Wipe your feet. Respect displays.	Return trays to the counter. Pick up trash.	Wipe your feet. Pick up trash.
Respect Yourself	Ask for help. Make good decisions.	Keep supplies in your locker. Report problems.	Choose food wisely. Wash your hands.	Watch your step. Stay seated.
Respect Learning	Be prepared. Be on time.	Go directly to class. Be prepared.	Eat in a timely manner. Listen to adults.	Be at the bus stop on time. Use time on the bus wisely.

Figure 6.1: Sample schoolwide behavior teaching matrix.

Visit **go.SolutionTree.com/RTIatWork** *for a free reproducible version of this figure.*

The manual *School-wide Positive Behavior Support: Getting Started Workbook* by the Center on Positive Behavioral Interventions and Supports (2010) outlines a recommended process for developing a schoolwide behavior expectations teaching matrix. The process includes the following steps:

1. Develop and list three to five positively stated rules or expectations that support the school's mission or purpose.

2. Identify and list all school settings in which rules are expected.

3. For each rule or expectation, provide at least two positively stated, observable behaviors such as "Walk with hands to yourself."

4. Develop a plan for teaching each expectation.

It is important to emphasize that this is a matrix to use for explicitly teaching behaviors that reinforce the mission and values and identified essential behaviors of the school. In order for a chart like this to be meaningful, it must be accompanied with a plan for how and when behaviors will be taught, retaught, and reinforced. As previously stated, classwide or classroom systems should support the behaviors on the schoolwide matrix.

The book *Uniting Academic and Behavior Interventions* (Buffum, Mattos, Weber, & Hierck, 2015) explains the process of teaching schoolwide behaviors at Tier 1.

> As a part of Tier 1, we:
>
> • Clearly define common, schoolwide behaviors that will be consistently accepted
>
> • Commit to explicitly teaching and modeling the behaviors we want students to exhibit
>
> • Identify how the behaviors we want to see will be positively reinforced as we modify behaviors and help students build better habits (p. 80)

Schoolwide systems supported by consistent expectations in classwide systems provide the foundation for more individualized behavior interventions at Tier 2 and Tier 3. Often the need for individualized support is mitigated by a well-constructed school and classroom behavior system. A classroom teacher who has a well-established system can often make adaptations to seating, time on task, reward systems, and routines for individual students without difficulty. Tier 3 interventions will not be successful in the absence of a system for teaching behavior at Tiers 1 and 2. Classroom behavior systems should establish and reinforce consistent behavioral expectations for all students in all areas of school.

Social and Emotional Learning

The skills taught in social and emotional learning (SEL) are the lifelong skills and attributes that are necessary to be successful in all areas of life. Teaching these skills is critical to a strong foundational program at Tiers 1 and 2. The primary focus of

SEL is to teach students of all ages how to build positive relationships, regulate their emotions, and make responsible decisions. This requires teachers to plan how the use of these skills will be integrated during the course of the school day. Many teachers initially teach these skills in direct lessons and then incorporate them into their ongoing class instruction. Some teachers reinforce SEL with role-playing situations or discussions during classroom meetings.

The considerations in figure 6.2 are intended to help educators make decisions on how to best teach and reinforce the social and emotional skills that are important to everyone.

Social and Emotional Learning Skills	Teacher Considerations
Self- Awareness Students understand their individual strengths and weaknesses and have strategies they use when experiencing difficulty. Students can identify what causes them difficulty and identify strategies that are helpful to them. Students can tell you what they are good at and what they do when they don't understand something.	How can you help students reflect on their progress as learners and identify strategies that are helpful to them? How do you encourage students to identify what is hard for them? Do you ask students to self-assess their learning? How do you provide frequent feedback regarding student performance and specific areas for growth? Do you ask students to use a journal or reflective thinking to respond to questions such as: • What was easiest for me to learn this week? Why? • What was most difficult about this assignment? Why? • What strategies did I use that helped me? Do you instill a growth mindset into students by focusing on what has not yet been accomplished and help them identify strategies to improve?
Self-Monitoring and Self-Management Students recognize when they are having difficulty and use self-management strategies to help them focus, complete assignments, manage frustration, and achieve goals. Students can tell you the strategies they use when they lose focus or have difficulty.	Do you introduce students to various strategies that they can use to: • Organize their work • Follow a schedule or timeline • Calm down (for example, count to ten, breathe deeply, use stress balls) • Increase focus and productivity (for example, use flexible seating, wear noise cancelling headphones) • Self-monitor time on task (for example, use timers)

Figure 6.2: Teaching considerations for social and emotional learning skills.   continued →

Social and Emotional Learning Skills	Teacher Considerations
Social Awareness Students have empathy, understand different perspectives, and treat others with respect. Students can express actions they take to treat others fairly and respectfully.	What do you do in your classroom to help students develop skills such as: • Listen to peers without interrupting • Respect others' opinions • Work cooperatively within a group • Participate in group discussions with varying opinions • Respect peers who are different than they are (for example, different backgrounds, abilities, races, or languages) • Show kindness and empathy
Decision Making Students make constructive choices. Students can tell you how they make personal decisions and how they make decisions when working with others.	How can you incorporate activities to build the following skills: • Develop good work habits • Accept responsibility • Develop determination and perseverance • Recognize poor choices and develop strategies to use in the future • Develop a plan to achieve a goal
Relationships Students develop positive relationships with peers and adults. Students have the ability to communicate and work cooperatively with others. Students can tell you what they do to ensure that others hear and understand their point of view.	What do you do in your class to promote: • Students working together toward a common goal • Students discussing and resolving conflict • Students using a process for listening to all perspectives

*Visit **go.SolutionTree.com/RTIatWork** for a free reproducible version of this figure.*

Schools that make the commitment to build a safe and respectful culture by having a comprehensive program for teaching behavior at all tiers of instruction will have the following systems and processes in place.

▽ Universal screening for behavior at Tier 1

▽ A process to use data for identification and progress monitoring regarding behavior

▽ Essential academic and social behavioral skills identified and explicitly taught

▽ Social and emotional learning integrated into schoolwide and classroom systems

▽ Teams that rely on data to problem solve and make decisions

▽ Teams that are proactive and use data to intervene before behaviors become severe

▽ Use the following four questions to guide interventions, which are based on the four critical questions of a PLC (DuFour et al., 2016).

    a. What do students need to know and be able to do?

    b. How will we know when they have learned it?

    c. What will we do when they haven't learned it?

    d. What will we do when they already know it? (p. 251)

▽ In a PBIS setting, we could rephrase these four critical questions as follows:

    a. How do we want students to behave?

    b. How will we know when they have learned how to behave?

    c. What will we do when they haven't learned how to behave?

    d. What will we do when they already know how to behave?

▽ Collective responsibility for meeting the needs of students with behavior issues, just as they do with those who have academic deficiencies

In their book *It's About Time: Planning Interventions and Extensions in Elementary School*, Buffum and Mattos (2015) discuss the challenge of collective responsibility for students with behavior problems as follows:

> The collective responsibility and collective commitment of a school are most evident when implementing programs designed for students with the most difficult academic and behavioral challenges. The leadership of a school must be prepared and remain committed to every student for a program such as this to be successful. As stated in *Revisiting Professional Learning Communities at Work* (DuFour, DuFour, & Eaker, 2008), "It is impossible for a school or district to develop the capacity to function as a professional learning community without undergoing profound cultural shifts" (p. 91). This culture will never be more evident or tested than when implementing Tier 3 behavior support. (p. 212)

Following are scenarios of three very different students: Nia, Wyatt, and Regen. (Nia's and Wyatt's names have been changed to protect their privacy. At the request of Regen's parents, Regen's real name is used.) We urge you to focus on the students' needs and the school's response rather than the students' ages. We can learn lessons from each scenario and apply them to any grade level. Consider the following as you read these scenarios:

▽ The collective responsibility of the school

▽ The systems and processes at Tiers 1, 2, and 3

▽ How the foundation at Tiers 1 and 2 supports Tier 3

Nia's Story

Nia was a second-grade student with a big smile, tremendous energy, and a dynamic personality. Like many little girls, she loved the color purple. Nia received Tier 3 support in reading but was not making progress in her classroom or in her intervention. Her classroom teacher and interventionists had tried all the strategies they knew to manage her behavior but were unsuccessful. The staff had no doubt that behavior was impacting Nia's progress.

The intervention team asked the behavior specialist who served the district to attend a problem-solving meeting. At the meeting, Nia's teachers explained that Nia's home situation was very chaotic and unstable. She frequently did not have food on weekends, and she was embarrassed because her clothes were often torn or dirty. There were times that she was unsupervised for nights or weekends. Her teachers kept extra clothes and snacks for her at school. Additional questioning revealed that her primary behavior issues centered on attention-seeking behavior, difficulty focusing, and verbal outbursts when she became frustrated. Her teachers had tried reward systems, student contracts, as well as morning and afternoon goal setting. Her teachers all agreed that Nia was trying but needed more intensive support.

Nia's intervention team, with the input of a behavior specialist, agreed that they would implement a system to teach her how to self-monitor her time on task and learn to calm down. The team knew this would have to be very intense at first. They modified the check-in/check-out model (described in detail later in this chapter; see page 147) to meet Nia's needs. Initially, a trained assistant met Nia upon arrival and at the beginning of every thirty-minute period to review how she would self-monitor.

A time-on-task observation revealed that she was regularly on task for four to five minutes, depending on the task, location, and so on. The intervention team members agreed that the classroom teacher would look at Nia or walk by her desk and give a thumbs up or down at five-minute intervals. The teacher would use a timer if needed. Nia would circle a happy face on her monitoring form each time the teacher gave her a thumbs up for being on task. If she was not on task, the teacher would give Nia a quiet reminder with a specific direction such as, "Eyes on me."

This level of focus was very hard for Nia, so at the end of thirty minutes, the assistant and Nia would review the number of happy faces, discuss what was difficult for her, review her goal, and then go to a quiet area in the classroom to practice a calm-down routine. This strategy would teach her how to remain calm and give her the attention she craved. In order to calm down, Nia would quietly count backward from twenty-five, do deep breathing by blowing petals off an imaginary flower, and then spend one minute with a purple bear the teacher let her keep in her book bin. After her calm-down, she would return to learning and begin the process again.

At the end of each day, the assistant would have a brief check-out meeting with Nia, and they would review her day and discuss the next day. The process of checking in, reviewing progress during the day, and checking out at the end of each day was specific and intentional. Each week, the teacher, check-in/check-out assistant, and behavior specialist monitored her progress with the goal of increasing the time between check-ins. By the end of the semester, Nia reached the goal of morning and afternoon check-in/check-out, four daily progress checks, and staying on task for twenty minutes.

There were times that things would happen at home that caused Nia to need more frequent reminders and calm-downs, so the team adjusted the check-in/check-out schedule. The goal was for her to learn how to monitor her own time on task and to have a way to calm down when frustrated. This is a slow and difficult task for a student who has very real issues compounded by a chaotic life at home. However, the school knew that this was Nia's reality and that in order for her to learn essential academic and social behaviors and perform on grade level in reading, it was necessary.

Nia entered third grade with the same home situation, but she was a different student. Due to her progress and the support of her school, her skills and her self-confidence were greatly improved. Her teachers communicated her check-in system—which was now only twice a day—to the third-grade team. That team started her routine on the first day of school.

Nia left elementary school in fifth grade on grade level in reading, attending to task with only reminders, and managing her own frustrations. Her future looked very different than it had at the beginning of second grade. She was prepared academically and behaviorally for the next chapter in her school career.

Wyatt's Story

Wyatt was a kindergarten student who was so aggressive that he required a one-to-one behavior assistant and regular (more than one time per day) class removal and an approved, safe physical restraint to keep him from hurting others. He was aggressive both at home and in school. Wyatt could not tolerate noise, change, or unstructured environments. He could do grade-level academic work with no problem. He had a visual schedule, as shown in figure 6.3 (page 128), that included icons for each segment of his school day and an individual behavior plan, complimented with frequent

continued →

home-school communication. The teachers and behavior assistant focused on teaching him anger-control strategies, calm-down techniques, and how to monitor his own behavior. The strategies they used were collaboratively developed with the behavior specialist. Wyatt was always provided a quiet area where he could go for redirection and calming down.

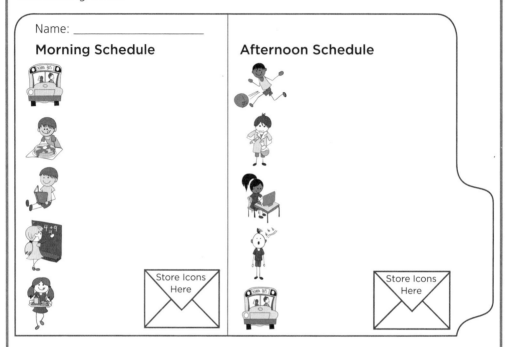

Source: Buffum & Mattos, 2015, p. 219.

Figure 6.3: Wyatt's visual schedule.

*Visit **go.SolutionTree.com/RTIatWork** for a free reproducible version of this figure.*

Each year brought new challenges for Wyatt. As he changed classes or campuses, there were new personalities and new routines to learn. Each of these changes caused a temporary increase in aggressive behavior and an adjustment to his program. Each summer he received a grade-to-grade transition plan that included sharing new visual schedules in advance, and a private tour of the building. The behavior specialist and behavior assistant regularly sought teacher input, reviewed data, and met for planning and problem solving. They met prior to the beginning of each school year, and monthly during the year, with the behavior intervention team. They also met any time a crisis occurred.

This level of coordinated planning between the campus leadership team and behavior intervention team allowed the school to anticipate and address potential behavioral problems. Any routine change, such as rearranging the classroom or altering the bell schedule, had to be considered and addressed. The behavior intervention team ensured that all team members had a process for communicating with the leadership team. The mission was to teach Wyatt strategies that he could learn and use independently to manage changes to his routine at home and at school. The behavior intervention team was proactive and worked with teachers to teach Wyatt how to manage upcoming changes. It was important for them to predict and prevent his outbursts rather than just reacting after a predictable event.

Over the years, as he moved from elementary to middle school, Wyatt developed the coping skills necessary for him to adjust to change. Most importantly, he learned how to self-regulate and calm down so as not to hurt others. He used his visual schedule independently to monitor his own schedule, which provided him needed structure. When he needed a quiet area for redirection, he had a procedure to take time for himself. His committed teachers believed that it was vital to teach the skills necessary to be a productive citizen. They viewed teaching self-management the same as teaching reading—having this ability would change his life. They knew that this goal was worth the time, perseverance, and dedication required.

Regen's Story

Regen and his smart, gracious mother taught the staff at Regen's school more than any college course or internship in education. They taught the staff the power of believing in all students and the danger of creating artificial barriers based on labels or preconceived notions. Regen's mother taught everyone the power of perseverance and the importance of celebrating small improvements. Regen's disabilities impacted all areas of academics, communication, and behavior.

Regen was initially in a self-contained elementary classroom. He was not challenged or provided academic work. He spent the majority of his day sitting, holding his favorite toy, listening to music, and rocking. Because Regen's school subscribed to the traditional approach of labels determining a student's academic placement and goals, his day was limited to the most mundane tasks. When discussing more rigorous goals, his mother's constant challenge to the school was, "Let him try, and let's see what he can do."

This sounds like a remarkably simple request, but because of Regen's differences, and a lack of understanding of how to proceed, teachers and administrators met the request with great skepticism. Regen's mother knew that Regen was not going to perform on grade level, but she also knew that he would maximize all his abilities by learning with his typical peers. The intent was not for him to be invited to a class and sit beside his peers; the goal was for him to be fully integrated, so he was a part of the class. Regen needed to have appropriate social skills so other students would develop relationships with him and accept him, and so he could learn along with them. His academic goals were individualized, but he could learn and maximize his level of achievement while his peers did the same.

continued →

Regen had to learn to tolerate noise, busy hallways, use a cafeteria line, order food, make eye contact, and greet people appropriately. He also had to learn to carry a backpack, sit at a desk, complete academic work, participate in art class, dress for physical education, go to pep rallies, and ride a bus. With the support of his family and a dedicated team of educators, he did it all!

School staff watched him grow from an elementary-aged student sitting in a corner playing endlessly with his favorite toy to a young man navigating a large high school (with support) and going to classes with his peers. They observed as he learned to talk to his peers, and as his peers initiated conversations with him, helped him, and accepted him as one of them. He was a part of the school family.

Every new experience required that Regen be taught appropriate behavior and the necessary coping and social skills for the situation. It was an hour-by-hour challenge. Often, he became frustrated and ripped posters from walls, screamed, ran from class, and became aggressive.

Teachers were frustrated, and the teacher and intervention teams had to ensure that his needs were balanced with the needs of all other students. Team members were determined that they could achieve success with Regen while simultaneously meeting the needs of all other students. This required collaboration, problem solving, and an ongoing review of formative data. Because Regen's goals were both academic and behavioral, it was necessary to ensure that the intervention team consisted of members with expertise in both areas. Teachers and intervention team members regularly problem solved and learned the skills necessary to communicate with Regen, collect and use formative data, and teach Regen how to be successful in school and in life.

Day by day, they peeled back the underlying causes of each issue Regen encountered in order to identify the specific skills needed for him to be successful. They then targeted and taught these specific skills. Regen's success was nothing short of life changing for him, his family, and those who served him.

The deeper success came from how Regen impacted the school culture. It is impossible to know how many other students and their families have benefited from the lessons the school learned while meeting his needs.

Regen reminded the entire staff to never assume that a student's limitations mean that he or she can't be successful in the general education classroom. All who worked with him came to realize the danger of placing artificial barriers on students because of traditional practices or assumptions about a student's potential. Like all great teams, Regen's teachers and administrators learned together, worked collaboratively, and stayed focused on their goals. Because of Regen, labels no longer define students in this school, and teachers have a system for teaching students needing intense support that they can replicate with others.

The students highlighted in these scenarios are clear examples of the power of collective commitment, systematic processes, and the work of collaborative teams. Nia's school had an intervention team in place and asked a district behavior specialist to be a part of the team for problem-solving behavior. Wyatt's school had an intervention team and a behavior intervention team, but because he was on track academically, the behavior intervention team addressed his needs. Regen needed both academic and behavioral support, so his school ensured that the intervention team included members with expertise in the area of behavior. The leadership team at each school was crucial for ensuring the systems, processes, and human resources were in place. The intervention or behavior intervention teams were critical for making long-term plans as well as on-the-spot adjustments for each student.

The Roles and Responsibilities of Teams in Behavior Interventions

As noted, all school teams are crucial to the success of students with varying academic and behavior needs and challenges. Their roles and responsibilities are outlined in the following sections.

Leadership Team

In the book *Taking Action,* Buffum et al. (2018) explain that an essential action of the leadership team at Tier 1 is to identify schoolwide academic and social behaviors that will be taught to all students. They state:

> Some behaviors and dispositions are universal; that is, they are not grade level or course specific. Instead they are essential for success everywhere on campus and beyond. These behaviors can be categorized into two categories: (1) academic behaviors and (2) social behaviors. (p. 139)

Academic behaviors are those that are critical to being successful in school or work. They include behaviors such as self-monitoring or the ability to know when you need to change behavior and motivation, and use organizational strategies.

Social behaviors are those we use when deciding how to act appropriately in social situations, such as using appropriate language, interacting verbally and physically with others, and respecting property.

It is the role of the leadership team to develop a process, communicate with all teachers, and identify the academic and social behaviors that are so important or essential that they should be explicitly taught to all students at Tier 1. For example, after identifying essential behaviors for central locations, such as the hallways, the cafeteria, and restrooms, teachers may plan a common lesson for teaching those behaviors during the first week of school and again at the beginning of the second semester.

At Tier 2, the leadership team must establish a process for identifying students needing additional time and support to learn the essential academic and social behaviors identified as well as plan for how students can receive the additional support needed. An important component of this process is identifying whether a student is having difficulty because of a skill issue or a will issue, which means the student has the ability or skill but has disengaged and refuses to complete assignments, comply with requests, and so on. Both issues require additional support, but in order for the intervention to be targeted, there should be a process to identify the underlying cause.

Identifying students who need intense intervention at Tier 3 is a critical role of the leadership team. A key component of identification is the determination of the process, schedule, and membership of the intervention team, which may also be referred to as the problem-solving or behavior team. This team's role is identifying and problem solving for students referred for Tier 3 support.

The leadership team plays a critical role in the area of coordinating human resources or human support at all tiers. For example, in the area of behavior, it is highly likely that the school will need staff members or community members with unique experience or expertise for problem solving and action planning. The leadership team has the capacity and the ability to coordinate schedules so intervention or behavior intervention team members can access resources, such as a school counselor or a community social worker. If the behavior intervention team communicates the need for additional expertise to the principal, who is a member of the leadership team, the principal can coordinate the various schedules and experts. Only a principal who serves on the leadership team has the power to clear the schedule of a campus counselor or invite community members to serve on committees.

Another example would be a situation in which a student's behavior changes dramatically after a traumatic event in his or her personal life. The leadership team has the ability to see the big picture of the student's behavior across all school environments and quickly determine that it needs to schedule a behavior intervention meeting. The leadership team has the power to coordinate the schedules of all who need to attend. This level of communication and collaboration between the leadership and behavior intervention teams allows them to address concerns quickly.

Intervention Team

The intervention team is critical to the success of students at Tier 3. As discussed previously, some schools elect to have a behavior intervention team specifically for the area of behavior that holds the same responsibilities as the intervention team. This team holds the responsibility of determining the needs of students based on gathering data, monitoring progress, and resolving issues and concerns. Team members have to identify students' needs, monitor ongoing data to determine trends in student behavior, and recommend changes as needed.

The membership of the intervention team is crucial. Schools frequently have standing members of this team as well as members whose expertise they might need periodically. The leadership team assumes the responsibility of finding the right team members as well as developing regular meeting schedules. They must ensure that teams are not only regularly reviewing progress but have a system for identifying students needing intense support and plan for unexpected in-the-moment meetings. This team should be dynamic and have access to members with expertise who can address diverse student problems, challenges, and issues.

Standing members of school staff can meet the needs of some students. However, students with complex needs may require professionals with a mental health or community service background. The availability of these members is critical if the intervention team believes that a student would benefit from services beyond school. This is often referred to as *wraparound support*.

The Need for Varied Team Expertise

In order to meet the ever-changing needs of the students highlighted in the previous scenarios, their schools relied on the expertise of proactive intervention teams that used student data and drew on each other's expertise. The students had layers of academic and behavior issues that required a team that could provide a wraparound support approach. Intervention teams could not look solely at academics, behavior, or school issues. They had to look at the whole student and how the issues he or she faced affected every element of his or her life.

Wraparound support must be flexible and address student needs individually and immediately. As mentioned earlier, the leadership team has the role of ensuring that the intervention team has the expertise necessary for addressing the myriad of issues students present as well as arranging schedules, meetings, and so on. Wraparound support may include alcohol and drug counseling, community transportation, housing assistance, food assistance, or a myriad of other issues. Therefore, it is important that the leadership team consider the varied services that may be needed by individual students and have a process for accessing this specialized expertise. These professionals work collaboratively with intervention team members when their services are needed.

In the case of Nia, there were numerous times that the intervention team came together with community partners to address issues such as providing welfare checks during school breaks; food for weekends and holidays; and providing toiletries, shoes, and clothing.

In the article "Wraparound: A Key Component of School-Wide Systems of Positive Behavior Supports" (2008), Lucille Eber states:

> The wraparound process is an essential component of school-wide positive behavior support if schools are to ensure success for students with complex needs across home, school and community settings.

She further explains the unique role that wraparound support can provide in a school:

> Wraparound plans organize and blend positive behavior support and academic interventions as needed to ensure success at school. Differentiating itself from traditional service delivery in schools, wraparound focuses on connecting families, schools and community partners in effective problem-solving relationships. (Eber, 2008)

Just as with all meetings that are necessary for systematic RTI processes, there should be a regular schedule planned to review students receiving wraparound support and then, if necessary, emergency meetings called. You can't meet the needs of students with the most significant challenges in a school by waiting for an emergency to call a meeting. Buffum et al. (2012) offer an analogy to illustrate this point:

> Imagine you visited your doctor and were told, "Your test results are in, and you are severely diabetic. You must begin taking daily insulin shots—without them, you could die." What is the likelihood that you would respond, "But doctor, you don't understand. I'm so busy; I don't have time to take insulin"? Not likely. Instead, you would probably take out your calendar, pencil in the insulin shots, and then build everything else around it. This is what schools must do to create collaborative time: make it the highest priority, pencil it into the schedule, then build everything else around it. (p. 40)

By being proactive, behavior intervention teams not only meet the goal of high levels of student achievement, they save valuable time by not continually reacting to a crisis that might have been preventable. They are doing what is necessary to maintain a safe and respectful school climate.

The leadership team can use the checklist in figure 6.4 for planning and improving behavior interventions at Tiers 1, 2, and 3.

How to Target Students' Behavior Needs

Targeting the needs of students who need additional time and support, interventions, or remediation in the area of behavior requires the same type of data analysis used in academics. We must consider multiple pieces of information, that when combined, tell teachers, interventionists, and intervention teams the *why* behind the behavior. All targeted interventions begin with understanding the root cause of the problem.

Action	Description	✔ Done	✗ Need to Do
Identify essential behaviors.	The leadership team leads the effort to identify the essential behaviors that teachers should explicitly teach to all students.		
Schedule schoolwide behavior instruction.	The leadership team works with teacher teams to establish a schedule for teaching essential behaviors to all students at the beginning of the school year as well as for reviewing and reteaching them during the school year.		
Establish a system or process for teaching essential schoolwide behaviors.	The leadership team ensures that a system for teaching what essential behaviors look and sound like in campus areas, such as hallways, bathrooms, cafeterias, and walkways, is in place and utilized as a part of teaching essential behaviors.		
Establish social and emotional learning as a part of schoolwide behavior instruction.	The leadership team works with teacher teams to establish a plan for how teachers will teach social and emotional learning schoolwide as well as in classrooms.		
Establish a system or process for teaching essential behaviors classwide.	Classroom teachers utilize a consistent system for teaching what essential behaviors look and sound like in the classroom.		
Identify students for Tier 2.	The intervention team has a system for collecting and using multiple types of information and data in order to identify students needing Tier 2 support.		
Ensure certain access to Tier 2.	The leadership team ensures a well-understood and systematic process is in place for determining students' targeted needs and providing targeted interventions.		
Identify students for Tier 3.	The intervention team has a system for collecting and using multiple types of information and data in order to identify students needing Tier 3 support.		
Provide targeted interventions at Tiers 2 and 3.	The leadership team regularly reviews student data to ensure that the specific types of interventions needed are in place.		
Establish a problem-solving and action-planning process for intervention teams.	Intervention teams have an efficient problem-solving process that results in targeted action plans.		

Figure 6.4: Teaching essential behavior skills team checklist.   continued →

Action	Description	✓ Done	✗ Need to Do
Establish a dynamic intervention team.	A dynamic intervention team with members who have varied types of background and experience is in place. The leadership team ensures that a process is in place to access the support of individuals with unique experiences that may be required to meet the needs of some students.		
Conduct universal screening for behavior.	The leadership team establishes a process for screening all students in the area of behavior and conducts these screenings at the beginning, middle, and end of the year. The leadership and teacher teams use this information to identify students needing closer attention and behaviors that need to be explicitly taught to all students.		
Document behavior.	The behavior intervention team uses behavior logs or other informal processes for regularly documenting the behavior of students receiving Tier 2 and 3 support for progress monitoring.		
Conduct functional behavior assessments to determine the reasons behind a student's behavior and target goals for improvement.	Select staff members understand how to conduct a functional behavior assessment and can do so in a reasonable timeframe. The completed assessment report should identify the specific concern, a review of all pertinent information (including the purpose or function of the behavior), observations of the student, and a summary statement.		
Monitor student progress.	A process is in place for regularly collecting, reviewing, and adjusting interventions based on progress monitoring.		
Ensure safety for all students.	A plan for ensuring the safety of all students is in place. Select staff understand de-escalation techniques and have been trained in what to do if students present a danger to themselves or others.		
Ensure supports are inclusive.	All students, including those with serious behavior needs, receive instruction in essential academic standards. If the school removes a student from the general education setting, a plan for reintegration is in place.		
Provide training and support for staff.	All staff receive training in teaching schoolwide behavior expectations and social and emotional learning. A comprehensive plan is in place for ongoing staff development for behavior just as it is for academics.		

*Visit **go.SolutionTree.com/RTIatWork** for a free reproducible version of this figure.*

Universal Screening for Behavior

Universal screening is the first critical step leadership teams must have in place for identifying students who need academic or behavioral support. A systematic process for identifying students needing immediate support or those who warrant careful observation is a key feature of universal screening.

Leadership teams should conduct universal screening for both academic and social misbehaviors. Alfie Kohn (as cited in Buffum et al., 2012) describes these behaviors as follows:

> *Academic misbehaviors* include behavior such as not paying attention, not completing assignments, missing class, using poor study habits, and so on. Often they are signs of lack of motivation, lack of knowledge of the "rules of school," or attendance problems.
>
> *Social misbehaviors* include behaviors such as acting out, using inappropriate language, or engaging in physical confrontations. These behaviors are quantitatively different from academic misbehaviors; academic misbehaviors appear as acts of omission aimed at avoiding a task or situation, while social misbehaviors may appear as acts of commission aimed at getting attention. (pp. 64–65)

In most cases, schools know the students who need intervention for behavior issues. For students who attended a school the year before, reports such as office discipline referrals, school safety surveys, and teacher or counselor referrals are all important pieces of information that schools can use as a part of a universal screening process. Many schools create a matrix comprised of the essential academic and social behaviors identified for Tier 1 and a process of utilizing discipline referrals as well as other types of reports to identify students needing more focused support to meet behavior expectations.

Data Review and Exploration

The OSEP Technical Assistance Center on Positive Behavioral Interventions and Supports (n.d.a) states:

> A data-based decision regarding student response to the interventions is central to PBIS practices. Decisions in PBIS practices are based on professional judgment informed directly by student office discipline referral data and performance data. This principle requires that ongoing data collection systems are in place and that resulting data are used to make informed behavioral intervention planning decisions.

Screening data should provide trends that answer questions such as the following.

▽ Are there students who have chronic attendance issues?

▽ Are there certain students who stand out for specific academic and social misbehaviors?

▽ What essential behaviors should be targeted to be retaught or reinforced at Tier 1?

▽ What are the behaviors to address at Tier 2?

▽ Who are the students who should be screened further for more individualized support?

There are several published screeners that enlist information from students, parents, and teachers to gauge behavioral risk factors. Many are effective, efficient, and easy to use. A good reference for this information is the website Positive Behavioral and Interventions and Supports (www.pbis.org/resource/systematic-screening-tools-universal-behavior-screeners). The authors encourage schools to consider their own resources and their ability to use current information and weigh the benefit of using outside resources, such as published screeners, in making the final decision regarding their system for universal screening. In making this decision, schools must be sure to consider both academic and social behaviors.

Identification and Determination of Intense Interventions

A comprehensive process for reviewing behavior data provides the information schools need to identify students who may need further evaluation. The information universal screeners provide, coupled with academic and behavior data from interventions at Tier 2, gives leadership and behavior intervention teams valuable information for identifying students needing intense intervention at Tier 3.

After carefully reviewing all information available related to student achievement, intervention teams often need additional information to identify students' targeted needs. We recommend using functional behavior assessments for this purpose. They provide the information that intervention teams need to design intense interventions. Heidi von Ravensberg and Allison Blakely (2014) describe the information as follows:

> To be considered technically adequate, an FBA must result in a summary statement that operationally defines the problem behaviors, describes the antecedents and consequences that predict and maintain problem behaviors, and states under what conditions the behavior is more or less likely to occur (Sugai, Lewis-Palmer, & Hagan-Burke, 2000). FBA is not a specific set of forms or fixed products; instead, it is a process of understanding environments to guide the development of contextually relevant interventions. (p. 3)

There are two types of functional behavior assessments used to gain more detailed information about students—practical and comprehensive. Sheldon Loman and Christopher Borgmeier (n.d.) describe practical assessments as follows: "[They] are used with students with mild to moderate problem behaviors (behaviors that are

NOT dangerous or occurring in many settings) and can be administered by school-based personnel (e.g., teachers, counselors, administrators)" (p. 6).

In their book *Simplifying Response to Intervention*, Buffum et al. (2012) offer the following eight steps for teams to use in completing a behavioral analysis to determine (1) the causes of a student's behavior and (2) the desired acceptable behavior:

1. Define and describe the behaviors.

2. Determine the consequence or reinforcement the student will receive.

3. Determine what the student is seeking (attention or avoidance).

4. Identify the behavior that immediately preceded the misbehavior.

5. Identify the environments that immediately precede the misbehavior.

6. Define an alternate behavior that is acceptable.

7. Determine the ultimately desired behavior.

8. Determine the reinforcement the student will receive for the desired behavior.

The information gained from completing a behavioral analysis provides schools with practical information about what triggers student misbehavior as well as strategies for teaching the appropriate behaviors.

The chart in figure 6.5 (page 140) shows this process. This type of detailed analysis of the causes of misbehavior allows behavior intervention teams to be prescriptive and proactive.

OSEP describes *comprehensive behavior assessments* in the following manner: "Comprehensive FBAs—Are used with students with moderate to severe behavioral problems; may be dangerous and/or occurring in many settings. They are used by trained professionals such as school psychologists and behavior specialists" (Loman & Borgmeier, n.d., p. 6).

The Effects of Academic, Health, or Home Issues on Behavior

It is critical that the behavior intervention team considers academic progress and any learning gaps as they problem solve and determine targeted interventions for students with behavior challenges. A strong system of academic intervention that employs the principles of the RTI at Work model will prevent or at least reduce many behavior issues. In *Effective Programs for Emotional and Behavioral Disorders*, Hanover Research (2013) states:

> In a recent study published in *Beyond Behavior*, researchers Cynthia Farley, Caroline Torres, Cat-Uyen Wailehua, and Lysandra Cook highlight "an increasing acknowledgment that strong academic instruction and interventions may be the first line of defense in working effectively with

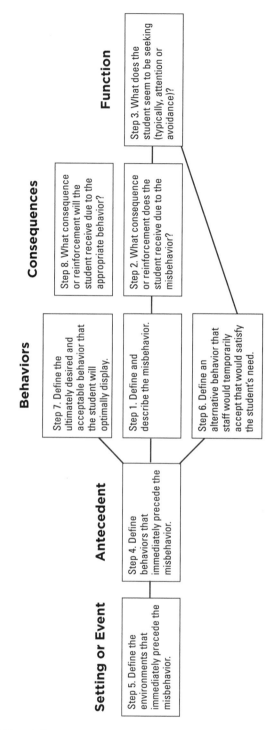

Source: Buffum et al., 2012, p. 121.

Figure 6.5: Behavior analysis protocol.

*Visit **go.SolutionTree.com/RTIatWork** for a free reproducible version of this figure.*

students with EBD." Other sources have echoed this sentiment, noting that "in the absence of sound academic instruction, the most effective behavior management systems in the world will do little to prepare students for school or later-life success. (p. 5)

Many students who have behavior challenges have the dual issue of academic failure. This is a critical consideration for intervention teams as they review data. They must give careful attention to all areas related to essential academic and behavior skills. The intervention team cannot be targeted in addressing behavior if it does not address issues related to academics, health, home, and English language.

Intervention teams must look at all available data and consider the following.

▽ What are the trends in academic performance and behavior performance, and is there a relationship?

▽ If the student presents academic issues, are they being addressed appropriately?

▽ Is the student making academic progress?

▽ When and where are the behaviors occurring? Does the time or location indicate a relationship with academic issues?

▽ How is the student's behavior impacting academic performance?

▽ Are issues related to health or home impacting academic performance or behavior?

▽ Are there attendance issues? If so, what is the cause?

▽ Have there been home visits or parent conferences? Have parents shared information that the team should consider?

Schools should not underestimate the value of parent conferences and information related to health and home in determining interventions. Kaylee (fictional name) is an example of such a case.

Kaylee's Story

Kaylee was a student receiving Tier 3 support in both reading and mathematics. She was not making progress, and her teachers complained about her negative attitude, lack of attention, and poor social skills. She refused to work in groups and was seen as a loner. The intervention team reviewed all of her information and felt they needed more.

Kaylee's parent would not return calls or attend meetings, so the campus counselor reached out to a mentor who frequently came to the school to eat lunch with Kaylee. After Kaylee visited with her mentor, whom she trusted, she related that there was no

continued →

food at home in the evenings or on weekends. A follow-up home visit revealed that the parent worked multiple jobs but failed to generate enough income to pay medical bills for one of Kaylee's younger siblings, pay rent, and have money for food. Due to the family's financial struggles, Kaylee was babysitting her siblings at night and going without food as well as her own prescription for medication to assist her in focusing at school. The school now knew the *why* behind the lack of effort and behavior and could begin to work with community support groups to solve the problems. Kaylee and her siblings were enrolled in a program with the local food bank that provided backpacks of food on weekends and holidays. A community service organization agreed to pay for Kaylee's prescriptions. As a result, the school began to see marked improvement in Kaylee's academic and behavior performance.

Progress Monitoring for Behavior

As part of initial action planning, the intervention team should consider how and when to monitor progress. Frequent monitoring of student progress, which includes progress on the stated goals as well as the student's current performance in relation to grade-level peers, is an essential function of intervention teams. The intervention team should establish regularly scheduled monitoring in order to be proactive in determining if students' interventions are working or not.

It is important that the intervention team has the data necessary to make appropriate judgments regarding why a particular strategy or intervention is or is not working. Data collection tools should be easy to complete and ask for documentation, including the following.

▽ Student name

▽ Date

▽ Location

▽ Time

▽ Targeted behavior or objective being observed

▽ Activity student was participating in at time of observation

▽ If the student was successful in meeting the goal

According to the Center on Response to Intervention at American Institutes for Research (n.d.b): "Progress monitoring is used to assess students' academic performance, to quantify a student rate of improvement or responsiveness to instruction, and to evaluate the effectiveness of instruction. Progress monitoring can be implemented with individual students or an entire class."

In order to determine whether a student is making progress and understand *why*, intervention teams must have actionable data. They need data that provide the information needed to answer questions such as the following.

▽ What is the current goal?

▽ Is the student improving?

▽ What is the student's current level of performance?

▽ How was progress assessed and when?

▽ What patterns or trends can we detect from the data?

▽ What are the triggers for misbehavior, such as location, time of day, and certain activities?

▽ What strategies will be helpful?

▽ Was the current plan or intervention implemented with fidelity?

▽ What are our next steps?

▽ Are any additional areas of expertise or community resources needed?

▽ If a change is needed, what is the targeted intervention that will address the need?

▽ How will progress be measured, by whom, and how frequently?

▽ When will we meet again?

▽ Who will distribute the new plan of action?

A system for reviewing multiple points of data in an ongoing manner provides intervention teams with the level of detail they need to make immediate and prescriptive decisions. When teams use convergent assessment, they are able to see trends and determine why students are being unsuccessful. This critical information guides decision making for interventions.

The "Behavior Observation Tool" reproducible (page 164) provides a simple format to help teams collect data on targeted behaviors in every classroom. This is a practical and user-friendly process for providing the intervention team information that allows them to detect trends across multiple settings. The tool in figure 6.6 (page 144) provides intervention teams with a guide to use in meetings for reviewing data, monitoring progress, and planning action steps.

Behavior Intervention Team Meeting Tool

Date: _____

Team Members: _____

Purpose: Review progress and current data, and problem solve for students at Tiers 2 and 3 scheduled for review or placed on agenda due to immediate need.

Agenda:

- Review norms.
- Review progress-monitoring data.
- Determine changes to be made.
- Review data for students referred for problem solving.
- Determine action plan for those students.
- Review list of students due for progress monitoring at next meeting.
- Create action items for any new members to invite to next meeting, data to collect, student observations, and so on.

Step 1: Review to determine progress and make changes for students currently being served with intensive behavior interventions.

Monitor Progress

Student	Current goals	Data	Progress Notes	Next Steps
	Review students' current goals and targeted behaviors.	List all data reviewed.	Areas of Improvement • What is working well and why? Areas of Difficulty • When and where are problematic behaviors occurring? • What are times of day or class periods for problem behaviors? • What are antecedents or triggers observed for problem behaviors?	List each action item and details such as the person responsible, timelines, follow up, and so on. If the team determines the current action plan isn't working, use the following problem-solving process to determine next steps.

Step 2: Problem Solving—Use a problem-solving process, such as the following, for students who do not currently have action plans or for those whose action plans are not working.			
Identify the Problem and Why It Is Occurring			
Student	**Current Data** Review and list all pertinent data regarding academic, behavior, health, and home issues.	**Problematic Behavior** Identify and prioritize the problematic behaviors.	**Determine Why** • When and where are problematic behaviors occurring? • What times of day or class periods do the problem behaviors occur? • What are antecedents or triggers observed for problem behaviors? • What are academic, health, and home issues to consider?
Brainstorm Solutions			
Current Interventions and Supports Discuss any interventions, services, or supports the student is currently receiving in or out of school.	**What Is and Isn't Working** Areas of Improvement • What is working well and why? Areas of Difficulty • When and where are problem behaviors occurring? • What are times of day or class periods for problem behaviors? • What are antecedents or triggers observed for problem behaviors?		**Possible Solutions** Discuss possible strategies, interventions, and supports.
Action Plan and Follow-Up			
Action	**Details** Who, When, Where	**Progress Monitoring** Data to collect, frequency of collection, and person responsible	**Date for Follow-Up**

Figure 6.6: Behavior intervention team meeting tool.

*Visit **go.SolutionTree.com/RTIatWork** for a free reproducible version of this figure.*

Self-Monitoring and Self-Management at Tier 3

Behavior issues that are so significant that they require intensive support at Tier 3 significantly impact student performance and are of great concern to teachers and school administrators. Although there are many social and academic behaviors addressed at Tier 3, among the most concerning to classroom teachers and administrators are those in the areas of defiance, anger, and aggression. Each of these issues hinge on the ability of students to develop lifelong skills of self-monitoring and self-management. Because developing these skills is critical in a person's life, we offer techniques that support students in acquiring the ability to manage their own behavior.

We emphasize the critical nature of developing these skills and the importance of explicit instruction. Teaching self-regulation and self-management takes time. The nature and complexity of the problems require a focused plan, ongoing monitoring, personalization, and adjustment. The commitment is worth the effort in that these are the misbehaviors that most hinder success in school and in life.

Self-monitoring and self-management include:

▽ Teaching students to recognize their emotions and what causes them and to create a plan for controlling their emotions and behavior

▽ Teaching students to use strategies to monitor a wide range of behaviors so they can learn to self-manage those same behaviors

▽ Teaching students to use strategies to calm themselves when they are becoming frustrated or agitated

▽ Teaching students to self-manage a wide variety of behaviors

Explicitly teaching self-monitoring and self-management is consistent with the components of a comprehensive program for intervening for behavior at Tier 3, which includes each of the following areas.

▽ **Prevention:** Make problem behavior irrelevant (environmental redesign and removal of triggers).

▽ **Teaching:** Make problem behavior inefficient (teach new skills and behaviors as alternatives).

▽ **Extinction:** Make problem behavior ineffective (minimize the reward for problem behavior by understanding the message being sent).

▽ **Reinforcement:** Make desired behavior more rewarding.

▽ **Safety:** Ensure safety for all (what to do in dangerous situations if needed).

The following practices include one or more of the previously listed criteria for teaching self-monitoring and self-management. We have found each of these strategies to be successful. We reference many of these practices in this chapter's featured student scenarios. Carefully consider each strategy, the individual students you serve, and how you might replicate these strategies in your school.

Check-In/Check-Out (CICO)

At Tier 2, check-in/check-out is a support structure that provides an adult for morning and afternoon check-ins with individual students regarding behavior goals. Students use a tracking sheet to monitor their progress during the day. The implementation of CICO requires the leadership team to establish the overall process, including the scheduling of necessary staff and coordinating with the behavior intervention team as they determine the behavior goals of individual students. If CICO is well-implemented at Tier 2, it will drastically reduce the number of students needing intense support at Tier 3. A well-established CICO program at Tier 2 ensures that the systems and processes for individual student success are in place.

Buffum et al. (2015) share the following about CICO:

> Within the process, students check in and check out with staff members with whom they have a relationship and who can coach and guide them through improving their performance. Check-ins and check-outs are brief, specific reflective pep talks that ask students to identify successes, areas for improvement, and goals.
>
> CI/CO works, but the process must be completed consistently, positively, and in the spirit of collective responsibility. It should be adjusted as students succeed or when more, or different, supports are determined to be necessary. The process produces data that can reveal progress to students and staff. It places responsibility on students to assess and monitor their own progress as they build better habits. It allows schools to be proactive in helping to improve student behavior. (pp. 83–84)

At Tier 3, CICO is individualized by providing a highly trained staff member for the student to check in with at the beginning of the school day, at identified times during the day, and at the end of the day. The intervention team can adjust the frequency and duration of contact with CICO support personnel based on student need. Some students may need a check-in at the beginning of the day and at the beginning and end of each class period as well as the end of the day. Other students may have certain classes or environments that are the most problematic and need the support personnel to stay in the class for a period of time at the beginning of the class period to help him or her get started and then return at the end of the period.

CICO is preventative and proactive by providing goal setting, monitoring, and redirection before problems escalate. At its heart, CICO teaches self-monitoring and self-management. It is a coordinated effort that helps students use a goal-setting sheet to monitor targeted behavior at frequent intervals.

This system provides:

▽ A manner to teach self-monitoring and self-management

▽ Increased structure

▽ Coordination between all adults

▽ A positive way to provide feedback and rewards

▽ Daily home–school communication and collaboration

▽ Student organization, motivation, incentives, and rewards

▽ An efficient manner to monitor student behavior

Each student highlighted in the scenarios at the beginning of this chapter had a CICO program personalized for him or her. Each student had different goals or targeted behaviors, and those goals changed as the needs of the student changed.

For example, consider Nia. Every school can identify with students who are significantly below grade level in reading, inattentive, and frustrated. However, Nia's team considered the impact of health and home and realized she needed to learn to deal with frustration and her desire for attention. Both of these needs were addressed in CICO simultaneously with the goal of teaching Nia to learn how to self-monitor and increase her time on task. Initially, her support was very intense with one-on-one check-in every thirty minutes. However, as she progressed, the team slowly increased the time between check-ins. The team adjusted her support when issues at home caused her to regress, but with the flexibility and personalization of CICO, Nia met her goals. Teachers working collaboratively and the problem-solving process utilized by the intervention team were instrumental in Nia's success.

Wyatt had a completely different issue addressed by CICO. He became highly agitated and aggressive if he could not predict his schedule. His goals were to learn to use a visual schedule and manage his schedule by monitoring *what I am doing now* and *what I will do next*, which taught him to self-manage his anxiety. His goals were quite different from Nia's; however, both were working on individual skills that taught them to self-monitor and self-manage their behavior. Both students were learning lifelong skills and using strategies that they could replicate in any environment.

Each student's program included the following.

▽ An identified CICO staff member to work with each day

Some students who use CICO at Tier 3 are escorted to class, and in some cases, the assistant stays in class for a period of time. This is dictated by the student's ability to self-monitor and self-correct. The intervention team bases the amount of adult assistance on student need. Ongoing data monitoring allows teachers and teams to see each student's trends in behavior. Support is adjusted as students' needs change.

▽ A staff member to meet them at the bus or school entrance in the morning

▽ A morning review of what went well or did not the day before

▽ A review of goals and strategies during the day

▽ Time and support adjusted based on need

▽ Identified calm-down areas in classrooms or the building

It is important that the look, feel, and function of calm-down areas outside of classrooms have the look and feel of an instructional setting. This allows students to calm down in a setting similar to a classroom and so they can easily transition back to class. The calm-down areas are often referred to as a *safe place* in reference to the students using them to reflect, calm themselves, and regain control.

▽ Plan for requesting calm down or using a calm-down area

For example, students might have a ticket that they could give to the teacher when feeling agitated. They could go to the calm-down area in the classroom for a period of time and then return to work. A student might need to leave class with the CICO support person and walk for ten minutes, use calm-down strategies that he or she had been taught, and then return to class. Calm down is not a way to avoid work; it is a manner of teaching students to self-monitor and self-manage behavior.

▽ Point or monitoring system used during the day

Students are monitored for their target behavior and receive points or teacher initials indicating their level of success on meeting their goal for that time frame. This assists students in developing the skill to self-monitor their own behavior and provides a reward for accomplishing their goal. If it is appropriate, students can take their point cards home to share with their families. At the end of the day, the student checks out with his or her assistant who monitors his or her performance. This cycle repeats itself daily.

▽ Intentional, planned CICO

Check-out at the end of each period or only at the end of the day depends on the students. Check-out is a review of the target behavior and a way to discuss strategies students can use to self-manage their own behavior.

The following CICO sheets are examples of simple tools that teachers can use to monitor students' behavior goals weekly (see figure 6.7) or daily (see figure 6.8).

Check-In/Check-Out Weekly Points

Date(s): _____

Student: _____

Weekly Goal/Target: _____

Great Job—2 points		Almost—1 point		Keep Trying—0 points	
Class Period	Monday	Tuesday	Wednesday	Thursday	Friday
1					
2					
3					
4					
5					
6					

Figure 6.7: Check-in/check-out weekly points.

*Visit **go.SolutionTree.com/RTIatWork** for a free reproducible version of this figure.*

Tracking System for Self-Monitoring Behavior

Teaching students to self-monitor their own behavior and knowing how and when to adjust their responses are the ultimate goals of behavior intervention. It is a necessary life skill. Teachers can use a behavior tracking system to teach students to self-monitor and self-correct specific behaviors. Teachers frequently use tracking systems to teach students to monitor and increase on-task behavior as well as decrease repetitive behaviors such as repetitious physical movements that interfere with the learning process.

Teachers give students a goal, such as: *I will remain quiet and look at the teacher while he or she is talking,* or *I will keep my hands lying flat on top of my desk.* The student will learn to monitor his or her target behavior at short intervals with that time frame gradually increasing. The teacher can use a cueing system, such as a timer or physical prompt, to indicate to students that it's time for them to monitor whether

Daily Behavior Goal Tracking

Student Name: _____

Date: _____

1 = poor   2 = fair   3 = good

Time Period	Student Score	Teacher Score	Total Score	Teacher Initial	Comments
8:00–8:15					
8:15–8:30					
8:30–8:45					
8:45–9:00					
9:00–9:15					
9:15–9:30					
9:30–9:45					
9:45–10:00					
10:00–10:15					
10:15–10:30					
10:30–10:45					
10:45–11:00					
11:00–11:15					
11:15–11:30					
11:30–11:45					
11:45–12:00					
12:00–12:15					
12:15–12:30					
12:30–12:45					
12:45–1:00					
1:00–1:15					
1:15–1:30					
1:30–1:45					
1:45–2:00					
2:00–2:15					
2:15–2:30					
2:30–2:45					
2:45–3:00					

Student Goals:

1. _____

2. _____

3. _____

You can do it!!

Daily Score: _____

Figure 6.8: Daily behavior goal tracking.

*Visit **go.SolutionTree.com/RTIatWork** for a free reproducible version of this figure.*

they are meeting their goal for that time period. The goal is for students to learn to monitor, manage, record, and assess their own behavior to promote self-regulation. Teachers can use the information in figure 6.9 to help students learn to self-monitor their behavior.

Self-Monitoring Steps	Actions or Considerations
1. Define the behavior to be addressed.	What is the specific targeted behavior? Be sure you know exactly what the desired behavior is. For example, *pay attention* is not targeted. The goal might be to *wait your turn, work on the assigned task without talking for five minutes*, or *stay in your seat for five minutes*.
2. Ensure that the student clearly understands the targeted behavior and expectation. Students should know specifically when and where you expect this behavior.	Teach students what the targeted behavior looks and sounds like. Do students understand well enough to give or recognize examples and non-examples of the behavior?
3. Develop a tracking system, such as a simple checklist, chart, or tally sheet, to let students know how and when to self-monitor.	What will be the frequency and process to track behavior? Will students use a tally sheet, a timer, or something else? Be sure students understand how to use the monitoring tool. Have them demonstrate performing the behavior and completing the tracking sheet.
4. Determine how you will cue or remind students to use their system.	Will you use a visual cue, verbal cue, physical cue, or a timer? Be sure students know what your cue is and what they are supposed to do when you use the cue.
5. Establish a plan to regularly discuss progress and goals with students.	How and when will you provide feedback to students?

Figure 6.9: Steps to help students learn to self-monitor.

Visit go.SolutionTree.com/RTIatWork for a free reproducible version of this figure.

Tracking systems are very individualized. Some students will need one-on-one assistance to learn this process, while others will be able to do it with reminders or visual cues from the teacher. Students receiving Tier 3 interventions may need to learn this type of monitoring in small groups or with a one-on-one assistant in the classroom. The students' level of cognition, language, and behavioral needs impacts the time frame for becoming independent.

Figure 6.10 shows an individualized tracking system teachers can use with students. Teachers can use the "Individual Behavior Tracking Sheet" reproducibles (pages 165–166) to create tracking forms for individual students.

Behavior Tracker

Student: _____

Goal: _____

Circle *On Track* or *Off Track* for each time period.

	On Track	Off Track
1.		
2.		
3.		
4.		
5.		
6.		
7.		
8.		

Daily Notes or Comments:

Figure 6.10: Individualized student behavior tracker.

Visit **go.SolutionTree.com/RTIatWork** *for a free reproducible version of this figure.*

Calm-Down Strategies

Students who experience chronic agitation, suffer from trauma, or display defiance often have difficulty or do not know how to calm down. Teaching students calm-down strategies gives them the ability to self-manage their behavior before it escalates out of control. As with all behavior strategies, explicit teaching of calm-down techniques is critical.

Many teachers have a calm-down area, such as a beanbag chair, in their classroom. In order for this area to be effective, teachers must teach students specific strategies to use in that area. Simply telling a student who displays chronic agitation or defiance to "take five minutes and calm down" when they don't understand how to calm down would be like telling students to read silently at their desks when they can't decode words. They have not developed the skill and must be taught what to do, and how to do it.

In Jessica Minahan's (2013) article "Teaching Self-Calming Skills," she outlines the following simple steps for teaching calm-down strategies.

1. **Teach the student how to identify his or her emotions:** When you notice signs of frustration, take the student aside and label the emotion. Explain how you know: "Your shoulders are high and hunched, and your fists are clenched. I can see you're frustrated." Over time, the student will learn to identify emotions without your cues.

2. **Teach the student self-calming strategies:** Students who are learning how to identify feelings of frustration for the first time may need frequent reminders to access certain strategies.

3. **Practice self-calming strategies with the student:** Like with any skill, practice is extremely important. Every day, when the student is calm, ask him or her to act out where he or she might go in the classroom when upset or frustrated, such as a quiet reading area or a beanbag chair or rug. The next time the student becomes frustrated, he or she can access that strategy.

Each of these steps and additional considerations for implementation are outlined in figure 6.11.

Steps for Teaching Calm-Down Strategies	Considerations or Actions
1. Identify the emotion.	Consider how you will teach students to identify their emotions. How will you teach students when they are becoming upset? Many teachers take the opportunity when students are calm to have them identify physical responses of being calm or upset. Students learn to identify how their body feels when they are becoming agitated and can identify the emotion. Some teachers use a visual symbol, such as a thermometer, to teach students how to identify when they are becoming upset.
2. Teach calm-down strategies.	What calm-down strategies will you teach students? What time of day or location is best for teaching this when students are calm? Teachers should have students practice several strategies and select four that they will use to calm down when upset. Teachers can create a visual cue for students to use when they are upset. Examples: • The flower—Have students pretend to hold a flower and blow the petals off the flower. They take a deep breath, hold it, and then blow the petals. • The walk—Have students take a short walk to cool off or calm down. This may be an escorted walk to the water fountain or around the classroom, depending on students' age and level of independence. • Take ten—Have students take ten long, slow, very deep breaths. • Be quiet and think—Have students silently count as high as they can, say the ABCs backward, or sing the ABC song. The goal is for students to be quiet and redirect their thoughts. • Pretzel squeeze—Have students hold their arms across their chest and squeeze and then relax to release tension.
3. Make a calm-down choice board students can use.	1. Use a visual cue for the four strategies students select or the ones you believe will be most effective. 2. Explain to students that they will be selecting one of these strategies to calm down when they notice they are upset. 3. Have students practice these strategies when they are calm.
4. Practice using the choice board with the student.	Be prepared to use the choice board. When students are upset, they can choose a strategy, or you can choose one for them. They may not do this right or agree to do it at first. This will take some time and continued practice when students are calm.

Figure 6.11: Steps for teaching calm-down strategies.   continued →

Steps for Teaching Calm-Down Strategies	Considerations or Actions
5. Reflect on the experience.	Reflecting with students after they have used their calm-down strategies is important. Students reflect on their choice and possible options for how to handle the situation that caused their anger or frustration. They can do this verbally or in written form. Students can reflect in a calm-down area where he or she can practice self-management. This area is often referred to as the *safe place*—a place to calm down, reflect, and gain self-control before returning to instruction.

*Visit **go.SolutionTree.com/RTIatWork** for a free reproducible version of this figure.*

Figure 6.12 shows a choice board that students can use to select a calm-down strategy. Figure 6.13 is a safe-place tool that students can use to reflect after they have implemented a calm-down strategy.

My Choice Board	
	Place my arms across my chest and squeeze.
	Take a short walk with an adult or in a location where I have permission to go independently.
	Silently say the ABCs backward.
	Pretend I am holding a flower and blowing on the petals.

Figure 6.12: Example choice board.

*Visit **go.SolutionTree.com/RTIatWork** for a free reproducible version of this figure.*

Safe Place Reflection Sheet

Name: _____

Date: _____

1. What was the problem? _____
   _____

2. What did I do to calm down? _____
   _____

3. Circle the activity I did.

   Think: "What can I do next time"?

4. What are some solutions? _____
   _____

5. What solution am I going to use? I'm going to _____
   _____.

Figure 6.13: Safe place reflection sheet.

*Visit **go.SolutionTree.com/RTIatWork** for a free reproducible version of this figure.*

Anger Control Strategies

Anger control is one of the most prevalent areas of misbehavior targeted at Tier 3. Students with anger control issues need to be taught explicit anger control strategies. As students learn to self-monitor their emotions and how to calm themselves, their anger and aggression become controlled. However, a student with anger and aggression also needs strategies he or she can begin to use while learning self-management. One of the most difficult situations for an educator is dealing with a student of any age who has lost control of his or her behavior and is aggressive. Having a clear set of verbal cues gives the teacher a plan of action and helps the student gain control.

The chart in figure 6.14 (page 158) outlines steps for teaching anger control as well as considerations for educators.

Steps	Actions and Considerations
Identify triggers or causes of outbursts.	Are there times of day, certain activities, or any other trends that help you understand the *why* behind the student's anger? Transition times, over-stimulation due to activity, or certain environments frequently cause students to lose control of their emotions, which quickly turns to aggression.
Teach students to recognize when, where, and why they are becoming aggressive.	Help students identify their emotion and the cause. This is the first step in learning to self-manage behavior.
Teach self-control strategies. Example: Stop and freeze! When students hear this, they freeze in place and do not move. They learn that they must be still until they have calmed down.	Students of all ages can learn: • How to put their hands down • How to stay silent • How to move away • How to walk away Teach students the verbal cues and practice using the strategies when students are calm.
Provide in-the-moment coaching.	Use verbal cues for in-the-moment coaching when students are upset.
Offer acceptable choices.	When students are angry or aggressive, offering two acceptable choices for in-the-moment coaching is sometimes helpful. Example: You can direct a student to "put your hands to your side," or "walk away and go to the beanbag chair now."
Create a plan for outbursts.	What will be the procedure if a student becomes aggressive in the classroom or in an open space? You should teach students what to do to create space between themselves and an angry or aggressive student. In order to calmly manage an outburst, have a plan in mind for what you will direct the class to do.
Establish a plan for a calm down and redirection after the event.	Students are learning to manage their own behavior. This takes time. Students should make a plan about how to calm down and how they can respond in the future. This time should be very intentional.

Figure 6.14: Steps for teaching anger control.

Visit go.SolutionTree.com/RTIatWork for a free reproducible version of this figure.

Buffum and Mattos (2015) discuss four strategies for teaching anger control.

1. Picture a stop sign and freeze:

   ▸ Stop and calm down.

2. The turtle technique (Joseph & Strain, 2010):

   ▸ Get your hands and feet still.

- ▸ Take three deep breaths and relax.

- ▸ Think of a plan to solve the problem or walk away.

3. The three Bs (McConnell & Ryser, 2005):

   - ▸ Be quiet.

   - ▸ Back away.

   - ▸ Breathe deeply three times.

4. Picture a relaxing scene:

   - ▸ Take three deep breaths.

Teachers teach students how to use these strategies when they are angry or upset. When students use one of these strategies, they complete a form that allows them to reflect on their choices and identify other possible solutions to use in the future, such as the Safe Place Reflection Sheet in figure 6.13 (page 157). If they become angry and do not use one of these options, then the teacher can reteach. This allows for instruction in problem solving. Figure 6.15 provides visual cues for teaching the anger control strategies previously listed.

STOP	Stop and Freeze
(turtle)	The Turtle Technique
(bee)	The Three Bs
(relaxing scene)	Picture a Relaxing Scene

Figure 6.15: Anger control strategies.

*Visit **go.SolutionTree.com/RTIatWork** for a free reproducible version of this figure.*

Conflict Resolution

Conflict resolution teaches students with behavior issues to develop the critical skills of problem solving, listening to others, and taking ownership of their actions. Many schools use conversation circles for teaching conflict resolution. The conversation circle brings the wider school community together to address a problem. Individual students with emotional or behavioral issues may not be able to participate in a large circle at first. In many situations, this process has to begin one-to-one between individual students. The leadership and intervention teams should discuss when and how to teach conflict resolution. Figure 6.16 shows steps for conflict resolution and considerations for educators.

Steps	Actions and Considerations
1. Take a breath and calm down.	Students should use a strategy to calm themselves to be prepared to listen to others' points of view.
2. Listen and discuss.	Students should learn a strategy to listen to others and then think about what they have said and ask clarifying questions. They should know that they are seeking to understand the other person's perspective. Many schools use "I" statements to teach this. Example: Student 1: When you _____, I feel _____ because _____. I wish you would _____. Student 2: I understand that when I _____, it made you feel _____ because _____.
3. Own it.	Students should be prepared to take responsibility for their actions. Taking responsibility means admitting that they were wrong or should not have done a particular action. They admit that they understand how it was hurtful to the other person.
4. Brainstorm together.	Students openly discuss how the situation could be handled differently by both parties in the future.
5. Make a plan.	Students discuss what they will do in similar situations in the future.
6. Shake on it.	One student acknowledges or apologizes for wrongdoing, and the other accepts the apology.

Figure 6.16: Steps and considerations for conflict resolution.

*Visit **go.SolutionTree.com/RTIatWork** for a free reproducible version of this figure.*

Safe and Inclusive Schools

We know that students learn essential academic skills best when they work with and learn from their peers. Behavior is no different. The authors recognize the challenge of balancing the goal of high levels of achievement for all students while maintaining a safe and respectful school environment. We also respect the rationale and the pressure that exist from parents and community members to remove the concern by removing the student. However, research clearly shows that schools are safer when comprehensive behavior support is integrated into a multitiered system of supports such as RTI at Work. A comprehensive program provides timely and targeted student interventions while simultaneously ensuring safety. The courageous and committed educators who accept this challenge deserve respect and support from the school community.

In *A Framework for Safe and Successful Schools*, Katherine C. Cowan, Kelly Vaillancourt, Eric Rossen, and Kelly Pollitt (2013) explain the relationship between school safety and the implementation of a system of academic and behavior supports as follows:

> The most effective way to implement integrated services that support school safety and student learning is through a school-wide multitiered system of supports (MTSS). MTSS encompasses (a) prevention and wellness promotion; (b) universal screening for academic, behavioral, and emotional barriers to learning; (c) implementation of evidence-based interventions that increase in intensity as needed; (d) monitoring of ongoing student progress in response to implemented interventions; and (e) engagement in systematic data-based decision making about services needed for students based on specific outcomes. In a growing number of schools across the country, response to intervention (RTI) and positive behavior interventions and supports (PBIS) constitute the primary methods for implementing an MTSS framework. Ideally though, MTSS is implemented more holistically to integrate efforts targeting academic, behavioral, social, emotional, physical, and mental health concerns. This framework is more effective with coordination of school-employed and community-based service providers to ensure integration and coordination of services among the school, home, and community. (p. 4)

We urge educators to consider the comprehensive nature of this type of support. When implemented fully at all tiers, RTI at Work provides the structure and processes necessary in both academics and behavior. It requires collective commitment, collaboration, and a system of interventions beginning at Tier 1. (In the next chapter, we will explore the best practices for academic support at Tier 3.)

> "Fortunately, most human behavior is learned observationally through modeling from others."
>
> —Albert Bandura

Conclusion

A comprehensive system of behavior and academic support provides the opportunity for all students to reach high levels of achievement. As practitioners, we know that this takes time, and each school faces different circumstances and levels of readiness for this work. We respect the challenges posed by students with significant behavior concerns and recognize the collective commitment required for success. However, as we learned from the students highlighted at the beginning of this chapter, this can change the lives of students we serve. We encourage schools to work together, believe in themselves, and believe in their students. It can be done!

Chapter 6 Action Steps

With your team, engage in the following action steps to review and implement the learning from this chapter.

1. This chapter is full of information, tools, and checklists regarding teaching students appropriate behavior. The real challenge here is knowing where to begin. In order to decide where to begin, ask the following questions:

   ▸ Do we have a school intervention team?

   ▸ Do we have the necessary varied expertise on this team?

   ▸ Have we determined the targeted needs of students with behavior issues?

   ▸ Once we determine these needs, have we identified intensive interventions that address them?

   ▸ Have we determined if behaviors are impacted by academic, health, or home issues?

   ▸ Do we have a way to effectively monitor the progress of our behavior interventions?

   ▸ Have we trained staff to effectively provide CICO support to students?

   ▸ Have we taught students how to monitor their own behavior?

   ▸ Have we taught students strategies to control their anger?

2. Reflect on the following questions to challenge your thinking and guide your processes:

   ▸ What do we really believe? If we believe that all students can learn and that behavior is critical to their success, how will we explicitly teach it to all students at every tier of instruction?

   ▸ What systematic processes do we have in place to determine the misbehaviors that need to be targeted and the specific students needing behavior intervention at Tier 2 and Tier 3?

▸ Do we have a system for teaching schoolwide behavior at Tier 1 that is supported by consistent classroom practices?

▸ Do we have a system for our leadership team or behavior intervention team to frequently meet, review behavior data, and respond accordingly?

▸ Does our system allow us to be proactive, or do we only respond after a significant incident?

▸ Do we provide the same level of training, planning, and focused attention to teaching behavior as we do to teaching academic skills?

▸ Do students have to be labeled to receive Tier 3 support?

▸ Do we have a simple and effective problem-solving process for all teams considering either academic or behavior concerns?

▸ Are students involved in setting goals and taught strategies to manage their own behavior?

▸ What do we do to ensure that all students feel respected and valued and have a positive relationship with staff members?

Behavior Observation Tool

Use this tool to monitor student progress in individual classrooms or to discover trends in behavior across the school by asking each teacher to complete it. You may add more goals in the empty spaces.

Student: _____

Date: _____

Teacher: _____

Behaviors listed are examples.

Academic Behaviors	Yes	Yes, With Help or Reminders	No	Making Progress
Participates and shows effort				
Follows class procedures				
Is compliant with directions from adults				
Organizes work with calendars, checklists, or folders				
Completes work as directed				
Social Behaviors	Yes	Yes, With Help or Reminders	No	Making Progress
Uses appropriate language				
Works well in groups				
Focuses and stays on task				
Keeps hands and feet to self				
Manages impulsivity (for example, waiting turns)				
Is on time to school and class				
Self-monitors with a timer				

Individual Behavior Tracking Sheet Example

3 = Great 2 = OK 1 = Oops!					
Name of student: Brian	Personal Space	Work On Task	Nice Words	Quiet Mouth	Raise Your Hand, and Wait to Be Called On
Time: 8:00–9:00 Ms. Jones Teacher or Adult	3	2	3	2	2
Time: 9:00–10:00 Ms. Jones Teacher or Adult	3	1	3	1	1
Time: 10:00–11:00 Mr. Rice Teacher or Adult	2	2	1	1	1
Time: 11:00–12:00 Ms. Carpenter Teacher or Adult	2	2	2	2	2 Yay! Back on track!
Time: 12:00–1:00 Ms. Morris Teacher or Adult	2	3	3	2	2
Time: 1:00–2:00 Ms. Jones Teacher or Adult	2	2	2	2	3

Comments:

Brian: Great job getting back on track with Ms. Carpenter!

page 1 of 2

Best Practices at Tier 3, Elementary © 2020 Solution Tree Press • SolutionTree.com
Visit **go.SolutionTree.com/RTIatWork** to download this free reproducible.

Individual Behavior Tracking Sheet

Use this tracking sheet to create individual student tracking forms. The far-left column should indicate the class or teacher, and the goal columns should indicate the targeted behaviors to be monitored for each time period or class.

3 = Great 2 = OK 1 = Oops! Name of student:					
	Goal:	Goal:	Goal:	Goal:	Goal:
Time: Teacher or Adult					
Time: Teacher or Adult					
Time: Teacher or Adult					
Time: Teacher or Adult					
Time: Teacher or Adult					
Time: Teacher or Adult					
Comments:					

Best Practices at Tier 3, Elementary © 2020 Solution Tree Press • SolutionTree.com
Visit **go.SolutionTree.com/RTIatWork** to download this free reproducible.

Academic Instruction at Tier 3

We often hear this familiar refrain from teachers who feel as if they are working without a support system to help them in serving students with the greatest challenges: "*I have never taught a student with these issues. I am not a special education teacher, and I don't know what to do. I am happy for her to be in my class, but I need help!*"

Tier 3 cannot happen in a vacuum in an intervention class down the hall. Tier 3 is the most intense system of support that is intended to accelerate learning the universal skills of reading, mathematics (number sense), writing, English language, essential social and academic behavior, and health and home. Students who receive intense support at Tier 3 also receive grade-level instruction in the essential standards. It is of paramount importance that all teachers at all tiers work collaboratively to ensure that the interventions at Tier 3 are yielding progress and the improvements are transferring to achievement in grade-level essential standards. This is not a job for one person, it is the responsibility of all teachers to work together in support of every student. Students and teachers win when we approach Tier 3 with collective responsibility.

In this chapter, we discuss the importance of building a strong academic foundation at Tiers 1 and 2, with a focus on designing and delivering instruction that utilizes best practices for students needing intensive intervention at Tier 3. We explore the importance of genuine collaboration, the roles and responsibilities of teams, high-leverage teaching practices, and the critical role of planning in advance for students with diverse learning needs.

The Foundation at Tiers 1 and 2

Student achievement is directly related to the quality of Tier 1 instruction. High-quality instruction that results in the goal of at least 80 percent of all students being successful at Tier 1 relies on many variables, but certainly the depth of focus and quality used in planning and delivering initial instruction are critical to this process. Teams must agree on common essential standards to provide the basis for learning targets and ongoing assessment for all learners. This process brings clarity and a focus to initial instruction, Tier 2 supplemental interventions, and the individual goals students have at Tier 3.

> "Children are the priority. Change is the reality. Collaboration is the strategy."
>
> —Judith Billings, Superintendent of Public Instruction, 1989–1997

There are commonly agreed-on essential targets that general education, special education, and interventionists all use for establishing unit, lesson, or intervention plans. Some students are ready for grade-level learning, and others may have already mastered the targets or have significant gaps to fill. Knowing and understanding what students must do to master grade-level essential learning provide the road map needed for planning and designing instruction.

The Four Critical Questions Essential to Student Learning

When used with intention and focus, the following four critical questions of a PLC ensure that teacher teams utilize the right thinking when determining essential standards, considering how to assess learning, and taking action as a result of reviewing pertinent data.

- What do students need to know and be able to do?
- How will we know when they have learned it?
- What will we do when they haven't learned it?
- What will we do when they already know it? (DuFour et al., 2016, p. 251)

These questions require focused discussion that results in instructional and intervention plans that address the needs of students at all tiers of instruction. Leadership teams and teacher teams should consider the following questions as they work to improve their collaborative processes.

What Do Students Need to Know and Be Able to Do?

▽ What are the essential standards, and what do those standards look like when vertically aligned through the grades?

▽ What will students know, understand, and be able to do to show mastery?

▽ Have teacher teams agreed on the step-by-step progression of learning for essential standards?

▽ Are teams consisting of general education, special education, and intervention teachers co-planning to intentionally support students with significant learning gaps?

▽ What types of learners can you predict may have difficulty?

▽ Are teams including special education teachers and interventionists working together to design Tier 1 instruction that addresses diverse learning needs?

How Will We Know When They Have Learned It?

▽ What are the mastery criteria of the standard?

▽ What do students have to do to demonstrate mastery?

▽ What is the frequency for monitoring student progress?

▽ What learning will be commonly assessed at the end of the unit?

▽ What learning will be assessed to determine progress mid-unit?

▽ What is the process for intervention teachers and general education teachers to discuss the progress students in intense interventions are making toward grade-level standards?

What Will We Do When They Haven't Learned It?

▽ Are teams collaboratively planning a response for students they predict will have difficulty?

▽ Are teacher teams using formative and end-of-unit data to ensure that interventions are targeted?

▽ Are teacher teams reassessing students to monitor their progress toward mastery of essential standards?

▽ Are intervention teams using a process to determine what is and is not working in order to ensure progress for students with significant learning gaps?

▽ Are Tier 2 interventions aligned to the essential standards?

What Will We Do When They Already Know It?

▽ How can teacher teams extend learning for students who have already mastered the learning targets?

▽ Are teacher teams planning in advance for students they predict will already know it?

Instructional Design for Diverse Learners

All classrooms have a wide variety of learners with varied interests, abilities, strengths, and challenges. Planning instruction with the mindset of providing equity for every learner requires teachers to approach planning from a proactive rather than a reactive perspective. Proactive teacher teams work from a belief that all students can be successful, and that instruction should be designed with their learning variances in mind. They consider students' unique learning needs and plan instruction in a manner that ensures that there is a pathway for each student to be successful. Teachers know the students in their class who are likely to experience difficulty; they know their learning needs and how they learn best. If they incorporate this thinking into designing instruction, students are more likely to be successful, and there will be fewer students who need intervention.

Figure 7.1 offers questions for teacher teams to consider and potential actions for them to take while planning instruction.

Planning Step	Guiding Questions for Teacher Teams	Actions to Take
Step 1: Analyze the standard and determine learning targets.	What will every student know, understand, and be able to do as a result of this unit of instruction?	Teams begin planning by reviewing the essential standard and answering the question: What do we want all students to know, understand, and be able to do as a result of this unit of instruction? Teams identify the specific learning targets and the criteria for success. For example, teams might choose to design scaled learning targets so all students are working toward mastering the same standard but at different levels of rigor. Teachers can scaffold instruction as students progress.
Step 2: Determine how we (teachers) will know students are learning the essential skills.	What will students be able to do to demonstrate mastery on the summative assessment? What skills should they be able to demonstrate mid-unit? How can students demonstrate their learning?	Consider the end-of-unit assessment and align at least one mid-cycle common formative assessment (CFA) to measure learning. Review the unit plan and schedule a time for a team data review after the CFA as well as when reteaching will occur mid-unit.

Step 3: Design the instructional plan. Teachers work collaboratively to design Tier 1 instruction with students' diverse learning needs in mind. Have a proactive plan that addresses learning variances and ensures students receive high-quality or best-first Tier 1 instruction.	What is the learning target, and how can we design instruction with all students in mind? What are students' unique learning needs? How do they learn best? How can we design instruction to maximize the success of all learners?	Align all instructional activities to the rigor level of the standard and to the assessment. Differentiate activities based on the types of learners in classrooms. The differentiated activities selected will likely help all students. For example, if you have students who have short attention spans, you may need to "chunk" the instruction into manageable pieces. You can do this by breaking the assignment into steps and numbering the page or presenting it one step at a time. You could color-code activities, work pages, or reading selections according to the order of completion, or use a graphic organizer that has the activity in sequential steps. This specifically addresses the needs of students who are easily distracted while helping most learners. Consider any students with individual goals and determine how those goals can be embedded into classroom activities, discussions, or learning stations.
Step 4: Determine a plan of action for addressing the needs of students who may not learn it the first time.	What are the learning targets and potential academic hurdles for students? What will we assess mid-cycle, when will we review data, and when will we reteach?	Know your learners and how they learn best. Utilize interventionists, special education teachers, and others who can share ideas. Plan in advance for students you predict will have difficulty. Be prepared with a ready-to-go plan for students you predict may struggle. Do not wait for them to fail. Be proactive. Data should be analyzed mid-unit to determine the targeted needs of students so teachers can intervene by the student, by the standard, and by the learning target. The number of students needing intervention at Tier 2 will be reduced by reviewing data, having a targeted plan, and intervening mid-unit.
Step 5: Determine activities to extend learning for students who have mastered the learning targets.	Is there a plan for students who have already mastered the essential skills being taught just as there is for those students who may not learn it the first time?	Use formative assessments to discover who may need learning extended. Look at the standard and learning target and determine the level of rigor or complexity by using a framework such as Norman Webb's Depth of Knowledge (DOK; Hess, 2013). Extend learning by designing activities at a higher level of rigor.

Figure 7.1: Steps and guiding questions for instructional planning.

Visit go.SolutionTree.com/RTIatWork for a free reproducible version of this figure.

To be proactive and maximize achievement at Tier 1, teams must use collaborative planning time to intentionally design instruction with all students in mind. Buffum et al. (2018) explain this concept in the following manner:

> It is important to remember that Tier 1 of RTI expects teachers and teams to understand how each student responds to instruction. The process of creating an essential standards unit plan positions teachers to not only react to student learning struggles, but more important, to proactively limit those struggles. This helps teachers to actualize the powerful premise: The best intervention is prevention. (p. 90)

Consider this quote as you read the following two scenarios that show the difference in how two teams approach planning initial instruction. As you read these scenarios, consider the thinking of the two teams and whether they plan proactively to prevent failure.

Team 1: The Engineers

Meeting: Collaborative Planning (fifty minutes)

Week 1 of nineteen-day unit

Team Members:

Team Leader—Brandon

Teachers—Carol, Reese, Hannah, Micah

Brandon: Good morning. I hope that everyone had a nice weekend! I wrote the essential standard on the board.

Carol: This is the persuasive writing unit. We have taught this for years, and for some reason it is always hard for students.

Brandon: Remember to open your unit plan so you can reference it while we plan.

Reese: Don't we always end this with them writing a persuasive essay?

Hannah: We do, and it always confuses them. I think we need some new ideas.

Micah: I am looking at a website; take a look at this idea. This is different and looks like something the students would enjoy.

Hannah: Look at this activity! It is great. I think my "low" students could do this.

Carol: I like all of them. I will make the handouts if you will find the articles we need.

Reese: It sounds like we have a plan.

Carol: So what are we going to do for an assessment? I think we are supposed to give a common assessment on day three.

Brandon: We have about ten minutes left.

Hannah: We could give them two topics and have them write an opinion paragraph with one piece of evidence.

Reese: That makes sense. Let's all bring them next time and see how the students are doing.

Carol: Everybody remember that if your special education students are having trouble, send them to Betty's room.

Reese: Yes, Betty said she would help with anything.

Brandon: Okay, our time is up. It took a while to find those things online, but they are great! Thanks!

Team 2: The Professors

Meeting: Collaborative Planning (fifty minutes)

Week 1 of a nineteen-day unit

Team Members:

Team Leader—Nikki

Teachers—Tom, Ethan, Elizabeth, Deandre

Nikki: Good morning. I hope that everyone had a nice weekend! Tom, do you have our essential standard?

Tom: Yes, if you look at the unit plan in your folder, you will see that the essential standard for this week is: *Write arguments to support claims in an analysis of substantive topics or texts, using valid reasoning and relevant sufficient evidence.* When I referenced the depth of knowledge (DOK) levels, this is a level 4 standard so we need to be sure everything is aligned.

Nikki: Let's take five minutes . . . Will everyone reference the DOK chart in your folder and then the learning targets in our unit plan? Are we still on track?

Ethan: I think we are on track with the targets. Can we move forward and look at the end-of-unit assessment and then discuss how we will assess with a quick check this week?

The team discussed the end-of-unit assessment in which students will combine all skills learned in the unit into a finished product.

They decided that on day three, they will use a short formative assessment to determine baseline persuasive writing skills by asking students to write a persuasive paragraph. They agreed that students who have difficulty focusing or organizing their thoughts would benefit by using a persuasion map template on the formative assessment. After further discussion, they determined that this option would be good for a large number of students. They agreed to allow students to choose either the persuasion map template or a traditional paragraph format. Ethan agreed to find a template and share it with the team.

continued →

Elizabeth: I have a rubric we used in the past for persuasive writing; let me show you. I think it is aligned with what we agree proficient work would look like when we did the essential standards chart.

The team referenced the original chart and agreed to use Elizabeth's rubric for evaluating the end-of-unit assessment.

Nikki: We have thirty minutes left, so let's determine when we will look at our assessment data and then plan our instructional activities.

Deandre: Let's be sure to build in reteaching. If we assess on Thursday, can everyone bring their data Monday and plan to reteach Tuesday? Since this is assessing baseline skills, we need to see where the whole group is.

Nikki: Great, I will put this on Monday's agenda. Is everybody good with this?

Elizabeth: For our initial instruction, we could have students look at two examples of really good persuasive writing. We could use something interesting like the *New York Times* article "Students Who Lose Recess Are the Ones Who Need It Most" (Lahey, 2014) or the *Boston Globe* article "School Suspensions Don't Work" (Bulley, 2014). These will help students understand what we are looking for and give them an exemplar. These articles may be difficult for some students, but we could initially have students work in groups and assign reading parts to minimize this issue.

Ethan: That's a great idea, and we could ask students to find evidence the authors used to support their claims as well as analyze how they wrote their introductory sentences.

Deandre: What if we followed that by giving students two topics to debate orally as an icebreaker, and then have them take two articles and write an opening paragraph with a statement of opinion and one piece of evidence? We need to be sure and teach each part of the rubric that we use on the assessment.

Nikki: We have about ten to fifteen minutes left. Let's address Rita and her reading level and how we can help our ADHD students. This could be really hard for them.

Tom: Students who have difficulty focusing might color-code as they go, such as highlighting the introductory sentence in blue and then highlighting the opinion statement in yellow. This helps them ignore extraneous information. In initial instruction, we could have students work in teams to complete a persuasion map for the two examples. This would help students who have gaps in reading or who have a hard time focusing.

Regarding Rita, I think she should have shorter articles that are at a lower reading level. I will find two and send them to you.

Deandre: My student, Natalie, will be able to do this on the first day. We need to go ahead and push her. She can go ahead and work on a five-paragraph format. I have a rubric and exemplars she can use. I will share them with everyone.

Nikki: Sounds like we are all set. I will email this to everyone. Be sure those who offered to share material send it no later than tomorrow afternoon.

Team 2: The Professors offer an example of the dialogue a team would have when planning and designing instruction with the needs of all learners in mind. The conversation responded to each of the four questions that guide the work of a PLC and considered the unique needs of the learners they serve.

The work of this team is an example of using the practices of Universal Design for Learning (UDL). As they planned instruction, they considered the learning variances in their class and purposefully designed plans with those students in mind. This method of planning instruction provides all learners equitable access to the content, regardless of their unique learning needs.

Designing instruction with UDL is much like the process that an architect might use when planning a new building. The initial design includes considerations for the patrons who will access the building and the various needs they might have. Architects have to plan for universal signage for patrons with different languages, ramps for those with physical challenges, and auditory prompts on the elevators for those with visual impairments. These features in the building design are necessary for some patrons and helpful to others.

This is the beauty of proactive planning with the needs of unique learners in mind. It provides equity and access to learning for some but is helpful for all.

Universal Design for Learning

Universal Design for Learning is a framework for planning and designing instruction in a manner that reduces barriers to learning for students with diverse learning needs. Utilizing UDL is a proactive way of planning initial instruction with the needs of all learners in mind. Instead of focusing on student deficits, teachers consider the students they predict may have difficulty and how they learn best. They use this information to design instruction that maximizes students' opportunities for success. Being proactive minimizes the need for modifying or changing instruction as a result of student failure.

This approach increases student achievement while reducing the amount of reteaching required. However, it is a very different way of planning and designing instruction than teachers have traditionally used. It requires collaboration, planning in advance, backward planning from the standard, and most importantly, intentionally planning for all types of learners. The time required to plan in this manner is well spent. However, it underscores the need to prioritize the curriculum by determining essential standards. By placing more emphasis on planning in advance, teachers will spend less time on designing reteaching.

In *Tool Kit on Universal Design for Learning*, the U.S. Department of Education (n.d.b) states:

> UDL is a framework with three guiding principles that parallel three distinct learning networks in the brain: recognition, strategy, and affect (Rose & Meyer, 2002). This framework is important because it reflects the ways in which students take in and process information. Using this framework, educators can improve outcomes for diverse learners by applying the principles below to the development of goals, instructional methods, classroom materials, and assessments. Use of these principles leads to improved outcomes for students because they provide all individuals with fair opportunities for learning by improving access to content.
>
> 1. Provide multiple and flexible methods of presentation to give students various ways of acquiring information and knowledge. Technically sophisticated (hi-tech) examples of this include using digital books, specialized software, and Web sites. Low technology (low-tech) examples include highlighted handouts, overheads with highlighted text, and cards with tactile or color-coded ink.
>
> 2. Provide multiple and flexible means of expression to provide diverse students with alternatives for demonstrating what they have learned. Hi-tech examples of this include online concept mapping software, which provides students with a graphic map to demonstrate learning, speech-to-text programs, and graphing to a computer, which collects data regarding students' learning progress. Low-tech examples include cooperative learning (asking the student to demonstrate his/her learning in small groups), think alouds (encouraging the student to talk about what s/he is learning), and oral tests.
>
> 3. Provide multiple and flexible means of engagement to tap into diverse learners' interests, challenge them appropriately, and motivate them to learn. Hi-tech examples include interactive software, recorded readings or books, and visual graphics. Low-tech examples include games or songs, performance-based assessment, and peer tutoring. (pp. 1–2)

When collaborative teacher teams, including special education and intervention teachers, come together to commonly plan units of instruction, all students benefit. All classrooms serve students with diverse learning needs. By predicting the types of difficulty learners may have and planning in advance to prevent failure, the outcomes for all students improve.

This way of thinking and planning benefits students with significant learning gaps including those with identified disabilities, while providing equal benefit to those who speak different languages, have difficulty focusing, and the many other learning variances seen across classrooms.

The Significance of Collaborative Teams

We cannot overstate the significant role of collaborative teacher teams in addressing individual student needs. These teams are the catalyst for substantive planning, data use, targeted prevention at Tier 1, and intervention at Tier 2. Whether in a small school in which there are single grade-level teachers planning around vertical standards, or a large school with multiple teachers per subject who commonly plan weekly units of instruction, teacher teams working collectively to achieve a common goal is of paramount importance. When all teachers assume the collective responsibility of high levels of achievement for all students, they work together with a sense of urgency to ensure student success. This level of collaboration greatly benefits students by having educators with varied backgrounds and expertise working together.

Barbara Ehren, Barbara Laster, and Susan Watts-Taffe (n.d.) explain the importance of genuine collaboration in RTI:

> Ideally, RTI is carried out within a context of true collaboration and shared expertise. In this sense, RTI is a very different way of conceptualizing general and special education, the link between the two, and the roles of other teaching specialists. Whereas general and special educators may be used to working independently of one another, or in separate silos, RTI calls for deliberate, intentional, ongoing collaboration—not to be confused with cooperation, which can involve working together without a shared purpose. We define collaboration as joining of forces, pooling of resources, and sharing of expertise in order to meet shared goals for instruction and assessment.

Collaborative planning with teachers in various roles (co-planning) requires focused dialog regarding learning targets, assessment, and unique needs of learners. The template in figure 7.2 (page 178) provides an example of a thought process to use when general education teachers and interventionists or special education teachers plan together.

This template includes two stages: preplanning and co-planning. In the preplanning stage, all teachers consider the unit to be discussed in collaborative planning in advance of the meeting and come prepared to develop an instructional plan. The general education teachers consider the targets, assessments, and the students they predict might have difficulty, and they are prepared to discuss the best way to teach and assess this unit. The special education teacher and interventionist are also prepared to discuss the unit details and have considered ideas to share that they think will benefit unique learners. They consider activities and strategies that benefit the learning needs of all students while considering individual needs and goals and how to address them.

In the co-planning phase, all teachers meet collaboratively and consider the essential standards, the learning targets, assessments, and the students they predict might have difficulty or may have already mastered the learning target.

This process does not require additional meetings or change the agenda for collaborative planning. It is intended for all teachers to consider the unit and needs of students in advance so when they come together, they are prepared to share their best ideas and have a proactive plan that addresses the needs of unique learners. Planning in this manner accesses the expertise of every teacher to support every learner.

Co-Planning Template		
Step 1 **Preplanning Considerations:** How can we plan and design instruction with the needs of all learners in mind?		**Step 2** **Co-Planning Considerations:** How can we use our collective skills, talents, and time to design and deliver instruction that maximizes the success of all students?

Collaborative General Education Team
 	
Based on our unit plan and determination of what all students must know to master the essential standards in this unit, we should consider the following:
 	
• Learning targets
• The essential student learning outcomes— what students will know, understand, and be able to do as a result of this instruction
• Students' unique learning needs
• The targets that will be assessed on formative and summative assessments
• Instructional activities and materials that will maximize the success of students with diverse learning needs
	Interventionists or Special Education Teachers
	
	Based on our unit plan and determination of what all students must know to master the essential standards in this unit, consider the following:
	
	• The best method for supporting this unit—coplanning, coteaching, sharing resources, or other?
	• The individual goals of the students I serve that align to this learning target
	• The current performance of each student I serve in relation to this target
	• How the students I serve learn best
	• The instructional strategies that will maximize the success of the students who may have difficulty
		All Team Members
		
		Based on our unit plan and determination of what all students must know to master the essential standards in this unit, consider the following:
		
		• Learning targets
		• The essential student learning outcomes—what students will know, understand, and be able to do as a result of this instruction
		• How to differentiate to maximize the learning of all of our students
		• How our students learn best
		• Strategies that maximize student success and address the learning variances in our class
		• Strategies that can be used with all students while specifically addressing students with unique learning needs. Examples of the types of strategies to consider:
		
		  - Increase the amount of white space in all documents
		  - Provide a variety of seating options
		  - Offer audio or visual options (outlines, unit organizers, graphics, text-to-speech software)

	• The individual goals of students and how they can be addressed in this unit of instruction	- Preteach vocabulary and symbols
		- Provide graphic representations of vocabulary
		- Provide lists of key terms
		- Offer all key information in primary language (for example, English, Spanish, American Sign Language)
		- Use illustrations, diagrams, and storyboards
		• Use examples and non-examples
		• Present information in incremental steps
		• Provide organizational tools such as checklists and timelines
		• Allow choice in type, design, or sequence of activities
		• Differentiate difficulty and complexity, such as the following:
		  - Learning menus and choice boards
		  - Tiered activities or tiered learning stations
		  - Frequent feedback to allow for self-correction
		  - Flexible grouping
		  - Self-checking stations
		The guidelines for UDL can be found at: http://udlguidelines.cast.org.

Source: Adapted from Wolfe & Hall, 2003.

Figure 7.2: Co-planning template.

*Visit **go.SolutionTree.com/RTIatWork** for a free reproducible version of this figure.*

As teachers co-plan they should reflect on the following questions in order to generate plans designed with all students in mind.

▽ How can we embed individual student goals into the overall instructional plan?

For example, if a student has an individual goal for communication, could teachers address it through specific questions or activities while the student participates in a group activity? The group activity is designed to benefit many types of learners, and the teacher plans to specifically address an individual goal during the activity.

▽ What are the barriers to learning for students, and how can we minimize or eliminate them?

▽ How does each student learn best, and how can we incorporate those strategies?

For example, if the learning target is to sequence the events of a story, some students might use a graphic organizer in which they write the events in order, some may draw graphic representations of the events, and some who have difficulty writing might need a template or software that allows them to sequence events without writing.

▽ What are the unique student needs to consider?

For example, if a student who is visually impaired is in the class, do we need to provide audio books which would also benefit students whose primary language is different?

▽ Are there other professionals that we should consult?

For example, should we consider speech pathologists, physical therapists, or teachers for students with visual impairments?

Roles and Responsibilities of Teams at Tier 3

The leadership team and intervention team hold the responsibilities for the critical roles of identification, determination, and problem solving for students with the greatest needs. The leadership team or guiding coalition has the role of ensuring that all schoolwide responsibilities are carried out, and the intervention team has the responsibility for determining students' targeted needs, monitoring progress, and ensuring proper intervention intensity.

General education and intervention teachers work collaboratively to design and deliver instruction, monitor progress, and contribute to the problem-solving process.

Leadership Team

The leadership team of a school assumes the responsibility for all schoolwide efforts. At Tier 3, the team must give these efforts greater focus and higher prioritization to ensure that systematic processes are in place, and to dedicate the necessary human and physical resources required to effectively identify the students with the greatest challenges, determine their needs, and monitor their progress. According to Buffum et al. (2018), the critical responsibilities or essential actions of the leadership team include the following:

1. Identify students needing intensive support.

2. Create a dynamic, problem-solving intervention team.

3. Prioritize resources based on greatest student needs.

4. Create a systematic and timely process to refer a student to the site intervention team.

5. Assess intervention effectiveness. (p. 282)

Implementing these essential actions requires that the leadership team has well-organized processes in place at Tiers 1 and 2 that support the necessary work at Tier 3. Teacher teams must use formative data, review progress, and have streamlined data collection at Tiers 1 and 2 in order for intervention teams to analyze a student's trends in learning and determine the next steps at Tier 3.

All students have access to all tiers of instruction, and all students have the goal of mastering essential standards. Practices must be systematic between the tiers of instruction to have a seamless process for identifying students' needs. This is the most important function of the leadership team. Buffum et al. (2012) state, "Of the five steps that comprise certain access, there is one step that a school must get right every time: *identify*" (p. 163). This quote signifies the paramount importance of the responsibilities the leadership team has in establishing a schoolwide system for identification.

By using multiple pieces of data, the team can see students with significant gaps in learning and trends in learning that will lead them to identify those students who should be referred to the site intervention team.

Chapter 6 (page 119) discussed the role of the leadership team in creating a dynamic intervention team with members possessing varied expertise. This is equally important for academics as it is for behavior. Some students have academic and behavior issues that are intertwined; other students have academic issues related to health or home that require a team with varied expertise. For example, a student who requires Tier 3 academic support and is beginning to experiment with alcohol or drugs would greatly benefit from having a counselor with a background in substance abuse serve on his or her intervention team. This expertise may not be available on the school campus, but with careful planning, a community agency might be able to attend meetings and offer support. This requires that the leadership team coordinate schedules to access those resources for students. The leadership team has a wide range of responsibilities critical to the success of Tier 3.

The checklist in figure 7.3 (page 182) can help the leadership team in achieving their responsibilities in regard to systematic processes and ensuring that all students are taught essential standards.

Systematic Processes			
Action	**Description**	**✔** **Done**	**✗** **Need to Do**
A multitiered system of interventions is in place to support high levels of learning for all students.	The leadership team ensures systematic processes for using assessment data to monitor student progress on the mastery of essential standards are in place. All students receive timely and targeted intervention based on data.		
Systematic processes are in place to ensure the timely and targeted identification of student needs.	The leadership team or guiding coalition ensures that a process is in place for using universal screeners, common formative assessments, and other measures of student progress to identify and determine students' targeted needs in a proactive and timely manner.		
Supplemental interventions are available at Tier 2 for all students.	Tier 2 interventions are centered on essential standards and available to any student based on his or her ongoing formative data.		
A dynamic intervention team is in place to determine the needs and monitor progress at Tier 3.	The leadership team ensures that an intervention team is in place. The intervention team should have access to members with varied expertise and a process for determining needs and monitoring progress on a regular basis.		
Tier 3 supports are available to all students, including those identified with disabilities. Special education is a part of Tier 3, but it is not the only intervention available.	Students receive intervention based on need, not on a label. A student may be served in any or all tiers simultaneously.		
There is a systematic and timely process in place to refer students to the intervention team.	All staff understand the process. It is timely and ensures that students are not waiting for long periods of time for teams to consider their needs.		
All interventions are matched to student need by type and intensity.	The intervention team makes individual determinations for the type of intervention. Students are not assigned to a one-size-fits-all intervention. The team determines interventions by the standard, by the student, and by the target. Intensity is based on student data, including student progress monitoring.		
Collaborative practices include general education teachers and special education teachers or interventionists planning and designing instruction together.	The leadership team ensures that all teachers have collaborative planning. Interventionists, including special education teachers and general education teachers, need to co-plan to support all learners in mastering essential standards. The leadership team supports teachers to be sure they have the necessary protocols and resources for their work.		

Teaching Essential Standards to All Students			
Action	**Description**	✓ Done	✗ Need to Do
Teachers regularly plan and deliver instruction designed for diverse learners.	All teachers regularly plan instruction using differentiated strategies to maximize student success. Teachers consider the needs of unique learners when designing initial instruction. Teachers understand the principles of UDL and receive training in differentiated teaching strategies.		
Teachers implement the teaching and assessing cycle.	The leadership team ensures that teachers have systematic processes to implement the teaching and assessing cycle. Teacher teams have the following: • Essential standards • Unit plans • Common formative assessments • A process for reviewing and using formative data • A process for identifying students needing Tier 2 supplemental intervention		
Teachers use multilevel instructional strategies to support students at all skill levels in mastering essential standards.	Teachers understand and use various differentiated strategies, such as multilevel grouping, and materials at varying levels of complexity to provide opportunities for students at all skill levels to work toward mastery of standards.		
The leadership team communicates and works with teacher teams to ensure that all students have access to essential standards.	All classes are designed to support mastery of essential standards by students at varying levels of ability.		
Interventions at all levels support students in attaining mastery of essential standards.	The leadership team supports the development of essential standard learning progressions that include the subskills or stepping stones for mastery of each standard. Teachers and interventionists use these progressions to determine goals and next steps and monitor progress.		

Figure 7.3: Essential academic skills leadership team checklist.

*Visit **go.SolutionTree.com/RTIatWork** for a free reproducible version of this figure.*

Intervention Team

The intervention team has the responsibility of determining students' needs, appropriate interventions, intensity of support, and progress monitoring. These duties are complex and require a collaborative approach. As mentioned previously, having members with varied experience and expertise allows the team to have representatives that can analyze data, problem solve, generate ideas for potential solutions, and understand the essential standards as well as students' current level of performance in order to determine a goal or next step in achievement.

Collaboration to Determine Targeted Needs at Tier 3

Collaborative problem solving to determine targeted needs includes evaluating all data and information related to the student and his or her learning needs. Critical pieces of information to consider include:

- ▽ Universal screeners
- ▽ Common formative assessments
- ▽ Intervention monitoring tools
- ▽ Social and emotional learning information
- ▽ Problem-solving tools and teacher information that shows what teachers have tried and what has and has not been successful
- ▽ Diagnostic data
- ▽ Medical information
- ▽ Classroom observations
- ▽ Time-on-task observations
- ▽ Family and caregiver input

The students requiring support at Tier 3 have significant learning gaps in universal or foundational skills. By using an efficient process for analyzing data, brainstorming, and problem solving, the intervention team can determine the intervention most likely to support students in closing their learning gaps in the universal skills identified for remediation.

According to Buffum et al. (2018), the six universal skills of learning include the following:

1. Decode and comprehend grade-level text.
2. Write effectively.
3. Apply number sense.
4. Comprehend the English language (or school's primary language).

5. Consistently demonstrate social and academic behaviors.

6. Overcome complications due to health or home. (p. 226)

It is important that intervention teams develop action plans that have a laser-like focus on remediating gaps in universal skills that place students on the path for success at their grade level. This requires that teachers align individual goals established at Tier 3 to the essential standards identified as critical for all students.

It is not uncommon to visit a school and, in discussing Tier 3, hear that "the individual goals are aligned to the standards" or that "our Tier 3 curriculum is aligned to the standards." The question is whether or not the goals and instruction are aligned to a universal skill and an essential standard identified by the grade-level teacher team as essential for all students.

For example, a Tier 3 intervention teacher may have a unit on rhyming words, and a third-grade student performing at the kindergarten level might have an individual goal in ELA intervention such as Common Core State Standard RF.K.2.A: "Recognize and produce rhyming words" (NGA & CCSSO, 2010). The teacher would be correct in stating that this goal is aligned to the standards, however, this would not be a standard that most grade-level teacher teams would identify as essential and is not associated with the universal skill of *decoding and comprehending at grade level*. The student would have a standards-aligned goal but would not be working on a skill preparing him or her for grade-level success.

Every teacher will likely agree that Common Core State Standard RF.3.3: "Know and apply grade-level phonics and word analysis skills in decoding words" (NGA & CCSSO, 2010) is an essential, universal skill. This standard appears in the Common Core State Standards in all grades K–5 with the associated grade-level supporting standards. This is an example of an essential standard that you would expect to find in all tiers of instruction, including the individual goals for students receiving Tier 3 remediation.

Teacher teams planning collaboratively with this standard can determine what students must do to demonstrate grade-level mastery, the specific phonetic skills required, and the progression of skills students should learn. This level of collaboration allows teachers to teach in a manner that places a student on the path for grade-level achievement.

The intervention team can use the tool in figure 7.4 (page 186) as a problem-solving form or agenda when determining an action plan addressing essential standards and skills.

Team Data Review: Action Plan

Use this tool to review data, determine targeted interventions, and monitor progress.

Student: _____

Meeting Date: _____

Step 1: State the Problem	Data reviewed: _____
• What are the students' needs?	Problem or concern:
	_____
	_____
	Trends in data:
	_____
	_____

Step 2:	Essential standard or standards assessed:
Analyze Data	_____
• What is the student's current performance level on learning targets?	Identified target skills: _____
	Current performance: _____
	Progress in interventions: _____
• What do the data say?	What has worked: _____
Brainstorm Solutions	What has not worked: _____
• What is the targeted need?	**Determine the Intervention**
• What strategy, support, or intervention should we try?	Action: _____
	_____
	_____
	_____
	_____
	Person responsible: _____

Step 3: Monitor the Plan	Goal: _____
• What are our success criteria, goal, and timeline?	Timeline: _____
	Date to reassess: _____
• When will we reassess?	Date to review progress: _____
• When will we meet to review?	Person responsible: _____
	Notes: _____
	_____

Figure 7.4: Team data review—action plan.

Visit **go.SolutionTree.com/RTIatWork** *for a free reproducible version of this figure.*

Strategies for Best Practice

In *High-Leverage Practices in Special Education* (McLeskey et al., 2017), the authors discuss high-leverage practices (HLPs) to be used in teacher preparation programs to provide special education teachers with effective practices to use with their students. They state that "The 22 HLPs are intended to address the most critical practices that every K–12 special education teacher should master" (McLeskey et al., 2017, p. 11). They explain that these practices are considered to be effective in both special education and general education classrooms. HLPs represent strategies or practices that will benefit all teachers serving students with significant gaps in learning.

Given the importance of collaboration between general education and all intervention teachers, it is important that staff serving students at Tier 3 understand and use the HLPs shared in this publication as baseline strategies and tools. The practices outlined in this document are instructional strategies or approaches that teachers can use across subject areas and benefit students with and without disabilities who are served at Tier 3.

Table 7.1 outlines the high-leverage practices that McLeskey et al. (2017) identify in the left column, and we include a brief description in the right column. We urge schools to work with all teachers planning and delivering instruction at Tier 3 to ensure that they understand and use these practices regularly.

Table 7.1: High-Leverage Practices for Special Education

Best Practice	Description
1. Collaborate with professionals to increase student success.	Collaboration between all members of the school team, including general education teachers, special education teachers, and interventionists, is intentional and ongoing to support mastery of students' academic and behavior goals.
2. Organize and facilitate effective meetings with professionals and families.	Individual teachers, teacher teams, and intervention teams organize meetings with families, colleagues, and other service providers through the use of agendas, meeting norms, and other tools to focus the meeting on achieving the meetings' stated purpose.
3. Collaborate with families to support student learning and secure needed services.	Teachers and intervention teams build positive and respectful collaborative relationships with families to support student learning.
4. Use multiple sources of information to develop a comprehensive understanding of students' strengths and needs.	Teachers use data from multiple sources, such as formal and informal assessments, curriculum-based assessments, observations, and student work, to create a comprehensive learner profile of student strengths and weaknesses.

continued →

Best Practice	Description
5. Interpret and communicate assessment information with stakeholders to collaboratively design and implement educational programs.	Teachers understand and communicate assessment information to team members in order to collaboratively develop targeted goals.
6. Use student assessment data, analyze instructional practices, and make necessary adjustments that improve student outcomes.	Teachers use ongoing formative data to monitor student progress, determine what is working and what is not, and adjust instruction accordingly.
7. Establish a consistent, organized, and respectful learning environment.	Teachers establish age-appropriate expectations, routines, and procedures within their classrooms that are positively stated and explicitly taught and practiced.
8. Provide positive and constructive feedback to guide students' learning and behavior.	Teachers provide ongoing goal-directed feedback to students as they work toward mastering their goals.
9. Teach social behaviors.	Teachers explicitly teach social behaviors aligned to schoolwide expectations. If students do not know how to perform a skill, it should be directly taught. We recommend explicitly teaching academic behaviors as well as social behaviors.
10. Conduct functional behavioral assessments to develop individual student behavior support plans.	Creating behavior plans and conducting functional behavior assessments is a process all teachers at Tier 3 should understand. (You can find more detailed information regarding functional behavior assessments in chapter 6, page 119). Behavior goals include teaching the student a pro-social replacement behavior.
11. Identify and prioritize long- and short-term learning goals.	Teachers use grade-level essential standards, assessment data, learning progressions, and other assessment information to make decisions about individual goals.
12. Systematically design instruction toward a specific learning goal.	Planning includes determining the skills and concepts necessary to achieve the identified goal and developing a clear path for student mastery.
13. Adapt curriculum tasks and materials for specific learning goals.	Teachers assess the individual needs of students and how they best learn. They select and adjust curriculum materials to maximize the opportunity for student success on the learning target.
14. Teach cognitive and metacognitive strategies to support student learning and independence.	Teachers teach cognitive and metacognitive strategies. These strategies support memory, attention, and self-regulation. Student goal setting and self-monitoring of progress are important to both learning and independence.

Best Practice	Description
15. Provide scaffolded supports.	Teachers use various types of verbal, visual, or physical assistance that supports students in performing skills they have not yet mastered. They gradually remove support as students master learning and become independent.
16. Use explicit instruction.	Teachers use explicit instruction to teach new skills. They model concepts or skills students need to master the content. They use examples and non-examples, highlight information, and remove extraneous information and other strategies to explicitly teach, model, and enhance student learning.
17. Use flexible grouping.	Teachers use various grouping strategies to teach specific goals or learning targets. Students may be in same or mixed ability groups based on the goal. Groups are used to target instruction for specific learning needs, foster collaboration, support varying abilities, and enhance vocabulary and comprehension.
18. Use strategies to promote active student engagement.	Teachers use a variety of strategies to promote active engagement. Strategies such as connections to real life, various grouping strategies, and technology are approaches a teacher might use to increase engagement.
19. Use assistive and instructional technologies.	Teachers evaluate and use instructional technology and assistive technology to promote student learning and independence.
20. Provide intensive instruction.	Teachers match the intensity of instruction to students' needs. They use grouping, systematic instruction, and frequent feedback as students learn.
21. Teach students to maintain and generalize new learning across time and settings.	Teachers use specific techniques to help students generalize and maintain learning over time. Teachers use strategies such as material reviews, practicing new skills in multiple environments, and using numerous examples and opportunities for practice in initial instruction.

Source: Adapted from McLeskey et al., 2017.

*Visit **go.SolutionTree.com/RTIatWork** for a free reproducible version of this table.*

Figure 7.5 (page 190) provides concrete examples and explanations of four of the high-leverage practices outlined in table 7.1. These examples demonstrate how high-leverage practices can be implemented in the classroom.

The best practice is described in the left column, the strategy is in the middle column, and a concrete example is in the right column. We encourage teachers to use or modify these examples to meet the needs of their students.

190 BEST PRACTICES AT TIER 3, ELEMENTARY

Best Practice	Strategy	Description or Example
Provide positive and constructive feedback to guide students' learning and behavior.	Provide positive and constructive feedback, which allows students to see what they are doing right and how they can improve. It gives them a path or strategy for accomplishing their goals. Student goal-setting is one way that teachers can provide explicit feedback. Student goal-setting should include: • Helping students have clear and meaningful targets • Establishing small yet meaningful goals • Creating a process for regular feedback	**Student Goal-Setting and Feedback Matrix** **Make It:** **S**pecific, Targeted, and Strategic **M**easurable **A**ttainable **R**esults Oriented **T**ime Bound Date: _____ Student Name: _____ Teacher Name: _____ Subject: _____ | Student Goal *I can…*	Timeline	Learning Targets	Activity, Quiz, or Self-Assessment	Grade, Mastery Percentage, or Specific Feedback
---	---	---	---	---
					  This tool includes a short-term goal *I can* statement, timeline, and learning targets. There may be several steps or progressions worded as *I can* statements that students take as they work toward mastery of a learning target. There is a place for students to track their own progress as well as for the teacher to log feedback. This could be amended to meet the needs of students in the following ways: • Use graphics for each step. For example, the "I can" statement might have a thumbs up, and the timeline might have a clock. • The progress check might be maintained by coloring bar graphs. • The feedback might be oral and provide examples.

		Example Cognitive Strategy
Teach cognitive and metacognitive strategies to support student learning and independence.	Cognitive strategies help students think strategically and organize their learning. These strategies help students organize their learning and increase their efficiency in approaching a task. The Tic-Tac-Toe Board described in the next column is an example of a cognitive strategy.	Create a Tic-Tac-Toe Board with activities or steps leading to mastery of a target. Students receive a timeline for completion. Include an activity tied to a student's goal in each block. Direct students to start at the center and then complete two additional tasks to complete a tic-tac-toe. After students complete the first series of three, direct them to tic-tac-toe in another direction. Task / Task / Task Task / ★ / Task (Task) Task / Task / Task
	Metacognitive strategies help students monitor and think about what they are learning. As students begin to understand how they learn, they will use these processes as they acquire new information. Examples include: • Checklists • Rubrics • Structured note taking • Graphic organizers • Think alouds	**Example Metacognitive Strategy** As students read or listen to nonfiction books, they look for the title and author, make note of important vocabulary, and think about new learning and questions. This process provides students a way to organize and think about their learning. **My Reading Notepad: Nonfiction Books** Students write or sketch notes to organize their thinking as they read. Book Title: Author: **Vocabulary Words**: Word / Meaning I Learned! Questions

Figure 7.5: Implementing high-leverage practices.

continued →

Best Practice	Strategy	Description or Example
Use strategies to promote active student engagement.	Teachers can increase student engagement by having students become actively involved in the learning process. Students should be involved in active listening, talking, writing, reading, and reflecting about learning. Teachers can accomplish this in a variety of ways, including: • Grouping strategies • Questioning strategies • Incorporating technology • Incorporating movement Monitor teacher talk time to no more than ten minutes paired with a minimum of two minutes of student processing time.	**Example Questioning Strategy** Numbered heads is a questioning strategy that involves all students. Students with significant academic challenges benefit from hearing the conversation of a group. This strategy is used to summarize information or come to agreement on an answer. Students work in groups. They can be in their regular teams or in new group formations of three to five. Each student has a number. • Teacher poses a question. • Students agree on the answer. • Teacher calls a number. • Teacher calls on one student from one group or all students with that number from all groups.

Teach students to maintain and generalize new learning across time and settings.	Students with academic and behavioral challenges have difficulty transferring skills and strategies from one setting to another as well as from one subject to the next. It is important to provide structures, such as checklists or other tools, to aid them in remembering to use the strategy in all classes. It is very helpful if teachers discuss the strategies in all settings and plan how they will commonly support their use.	It is very helpful to have a checklist or reward system that reminds students as well as all teachers to use important strategies. Teachers can create a simple checklist with important vocabulary, academic, or behavior strategies. They can use this checklist as a daily reminder or reward system for students.

Strategies to Remember

Strategies or Vocabulary I Am Supposed to Use Each Day

Class Period or Setting	Great Job!	OOPS!

Source: Adapted from McLeskey et al., 2017.

*Visit **go.SolutionTree.com/RTIatWork** for a free reproducible version of this figure.*

Teachers and students can use the Student Goal-Setting and Feedback Matrix in figure 7.6 as they implement student goal setting and provide feedback. The description of this strategy in figure 7.5 (page 190) offers suggestions for how teachers can modify it for individual students.

Student Goal-Setting and Feedback Matrix

Make It:

Specific, Targeted, and Strategic
Measurable
Attainable
Results Oriented
Time Bound

Date: _____

Student Name: _____

Teacher Name: _____

Subject: _____

Student Goal I can...	Timeline	Learning Targets	Activity, Quiz, or Self-Assessment	Grade, Mastery Percentage, or Specific Feedback

---

Figure 7.6: Student goal-setting and feedback matrix.

*Visit **go.SolutionTree.com/RTIatWork** for a free reproducible version of this figure.*

Students use the far-left column to track their small steps toward mastery of a learning target. They can include more than one *I can* statement for each learning target. These statements are intended to be student-friendly examples of the learning targets. For example, the learning target *Tell about a topic or name a book* may have multiple *I can* statements, such as *I can identify a topic* and *I can tell you the topic of the book I am reading.*

Students use the activity, quiz, or self-assessment column to indicate what they are using to gauge progress. The teacher and student discuss this when establishing the goal. They can measure progress with a quiz or assessment, or informally, such as students self-assessing their own progress.

The teacher completes the grade, mastery percentage, or specific feedback column as he or she provides specific feedback. Feedback should include an explanation to students regarding what they did correct, how they can improve, and specific steps to take toward their goal. The teacher may make a simple note on the form, but it should be accompanied with an explanation to help the student improve.

Referenced in figure 7.5 (page 190), figure 7.7 shows an example of a metacognitive strategy for students to use as they are reading. This helps students to organize and document and reflect on their learning. As students develop the habit of reflecting on learning, they begin to notice how they learn best and regularly use strategies they find helpful.

My Reading Notepad: Nonfiction Books

Students write or sketch notes to organize their thinking as they read.

Book Title:

Author:

Vocabulary Words

Word	Meaning

I Learned!

Questions

Figure 7.7: My reading notepad—nonfiction books.

*Visit **go.SolutionTree.com/RTIatWork** for a free reproducible version of this figure.*

Also referenced in figure 7.5, figure 7.8 (page 196) shows an example of how teachers can help students generalize their learning across different settings. As students practice using targeted strategies, it will increase the frequency that they are regularly used.

Strategies to Remember

Strategies or Vocabulary I Am Supposed to Use Each Day

Class Period or Setting	Great Job!	OOPS!
	⭐	😮
	⭐	😮
	⭐	😮
	⭐	😮
	⭐	😮
	⭐	😮
	⭐	😮

Figure 7.8: Strategies to remember.

*Visit **go.SolutionTree.com/RTIatWork** for a free reproducible version of this figure.*

As with all decisions regarding interventions, determining time and intensity should be based on the needs of individual students and their data. Students' needs are greater at Tier 3; therefore, teachers must intensify the intervention. They can do this in various ways, including the following.

1. **Increase time:** Increase instructional time per week in both duration and frequency.

2. **Use smaller group sizes:** Create groups in Tier 3 that are smaller than groups in Tier 2.

3. **Monitor progress:** Measure student progress more frequently and in a way that is more individualized.

4. **Slow the pace:** Ensure the pace of instruction is slower and more deliberate so skills are introduced, taught, and practiced over a series of focused lessons.

5. **Offer targeted skills:** Provide explicit, targeted instruction on a focused set of skills.

6. **Provide repeated practice:** Offer repeated opportunities for practice in multiple environments.

Intervention teams should make all decisions regarding intervention intensity based on data. As intervention teams work in collaboration with teachers to monitor progress, they can adjust all facets of the instructional program, including time and intensity, based on students' need.

Conclusion

Approaching learning through the UDL lens provides the process for collaborative teacher teams to plan in advance for the needs of all learners. We have had the experience of working with students who face significant obstacles and have seen the amazing results when the school changed its mindset from "They can't" to "What can we do to make it possible?" We urge all schools to resist the urge to define students based on labels or presumptions of what they can or can't achieve. By removing barriers and increasing support, schools can see students achieve beyond what many may have thought possible.

> "Test scores and measures of achievement tell you where a student is, but they don't tell you where a student could end up."
>
> —Carol Dweck

The RTI at Work model referenced throughout this book is the framework for implementing successful educational practices with all students. It is grounded in strong Tier 1 instruction and using data to intervene by the student and by the skill at every tier of instruction. It is a best practice approach for every student. Implementing this model requires a shift in thinking from reacting and labeling students after they fail to a proactive model implemented with a sense of urgency and collective responsibility for all students to reach high levels of learning.

We encourage all teacher and intervention teams to believe in their collective power, believe in themselves, and believe in their students. Start with a dream . . . make a plan . . . and work together to see it become reality.

The last chapter offers leadership, intervention, and teacher teams practical, job-embedded learning activities as they work together to improve the implementation of Tier 3 interventions. We urge all teams to embrace the opportunity to design a system in which the goal of every student and teacher can be realized—high levels of learning for all.

Chapter 7 Action Steps

With your team, engage in the following action steps to review and implement the learning from this chapter.

1. As you move forward with implementing Tier 3 interventions, Buffum et al. (2018) suggest asking yourself the following questions.

    a. **Targeted:** What exactly is the intervention's purpose? What specific skill, content, or behavior should students learn by the end of the intervention? If you can't specify this, it's a clear indication that the intervention is not targeted enough. To remedy this problem, make the intervention more focused.

    b. **Systematic:** Is there a systematic process to identify every student who needs help in the intervention's targeted area? Once identified, can all the students that need the intervention actually receive the intervention? If a team answers *no* to either of these questions, what steps can you take to make the intervention more systematic?

    c. **Research-based:** What research or evidence validates that the intervention has a high likelihood of working? If you can't cite any, then discontinue the practice and study better practices to reteach the targeted outcome.

    d. **Administered by a trained professional:** Who is currently administering the intervention? Are they properly trained and competent at this task? If not, does the school have staff who are better trained, or can the school provide the staff member additional training and support to become more effective?

    e. **Timely:** How long does it take to identify and place students in the intervention? We suggest it should not take longer than three weeks.

    f. **Directive:** Are targeted students required to attend? If not, what steps can you take to ensure students needing help are present for the intervention? (p. 256)

2. Consider how teacher teams can use instructional strategies offered in this chapter to build a bank of ideas that they can readily access when designing instruction. This might be an electronic tool, such as a Google spreadsheet, and does not have to be lengthy. As teachers gain comfort in utilizing a few of the high-leverage practices outlined in this chapter, they can continue to add to their bank of ideas.

Personalized Learning for Teams

I n this chapter, we provide learning activities that allow leadership teams, teacher teams, intervention teams, and individual teachers to apply the learning in this book. These tools and activities are intended to deepen your learning and support the implementation of practices discussed in earlier chapters. The activities are designed for:

▽ Monitoring the implementation of action steps

▽ Applying your learning and providing tools for immediate use

▽ Building shared knowledge

Each activity provides an explanation of who it is for, why it is important, suggestions for how to use it, and a description of its connection to Tier 3.

Allowing practitioners the opportunity to learn and apply the concepts and principles of this book moves the reader from learning to doing. As stated in the seminal work of DuFour et al. (2016), "Most educators acknowledge that our deepest insights and understandings come from action, followed by reflection and search for improvement" (p. 9).

It is our intention that the following activities allow educators and the collaborative teams they work with to learn and continue to improve so that together, they can meet the common goal of high levels of learning for all students.

As DuFour (2015) states: "Any school dedicated to ensuring all students learn at high levels must stop debating what they *think* students can or can't do and instead change the question to this: *How will we get every learner there?*" (p. 205).

Activity 1: Planning Instruction for All Students

This activity is designed to support efficient and effective collaborative lesson planning. The Collaborative Planning for All Students Agenda in figure 8.1 (page 202) provides a process for collaborative teacher teams to hold instructional planning meetings that are efficient as well as effective in designing instruction that addresses the needs of all learners.

> "A single leaf
> working alone
> provides no shade."
>
> —Chuck Page

Review the first paragraph under Instructional Design for Diverse Learners (page 170) in chapter 7. The tool in figure 8.1 provides a structure for teachers to use when they are collaboratively planning instruction that accomplishes the goal of meeting the needs of students with varied interests, abilities, strengths, and challenges.

The four critical questions of a PLC (DuFour et al., 2016) guide the discussion in this agenda.

1. What do students need to know and be able to do?
2. How will we know when they have learned it?
3. What will we do when they haven't learned it?
4. What will we do when they already know it? (p. 251)

By using the agenda in figure 8.1, collaborative planning will have the following outcomes.

▽ A complete understanding of the essential standards being addressed in the instructional plan

▽ A reflection on the mastery criteria of the summative and any mid-unit assessments

▽ An instructional plan that considers students' unique learning variances

▽ A plan for those students who may continue to need support after initial instruction

▽ A plan for those students who need extended learning opportunities

Why It Is Important

It is essential that teacher teams have both the time and the structure necessary for effective collaborative planning. The agenda provides a protocol teacher teams can use to ensure that the time they spend in planning results in a plan of instruction that maximizes the success of every learner.

How to Use This Activity

Teams can use this activity to develop a meeting agenda that ensures their instruction is aligned to the standards as well as the assessments. Discussion should lead to a unit of instruction planned with all students' needs in mind. Teams may be comprised of all general educators or include interventionists or special education teachers. The agenda can be personalized to meet the needs of any team.

1. Using the agenda in figure 8.1 (page 202), teams should begin by reviewing the following.

    ▸ **Roles and responsibilities:** Teams should consider the roles and responsibilities their team needs to ensure their planning meetings are efficient. Many teams assign roles, such as facilitator, note taker, data facilitator, resource manager, and so on. They can build team capacity by rotating roles and responsibilities among team members periodically.

    ▸ **Meeting norms:** The development and use of norms are critically important to effective and efficient meetings. Teams should review norms at each meeting.

    ▸ **Pertinent data:** All team meetings may not have data to be discussed. It is important that teams have a schedule and allow time for data review after common assessments.

2. Before designing instruction, teams should consider and discuss critical questions one and two of a PLC.

    ▸ **What do students need to know and be able to do?** Teams should have a common understanding of what students should know, understand, and be able to do as a result of instruction. The standard and the learning targets should be outlined prior to designing assessment and instruction. Some schools analyze and unwrap standards at the beginning of a semester or on a professional development day. If this has been done in advance of the meeting, discussion should include a reflection on prior work to bring the expectation of the standard to the forefront of instructional planning.

    ▸ **How will we know when they have learned it?** If teams have developed a common, end-of-unit assessment, they should review it to ensure that they identify learning targets and plan instruction aligned to the assessment. If teams have not developed a common, end-of-unit assessment, they should determine what learning will be assessed in a summative assessment and what will be assessed mid-cycle. All team members should have an understanding of what students should be able to do mid-unit and end-of-unit to demonstrate mastery prior to designing instruction.

3. Develop the instructional plan to proactively support students predicted to have difficulty. Plan initial instruction so it aligns to the standard and the assessment and maximizes the opportunity for success of all learners.

    ▸ **What will we do when they haven't learned it?** Some students may continue to struggle after initial instruction. Teachers should consider what else can be done to maximize each student's opportunity for success.

    ▸ **What will we do when they already know it?** Instructional plans should consider the needs of students who may have already mastered the learning target and require learning extensions.

4. Assign follow-up tasks to team members, such as locating materials or sharing team documents with colleagues.

Collaborative Planning for All Students
Meeting Norms
_____
_____
_____
Roles and Responsibilities
Facilitator: _____
Time keeper: _____
Recorder: _____
Other:
_____
_____

Agenda	Time
1. Review the following:	
• Team member roles and responsibilities	
• Meeting norms	
• Pertinent data (when applicable): pre-assessments, common formative assessments, or summative assessments	

2. Before designing instruction, teams should consider and discuss critical questions one and two of a PLC:	
What do students need to know and be able to do? • Analyze the standards to ensure that all team members understand the required learning of each essential standard in the unit. If you have done this in advance of the meeting, briefly review your work. • Determine learning targets. If you have determined these previously, briefly review them.	
How will we know when they have learned it? • Collaboratively agree on the summative and mid-unit assessments you will use during the unit of instruction. If you have previously determined the common, end-of-unit assessment, briefly review it.	
3. Design instruction for all students. Consider specific students and their unique needs. What strategies can be utilized to address the unique learning needs of your classrooms? Consider students that you predict may have difficulty and proactively address their needs.	
What will we do when they haven't learned it? • Have a plan in place for students who may continue to struggle after initial instruction. Consider strategies to provide additional explanation or alternate means of presentation, such as hands-on activities, videos, graphic organizers, and so on.	
What will we do when they already know it? • Include strategies for those students who need their learning extensions.	
4. Assign follow-up activities to team members. Is there a need for specific books and materials? Who can locate and access these items, and when? Is there a need for ideas or strategies to use with specific students? If so, who will provide these, and when?	
Total Time for Meeting	

Figure 8.1: Collaborative planning for all students.

*Visit **go.SolutionTree.com/RTIatWork** for a free reproducible version of this figure.*

Connection to Tier 3

Working as a team to consider the needs of all students ensures that those with the greatest needs will have plans in place to maximize success. If the team includes interventionists or special education teachers who serve specific students, then plans can be aligned so all staff members are working toward the same goal and utilizing similar strategies.

Activity 2: Teaching Essential Academic and Social Behaviors

This activity is designed for individuals, teacher teams, or a site intervention team. It is intended to engage educators in problem solving to determine interventions to address both social and academic behaviors.

Why It Is Important

All educators at all tiers of instruction have students who have social and academic behaviors that interfere with learning. Many of these students also require academic intervention. It is important that teacher teams problem solve and determine how to explicitly teach essential behaviors.

How to Use This Activity

Teacher teams or individual teachers can use this activity for continued learning. It is intended to engage participants in a problem-solving and action-planning process that can be modified to meet their needs. As you read the following scenario, Ashton's Story, highlight the points that stand out to you.

Ashton's Story

Ashton is a student with poor social and academic behaviors. She is unmotivated, unengaged, and does not complete or organize her work. She is failing all subjects. When she is frustrated, she uses inappropriate language, walks away from teachers when they are talking, or tears up her work. She sometimes leaves class without permission but does not leave the school building. Teachers usually find her sitting alone in a hall away from others. Her teachers are frustrated and do not know what to do.

Ashton's universal screener and essential standard benchmark assessments indicate that she is three years below level in mathematics. She has not memorized basic mathematics facts and has difficulty with calculations. She is currently in a mathematics intervention at Tier 3 four times per week for thirty minutes. She is making progress, but it is slow.

Her reading level is below average but is within one year of grade level. She enjoys art and does well with oral directions or prompts. When teachers break her work into small components or chunks, it is helpful for her.

---

1. Based on the scenario, discuss or make note of the following.

   ▸ What is working, or what have teachers tried?

   ▸ What are the behaviors that need to be targeted?

   ▸ What seems to be the cause or trigger for misbehavior?

2. Read and discuss:

   ▸ Review the three scenarios about Nia, Wyatt, and Regen in chapter 6 (pages 126–130). As you read, highlight strategies that stand out to you. Some strategies can be used with students of all ages and skill levels.

   ▸ Read the section Self-Monitoring and Self-Management at Tier 3 in chapter 6 (page 146).

   ▸ Discuss the CICO strategy featured in chapter 6 (page 147). Consider whether it would be an option for Ashton. Do you feel that CICO would be helpful in reducing her frustration? If Ashton were in your school, how might you personalize a CICO system for her? Consider figure 6.7, Check-In/Check-Out Weekly Points (page 150). What would you identify as a targeted goal, and how might you use this in your school?

   ▸ Read the section Calm-Down Strategies in chapter 6 (page 154). Discuss the considerations or actions related to teaching the three steps:

      - Teach the student how to identify emotions.

      - Teach the student self-calming strategies.

      - Practice self-calming strategies with the student.

3. Take action:

   ▸ Refer to figure 6.6, Behavior Intervention Team Meeting Tool (page 144). Read and discuss the tool and note how it can be used for an initial meeting or as a follow-up to monitor progress. Use this process to create a mock action plan for Ashton.

After considering these questions for Ashton, repeat the process for one of your own students.

Connection to Tier 3

As the site intervention team develops an action plan, they must consider how to implement it in all environments (for example, general education, interventions, physical education) and who will monitor student progress. Communication and collaboration between all staff responsible for implementing the action plan are critical. You can use this activity to improve action-planning or progress-monitoring processes for students needing behavior intervention at Tier 2 or Tier 3.

Activity 3: Using Collaborative Structures to Ensure High Levels of Learning at Tier 3

This activity is designed for members of the leadership team or guiding coalition. It is intended to help these teams in identifying essential action steps as well as their next steps in achieving the goal of high levels of achievement for all students. We encourage teams to use this tool at the beginning of each school year and at mid-year to develop long- and short-term goals.

Why It Is Important

It is important for teams to commit to continual improvement. As team members change and the school improves, taking the time to reflect on progress as well as work together to determine the next steps to take is important for sustaining change and ongoing improvement.

How to Use This Activity

Figure 8.2, Leadership Team Reflection Tool, is designed for members of the leadership team or guiding coalition as they consider their work, their goals, and the actions to prioritize for a given time period.

Teams should discuss and come to a common agreement of the meaning of the success criteria. They should ask themselves, "What would this look and sound like in my school?" The team should carefully consider where they are in implementation and make note of their current actions as well as next steps.

Connection to Tier 3

The success criteria in figure 8.2 are important to laying a firm foundation at Tiers 1 and 2, and they reflect the beliefs and actions necessary to implement RTI at Work at all tiers. Tier 3 is directly supported by all actions included in this tool.

High Achievement for All Learners
Check Yourself
Do We Have a Firm Foundation at Tier 1 and Tier 2?
The leadership team reviews the following criteria to help them determine next steps in achieving the goal of high levels of achievement for all learners. The success criteria in the left column are areas critical to creating a firm foundation at Tier 1 and Tier 2. As leadership teams discuss the practices listed in the left column, they make note of their current practices and next steps in the right column.

Foundational Success Criteria	Practices Currently in Place and Next Steps for Our Team
Beliefs and Culture	**Beliefs drive the practices of the school.**
The school values collaborative decision making.	
All staff see all students as their responsibility.	
Learning is the fundamental purpose of the school.	
Leaders at all levels continuously use data to improve teaching and learning.	
Collaborative Practices	**Collaborative teams work for the common purpose of high levels of achievement for all learners.**
Grade or subject-level educators regularly collaborate with interventionists and special educators to align practices.	
All teachers have regularly scheduled collaborative time for planning and data review during the school day.	
Teachers use collaborative practices such as co-planning, commonly developed assessments, co-teaching, or partner teaching.	
The school uses partnerships with outside agencies to allow for wraparound services.	
"All Means All" Academic Instruction	**The school uses inclusive practices to improve achievement of all learners.**
The RTI at Work model is in place at all tiers of instruction.	
Students receive support, including intense interventions based on identified needs, not labels.	
Teams match intense interventions to the type and intensity of student need.	
All work, including instructional planning, is guided by the four critical questions essential for learning (DuFour et al., 2016): 1. What do students need to know and be able to do? 2. How will we know when they have learned it? 3. What will we do when they haven't learned it? 4. What will we do when they already know it? (p. 251)	

Figure 8.2: Leadership team reflection tool.

continued →

"All Means All" Academic Instruction	The school uses inclusive practices to improve achievement of all learners.
Staff understand and use the principles of UDL when planning.	
Teachers consistently use flexible grouping to increase student engagement and participation in learning.	
Differentiation and UDL are common practices in all classrooms.	
Teacher teams design Tier 3 interventions to support students in achieving essential standards.	
All students receive instruction in grade-level essential standards.	
"All Means All" Behavior Instruction	**Positive behavior support is in place at all tiers of instruction.**
The RTI at Work model includes both academic and behavior supports at all tiers of instruction.	
Leadership and teacher teams have identified all essential behavior skills.	
Universal screening includes assessment of academic and social behaviors.	
The leadership team has developed a matrix for teaching behavior schoolwide.	
Schoolwide behavior instruction occurs multiple times per year in order to reinforce, reteach, and address the needs of students new to campus.	
Teachers explicitly teach behavior, including self-monitoring and self-management at Tiers 2 and 3.	
The intervention team has a process to identify, action plan, and progress monitor for behavior.	
Educator Supports	**Educators at all levels receive the support necessary for the implementation of PLC at Work and RTI at Work practices.**
New initiatives are limited to those necessary for teams to grow and learn in the implementation of PLC at Work and RTI at Work practices, which includes topics such as high-impact instruction, assessment, use of data, and collaborative practices. Those topics critical to success receive sustained staff development.	
All staff are provided targeted PD as needed to meet student achievement goals.	

Collaborative teams are encouraged to use action research to find and implement best practices.	
Data-Informed Practices	**Staff use data regularly for the purpose of continual improvement.**
The leadership team uses data to monitor school progress, guide instructional practices, and make school decisions.	
A system for monitoring student progress on essential academic and behavior standards is in place beginning at Tier 1.	
Universal screeners are in place for reading, math, and behavior.	
Common formative assessment results are used to adjust Tier 1 instruction and determine Tier 2 interventions.	
Teachers and the interventional team regularly monitor student progress in interventions for behavior and academics.	
The effectiveness of interventions is regularly reviewed.	

*Visit **go.SolutionTree.com/RTIatWork** for a free reproducible version of this figure.*

Activity 4: Determining Learning Progressions

This activity is designed for vertical teams, including general education teachers, curriculum specialists, interventionists, special education teachers, and others who may use learning progressions to align instruction across all tiers of instruction, determine goals, and monitor progress for individual students.

Why It Is Important

It is critical that all students are working on the same path toward mastery of essential standards. Learning progressions allow teams and teachers to work collaboratively and determine if a student is making progress toward mastery of an essential standard. It ensures that interventions are focused on skills determined to be essential for grade-level mastery.

How to Use This Activity

This activity should be used by teams of teachers and interventionists who are responsible for ensuring that interventions are aligned to the same essential standards as general education. It is intended to provide teachers with a hands-on learning opportunity as they develop a learning progression.

In this activity, participants develop a learning progression for one essential standard. They begin by identifying the critical subskills leading to mastery in one grade. They should select either the lowest or highest grade that applies to the standard. Typically, elementary grades begin with either kindergarten or grade 5. Secondary teams might begin with either grade 6 or grade 12. After completing a progression for one grade, participants repeat the process vertically. The vertically aligned progression of skills provides all teachers a list of critical skills that they can use to set goals, plan, and assess.

1. Review the section Establishing Learning Progressions in chapter 5 (page 100). Figure 5.3 (page 103) provides an example of how the process can be used for individual student goal setting. As seen in this example, teams should consider a student's current level of performance (where I am now) as well as his or her current grade level (where I am going) in determining the range of grades to include for individual goal setting.

2. Discuss the information and the process for developing a learning progression. How would this help you? How would it help students?

3. With teammates, agree on an essential standard aligned to a universal skill a student would address at Tier 3. You will use this standard in this activity.

> "Excellence is a continuous process and not an accident."
>
> —A. P. J. Abdul Kalam

For example, the team agrees on an essential standard for this work, such as Common Core State Standard W.3.1: "Write opinion pieces on topics or texts supporting a point of view with reasons" (NGA & CCSSO, 2010). This standard appears in the Common Core State Standards in all grades, kindergarten through grade 5.

Use the standard selected and complete the tool in figure 8.3 for either the lowest or highest grade. For example, a team who used the standard referenced would begin with either kindergarten or grade 5, and then replicate the process in the other grades. The team would then have a list of all essential skills for that standard K–5 that members could use for individual goal setting and progress monitoring. Be sure to include vertical team members with knowledge of this standard.

Consider your next steps. What essential standards will you use, and what will the process be for your team to move forward determining and using learning progressions?

Essential Standards for All Learners

Directions: Teacher teams work together to determine the skills that are critical stepping stones for a student to achieve mastery of the essential grade-level standard. Start this process with one grade level, and then continue with a vertical alignment lowest to highest grade or highest grade to lowest grade.

Essential Standard:

_____

_____

You do not have to list all skills. Include those that are critical stepping stones. Skills should be those that are commonly agreed to be the skills that students will typically master on their path toward the grade-level essential standard. There is not a set number of subskills that have to be determined.

Include how mastery may be determined or what this would look like in order for students to be assessed.

As you assess students, indicate where they are currently performing, and use the next highest skill as their personal goal.

Skill Essential Subskills Leading to Mastery of Standard	Mastery Criteria What Students Will Be Able to Do to Demonstrate Mastery

Figure 8.3: Determining a grade-level learning progression.

*Visit **go.SolutionTree.com/RTIatWork** for a free reproducible version of this figure.*

Connection to Tier 3

Learning progressions provide teachers with a clear path to align interventions at Tier 3 to grade-level essential standards. Using this progression for goal setting and progress monitoring gives students the opportunity to show their progress toward grade-level mastery.

Activity 5: Determining Team Membership

This activity is designed for the leadership team to ensure that team members on the leadership and intervention teams reflect a wide variety of talent, expertise, and skill.

Why It Is Important

The leadership and intervention teams require diversity of talent, experience, and background to fulfill their responsibilities effectively. Utilizing this activity and discussing who serves on the team ensure members reflect the broad range of talent needed.

How to Use This Activity

This activity could be a part of continued learning regarding the roles and responsibilities of teams. Individuals or teams should read the section in chapter 3, Considerations for Team Membership (page 53) and reflect on the team member characteristics outlined in this section.

> "The strength of a team is each individual member. The strength of each member is the team."
>
> –Phil Jackson

Connection to Tier 3

Team membership should include members who have a background and passion for students needing intense intervention. By selecting some members who have the skill and passion for working with students needing academic or behavior intervention at Tier 3, teams will be better prepared to fully implement RTI.

The leadership team can use figure 8.4 to help them gather information about staff and select teams with a variety of expertise. This tool could be used by the leadership team in determining the broad base of individuals asked to serve on both teams. The form could be shared, and all staff asked to complete their information. This allows the leadership team to see the wide range of skills available.

Current Grade Level and Courses	Name	Years Taught in Grade Levels and Courses	College Major and Minor	Specialized Trainings	Educational Passions
Fifth grade	Mario Gomez	Ten years Two at second grade Four at kindergarten Four at fifth grade	Education of the Deaf and Hard of Hearing Minor: Learning Handicapped	Differentiation for the Autistic Child Reading Engagement for All RTI training	Pulling for the underdog Co-curricular coaching

Figure 8.4: Staff background sheet.

*Visit **go.SolutionTree.com/RTIatWork** for a free reproducible version of this figure.*

Activity 6: Targeting Individual Student Needs

This activity is designed to support intervention team members in determining the needs of students at Tier 3. It can be used with individual students or shared with the leadership team as they reflect on the needs of all students at Tier 3.

Why It Is Important

For interventions to be effective, intervention teams must consider data, determine students' targeted needs, as well as outline who will provide the intervention and a process for monitoring progress. Teams need an efficient process for doing this important work.

How to Use This Activity

This activity can be used when teams are learning the purpose and role of the intervention team or deciding on an organizational tool to document individual interventions.

1. Read the section in chapter 5, Identifying and Targeting Needs at Tier 3 (page 95).

2. Analyze the Intervention Team Worksheet in figure 8.5. Notice the focus of this process on developing a detailed individual action plan based on multiple pieces of data. The team's problem-solving process should result in detailed action plans.

3. Consider a student you currently serve. Use figure 8.5 to create an action plan for this student.

4. Compare the discussion used in completing figure 8.5 and any differences to the action-planning process you have now.

5. How might you use or modify the worksheet in figure 8.5?

Connection to Tier 3

The tool in figure 8.5 helps teams determine specific goals for students. This is a critical decision for teams determining interventions at Tier 3. Often, students have multiple needs, and the intervention team needs to prioritize those needs to determine a small number of individual goals to monitor in incremental steps.

This process asks teams to consider the information necessary to create a detailed action plan. Considerations include:

▽ Using convergent data or multiple pieces of information to provide an understanding of why the student is having difficulty

▽ Determining the strategies to be used

Intervention Team Worksheet

Student Name: _____

Grade Level: _____

Date of Intervention Team Meeting: _____

Design Considerations for Each Student Needing Tier 3 Interventions

For this student, what specific skill or behavior deficits do the data indicate?

Notes (Be specific as to the team's outcome or decision):

What are the intervention strategies or programs to address these specific skill or behavior deficits? (When possible, use research-based strategies.)

Notes (Be specific as to the team's outcome or decision):

What are the intervention delivery grouping and scheduling to ensure the necessary time and intensity to accelerate learning?

Notes (Be specific as to the team's outcome or decision):

Who will provide remediation during Tier 3 intervention time? (Most qualified available)

Notes (Be specific as to the team's outcome or decision):

What are the data to be reviewed, the method for collecting the data, and duration between data points for progress monitoring (for example, progress monitoring bi-weekly using a running record)?

Notes (Be specific as to the team's outcome or decision):

What are the expected outcomes of Tier 3 intervention and the specific goals that this student will be striving to meet?

Notes (Be specific as to the team's outcome or decision):

What are the schedule and process for intervention and core teachers to collaborate regarding this student's progress and strategies?

Notes (Be specific as to the team's outcome or decision):

Figure 8.5: Intervention team worksheet.

*Visit **go.SolutionTree.com/RTIatWork** for a free reproducible version of this figure.*

   ▽ Identifying how students will be grouped to ensure that the intervention is intensive

   ▽ Establishing the frequency of progress monitoring

   ▽ Determining goals and outcomes

Activity 7: Leadership Team Monitoring Plan

This activity is designed to provide the leadership team with an easy-to-use process for monitoring the implementation of established goals and actions related to Tier 3 interventions. Each goal has a place for the team to document the evidence they will use to determine progress, who is responsible, and a timeline for monitoring.

Why It Is Important

The volume of work required to establish the RTI at Work process entails a wide range of people with varying roles and responsibilities. It is essential to determine a monitoring process while identifying goals.

How to Use This Activity

You can use figure 8.6 with any of the goals or actions established by the leadership team. Although it is specifically designed for Tier 3, you can use it for other goals associated with the implementation of RTI at Work. You can replicate this tool in an electronic form or maintain it on paper. Many schools keep a document, such as a running log, that the leadership team uses to organize, support, and monitor progress on established goals and actions.

Connection to Tier 3

The responsibilities of leadership teams are voluminous. It is imperative that the actions necessary to implement Tier 3 interventions remain organized and move forward in order to meet the collective commitment to students.

Figure 8.6 allows leadership teams to delineate their goals and the evidence they will use to determine progress. It also allows them to identify the person responsible for monitoring as well as a progress review date. Teams should have an established process and timeline for reviewing progress on each goal.

Activity 8: Getting to Know Our Learners

This activity is designed for collaborative teacher teams. Teams use this activity to apply the principles of UDL introduced in chapter 7, Academic Instruction at Tier 3 (page 167).

Working the Plan

Goal:

Evidence	Who Will Monitor and When

Goal:

Evidence	Who Will Monitor and When

Goal:

Evidence	Who Will Monitor and When

Figure 8.6: Working the plan.

*Visit **go.SolutionTree.com/RTIatWork** for a free reproducible version of this figure.*

Why It Is Important

All classrooms have students with a wide variety of learning needs. If teachers and teacher teams consider those needs in advance, they can incorporate many types of supports to facilitate student success in initial instruction. This proactive and efficient way of designing instruction utilizes the talents and skills of the entire team for the benefit of students at all tiers of instruction. For example, if a collaborative team of three teachers knows that they each have one or more students with significant gaps in reading, they can pre-plan for how they will address that issue related to each new unit of instruction.

The team may determine that a new unit has a significant amount of new vocabulary. Their discussions might lead to the team deciding that certain vocabulary needs to be pre-taught, or teachers may decide that they will support students who struggle in reading by incorporating technology or graphic organizers, or using shared reading in group work. This process incorporates the best thinking of the entire team and creates equitable instruction across classrooms.

How to Use This Activity

Teacher teams can use this activity when designing instruction with the needs of all students in mind.

1. Read this section in chapter 7, Universal Design for Learning (page 175).

2. Discuss what stands out to you in this section.

3. Pay particular attention to the final paragraph of the section that reads: When collaborative teacher teams, including special education and intervention teachers, come together to commonly plan units of instruction, all students benefit. All classrooms serve students with diverse learning needs. By predicting the types of difficulty learners may have and planning in advance to prevent failure, the outcomes for all students improve. This way of thinking and planning benefits students with significant learning gaps including those with identified disabilities, while providing equal benefit to those who speak different languages, have difficulty focusing, and the many other learning variances seen across classrooms.

   ▸ How does this compare to how you currently work? If you do not currently do this, what could you and your team do to replicate this thinking?

   ▸ Review the tool in figure 8.7, Who Are Our Learners, and What Are Their Needs? Figure 8.8 (page 220) provides a completed example.

   ▸ As a team, discuss the students you currently serve. What type of learning needs do they have? What should you consider in all instructional planning? For example, do you have students with large gaps in reading or difficulty attending to tasks? Consider how these students learn best and the type of instructional strategies that could be regularly used to support them.

The tool in figure 8.7 is intended to assist teacher teams in planning in advance for the types of learning variances students present. They can use this process to consider similar learning needs of students in more than one classroom as well as to plan for

List the Types of Learning Variances You Must Consider in Planning	Example: Below Grade-Level Readers	Example: Inattentive Students	Example: Students Whose Primary Language Is Not English
List Students			
How They Learn Best			
Considerations for Differentiation			
How This Will Support Student Success			

Figure 8.7: Who are our learners, and what are their needs?

*Visit **go.SolutionTree.com/RTIatWork** for a free reproducible version of this figure.*

individual students. The goal is for teacher teams to have an easy process they can incorporate into their planning time that supports the needs of diverse learners.

Connection to Tier 3

This collaborative process provides teachers with the best thinking of their entire team in order to have proactive plans in place to address learning variances. When teachers consider the needs of all learners in advance, including those receiving intense interventions, the students with significant learning gaps benefit, as well as the whole class.

This process is not intended to produce an exhaustive list of ideas or name every student with a minor problem. It is intended to outline the major areas in which

List the Types of Learning Variances You Must Consider in Planning	Example: Below Grade-Level Readers	Example: Inattentive Students	Example: Students Whose Primary Language Is Not English
List Students	Kim, Will	Jaime, Christopher, Brianna, Jasmine	Maria, Rosa, Javier
How They Learn Best	• When working and discussing in groups • When graphics are used with text	• When activities are step by step • When they can move during class • When there is limited information or number of pages at a time	• When explanations or clarifications are in Spanish • When text and explanations include graphics
Considerations for Differentiation	• Incorporate group reading/ discussion strategies. • Use graphic organizers. • Use graphic representations when presenting new vocabulary.	• Break work into small increments or chunk assignments. • Use overview or unit organization sheet. • Use stress balls or other objects to reduce fidgeting. • Alternate seating such as floor space, table space, standing tables, or stools. • Include increased white space on handouts.	• Utilize technology and group work to incorporate discussion and reinforcement in Spanish. • Use graphic representations when presenting new vocabulary.
How This Will Support Student Success	• Improves comprehension by reducing the impact of reading challenges	• Organizes assignments • Reduces distractions by increasing white space on handouts • Provides for movement	• Reduces the impact of language on comprehension

Figure 8.8: Who are our learners, and what are their needs? example.

*Visit **go.SolutionTree.com/RTIatWork** for a free reproducible version of this figure.*

students have difficulty, and provide a list of strategies that you can regularly incorporate into instruction. It is a simple and doable manner for teams to think proactively about the needs of students.

Conclusion

The words of DuFour et al. (2016) provide the rationale for this chapter:

> If the organization is to become more effective in helping all students learn, the adults in the organization must be continually learning. Therefore, structures are created to ensure staff members engage in job-embedded learning as part of their routine work practices. (p. 11)

This chapter was written to provide educators with tools for their continued learning as they work to fulfill the mission of high levels of learning for *all* students. This mission requires that educators embrace working and learning together to ensure that they are equipped to utilize practices that maximize student success.

Chapter 8 Action Steps

With your team, engage in the following action steps to review and implement the learning from this chapter.

1. Utilize tools, such as Figure 1.2, RTI Alignment at Tiers 1, 2, and 3 (page 26), and Figure 7.3, Essential Academic Skills Leadership Team Checklist (page 182), to determine areas for growth. Identify activities in this chapter or other chapters in the book that will support you in meeting your goals.

2. Commit to job-embedded learning. By using the structures, processes, and tools in this book, the leadership team, intervention team, and teacher teams can learn as they work.

3. Use student data regularly and for the purpose of identifying targeted areas for individual, team, and school improvement. Use the information the data provide to guide goal setting and targeted professional learning.

Final Thoughts

Throughout this book, we have shared stories of amazing schools, students, families, and educators whom we have had the honor to work with. Our mission was to use our collective experience, research, and examples of the RTI at Work process to help all collaborative teams ensure high levels of learning for all students. We will leave you with these final thoughts about the journey we believe is the most exciting one a school can take—working as a collective, collaborative team to ensure that every student leaves school with the essential skills necessary to fulfill their hopes and dreams in life.

▽ **Understand the mission and vision of your school and team:** It is imperative that you take the time to be crystal clear on your beliefs, mission, and vision. Every day brings numerous opportunities for you to voice and take action on a mission of high levels of learning for all. We urge every team to ask themselves what the school, classrooms, and meetings will look and sound like when this mission guides all actions. In order for a mission and vision to become reality, it takes clarity and commitment. It must become a habit to reflect and ask whether individual actions and discussions are consistent with common commitments.

▽ **Share a collective commitment:** The commitment of every employee to every student is paramount if you are to achieve the goal of high levels of learning for all students. Labels such as *special education student, low-income student, low reader,* or *should be in special education* should be replaced with *all students are our students* and a common acceptance that every student can and must learn essential standards.

▽ **Always put *why* before *what*:** Clearly understand and communicate why this is vital life-saving work, and be sure that this is communicated in relation to every new process or procedure.

▽ **Establish systems and processes:** The RTI at Work process creates a systematic process at all tiers of instruction that improves the education of every student. You may choose to use the questions, tools, and examples in this book to continually improve how each tier works and supports improved achievement. We encourage you to regularly monitor and ask about the progress of students served by Tier 3 interventions. Building an effective system that improves the progress of students with the greatest need yields success for *all* learners.

▽ **Learn by doing:** As mentioned earlier, we have had the opportunity to learn with the best teachers, principals, superintendents, parents, and educators. We stand in awe of the teachers and teams who do this incredible work each day. The success stories of the students we shared are due to the hard work, perseverance, and willingness to learn, make mistakes, and challenge the status quo of teams who served them. We must view working as a PLC and implementing a system of interventions as a continual process of growth and improvement. Students change, needs change, and we must continue to change and learn. We urge you to start. Start and agree to get better. You will make mistakes, *but you will improve.*

▽ **Learn together:** As you and your team search for solutions to the challenges you face, we urge you to remember to use all the resources available to you, including the valuable website www.allthingsplc .com. The schools listed on this site have been named as model PLCs after a rigorous review of their school data, systems, and processes. Every school provides specific information about its intervention system. Utilizing this site is a great way for teams to do action research.

▽ **Work as a team and believe in yourself, your team, and your students:** There will be days when you doubt if you have the capacity to achieve your goals. Schools are busy and complex places that bring new challenges every hour of every day. It is inevitable that you will experience many opportunities to give up, stop, or take a detour. As a team, you must support each other, believe in this very important work, and support your students. As a team, you must maintain the commitment to

> "A challenge only becomes an obstacle when you bow to it."
> —Anonymous

continually move forward and understand that every person is responsible for leading this work. The principal, teachers, the central office, or any staff member cannot achieve this alone—and one person cannot cause it to fail. As team members, with a common vision and common commitment, you must each lead, support, and influence this mission.

We believe in you and in your power to do great things for *our students*!

Resources and Tools

Table A.1 provides tools and resources you can find throughout this book. Use this chart to help you and your team find the appropriate tools for the task.

Table A.1: Resources and Tools

Chapter	Tool	Purpose
Chapter 1 (pages 26–28)	Figure 1.2: RTI Alignment at Tiers 1, 2, and 3	Tool to analyze processes at each tier and check for alignment with Tier 3
Chapter 2 (page 35)	Figure 2.1: Team Collective Responsibility Survey	Tool to collectively analyze the collective responsibility of the staff for the purpose of determining areas of staff growth
Chapter 2 (page 41)	Figure 2.2: Dreams and Commitments	Tool for considering the actions and practices we hope are in place at the schools our own children attend and commit to replicating for the students we serve
Chapter 3 (pages 68–69)	Figure 3.3: 1-2-3 Action Planning	Tool to determine the professional development and coaching needed for established goals as well as how and when to monitor progress
Chapter 3 (page 69)	Figure 3.4: Monitoring Our Progress	Action-planning tool for teams to monitor their progress toward agreed-on goals
Chapter 3 (page 70)	Figure 3.5: Roles and Responsibilities for Teams at Tier 3	Tool to help establish leadership and intervention teams at Tier 3 and the roles and responsibilities of team members
Chapter 5 (page 97)	Figure 5.1: Intervention Team Problem-Solving Process	Tool offering a process for intervention teams to use to efficiently and effectively determine targeted interventions
Chapter 5 (page 114)	Figure 5.7: Tier 3 Team Data Analysis Considerations	Tool offering considerations for the leadership team in determining if the process at Tier 3 is timely, targeted, and systematic

continued →

Chapter	Tool	Purpose
Chapter 6 (pages 135–136)	Figure 6.4: Teaching Essential Behavior Skills Team Checklist	Tool providing actions for the leadership team to consider in improving interventions for behavior at Tiers 1, 2, and 3
Chapter 6 (pages 144–145)	Figure 6.6: Behavior Intervention Team Meeting Tool	Tool offering a process for intervention teams to use when reviewing progress, problem solving, and developing an action plan
Chapter 6 (page 150)	Figure 6.7: Check-In/ Check-Out Weekly Points	Check-in/check-out tracker to monitor progress by class period for weekly goals
Chapter 6 (page 151)	Figure 6.8: Daily Behavior Goal Tracking	Form to help with daily goal tracking by time period
Chapter 6 (page 153)	Figure 6.10: Individualized Student Behavior Tracker	On- and off-track goal tracker using icons
Chapter 6 (pages 155–156)	Figure 6.11: Steps for Teaching Calm-Down Strategies	Tool for students and teachers to use when teaching calm-down strategies
Chapter 6 (page 157)	Figure 6.13: Safe Place Reflection Sheet	Tool for teachers and students to use for students to reflect on what upset them, how they calmed down, and what they will do next time
Chapter 6 (page 164)	Behavior Observation Tool	Tool for teachers or support staff to use to observe students and determine student progress on behavior goals
Chapter 6 (page 165)	Individual Behavior Tracking Sheet Example	Completed example of Individual Behavior Tracking Sheet
Chapter 6 (page 166)	Individual Behavior Tracking Sheet	Sheet to track individual goals and ratings by time period; may add icons if needed
Chapter 7 (pages 178–179)	Figure 7.2: Co-Planning Template	Preplanning outline for teachers to use when planning for students' unique learning needs; use in advance of collaborative planning
Chapter 7 (pages 182–183)	Figure 7.3: Essential Academic Skills Leadership Team Checklist	Checklist that gives the leadership team a way of analyzing Tier 3 interventions to ensure they are systematic and include the structures and processes necessary for students to master identified essential standards
Chapter 7 (page 186)	Figure 7.4: Team Data Review—Action Plan	Action-planning tool for the intervention team to use as they review data to determine targeted interventions or monitor progress
Chapter 7 (page 194)	Figure 7.6: Student Goal-Setting and Feedback Matrix	Matrix for students to set individual goals, track their own progress, and receive feedback from their teacher or make notations about self-assessment
Chapter 7 (page 195)	Figure 7.7: My Reading Notepad— Nonfiction Books	Tool for helping students take notes when reading nonfiction books; an example of how teachers can teach students to think about how they learn so they can begin to replicate the strategies with new learning

Chapter	Tool	Purpose
Chapter 7 (page 196)	Figure 7.8: Strategies to Remember	Tool that supports students generalizing specific strategies that are successful in one class or intervention across other environments, classrooms, or subjects
Chapter 8 (pages 202–203)	Figure 8.1: Collaborative Planning for All Students	Concept map offers teams a structured discussion process to guide them to plan in advance for unique learners; the process ensures alignment to standards and assessment
Chapter 8 (pages 206–209)	Figure 8.2: Leadership Team Reflection Tool	Checklist that provides a list of practices teams can use as a guide for goal setting and implementing Tier 3
Chapter 8 (page 211)	Figure 8.3: Determining a Grade-Level Learning Progression	Process that supports teams developing learning progressions; provides suggestions for a process to follow
Chapter 8 (page 213)	Figure 8.4: Staff Background Sheet	Tool for collecting information about a staff's special skills and interests; use when determining leadership or intervention team membership
Chapter 8 (page 215)	Figure 8.5: Intervention Team Worksheet	Intervention team members use this process to document the details of interventions for individual students.
Chapter 8 (page 217)	Figure 8.6: Working the Plan	Tool to help the leadership team monitor goals and progress in implementation of Tier 3 interventions
Chapter 8 (page 219)	Figure 8.7: Who Are Our Learners, and What Are Their Needs?	Framework that teams can use when discussing students' unique learning needs; use information to proactively plan for all learners.
Chapter 8 (page 220)	Figure 8.8: Who Are Our Learners, and What Are Their Needs? Example	Completed example of figure 8.7: Who Are Our Learners, and What Are Their Needs?

References and Resources

Achieve. (2015). *The role of learning progressions in competency-based pathways.* Accessed at www
.achieve.org/files/Achieve-LearningProgressionsinCBP.pdf on August 15, 2019.

AllThingsPLC. (n.d.a). *All things PLC, all in one place.* Accessed at www.allthingsplc.info on August
8, 2019.

AllThingsPLC. (n.d.b). *White Oak Primary School.* Accessed at www.allthingsplc.info/evidence
/details/id,1365 on August 15, 2019.

ASCD Guest Blogger. (2010). *Effective schools for the urban poor (1979).* Accessed at http://inservice
.ascd.org/effective-schools-for-the-urban-poor on August 11, 2019.

Bailey, K., & Jakicic, C. (2012). *Common formative assessment: A toolkit for Professional Learning
Communities at Work.* Bloomington, IN: Solution Tree Press.

Barnes, E. W. (2017). New Supreme Court decision benefits students with IEPs. *Edutopia.* Accessed
at www.edutopia.org/article/new-supreme-court-decision-benefits-students-iep-elizabeth-w
-barnes?utm_source=SilverpopMailing&utm_medium=email&utm_campaign=042617%
20enews%20buildastudent%20remainder&utm_content=&utm_term=fea4hed&spMailing
ID=17099132&spUserID=NDAwNzE3ODIyMTcS1&spJobID=1002227222&spReportId
=MTAwMjIyNzIyMgS2 on August 15, 2019.

Bongiorno, D. (Ed.). (2011). *Early childhood education: Response to intervention in primary grade
reading.* Accessed at www.naesp.org/sites/default/files/Primary_Reading_0.pdf on August 15, 2019.

BrainyQuote. (n.d.a). *Albert Bandura quotes.* Accessed at www.brainyquote.com/quotes/albert
_bandura_788120 on August 11, 2019.

BrainyQuote. (n.d.b). *Tony Fadell quotes.* Accessed at www.brainyquote.com/authors/tony-fadell
-quotes on August 11, 2019.

Brantlinger, E. A. (Ed). (2006). *Who benefits from special education?* Mahwah, NJ: Erlbaum.

Brown-Chidsey, R., Bronaugh, L., & McGraw, K. (2009). *RTI in the classroom: Guidelines and
recipes for success.* New York: Guilford Press.

Buffum, A., & Mattos, M. (Eds.). (2015). *It's about time: Planning interventions and extensions in
elementary school.* Bloomington, IN: Solution Tree Press.

Buffum, A., Mattos, M., & Malone, J. (2018). *Taking action: A handbook for RTI at Work.*
Bloomington, IN: Solution Tree Press.

Buffum, A., Mattos, M., & Weber, C. (2012). *Simplifying response to intervention: Four essential
guiding principles.* Bloomington, IN: Solution Tree Press.

Buffum, A., Mattos, M., Weber, C., & Hierck, T. (2015). *Uniting academic and behavior interventions: Solving the skill or will dilemma.* Bloomington, IN: Solution Tree Press.

Bulley, D. (2014). *School suspensions don't work: It's time for something better.* Accessed at www .bostonglobe.com/magazine/2014/12/21/school-suspensions-don-work-time-for-something -better/kXQMRlfBWccB8hPduwoHTK/story.html on December 17, 2019.

Carnevale, A. P., Strohl, J., Ridley, N., & Gulish, A. (2018). *Three educational pathways to good jobs: High school, middle skills, and bachelor's degree.* Washington, DC: Center of Education and the Workforce, Georgetown University.

CAST. (2011). *Universal design for learning (UDL) guidelines: Full-text representation.* Accessed at https://wvde.state.wv.us/osp/UDL/4.%20Guidelines%202.0.pdf on August 15, 2019.

CEEDAR Center. (n.d.). *High-leverage practices crosswalk.* Accessed at http://ceedar.education.ufl .edu/wp-content/uploads/2017/11/HLP-Crosswalk-with-PSEL1.pdf on August 11, 2019.

Center on Instruction. (2006). *Intensive reading interventions for struggling readers in early elementary school: A principal's guide.* Accessed at www.fcrr.org/Interventions/pdf/Principal'sGuideto Intervention.pdf on August 11, 2019.

Center on Positive Behavioral Interventions and Supports. (2010). *School-wide positive behavior support: Getting started workbook.* Accessed at www.pbis.org/common/cms/files/pbisresources /SWPBS_team_workbook_ver_oct10_2012.docx on January 19, 2019.

Center on Response to Intervention at American Institutes for Research. (n.d.a). *The essential components of RTI.* Accessed at www.rti4success.org on August 11, 2019.

Center on Response to Intervention at American Institutes for Research. (n.d.b). *Progress monitoring.* Accessed at www.rti4success.org/essential-components-rti/progress-monitoring on August 11, 2019.

Center on Response to Intervention at American Institutes for Research. (n.d.c). *Universal screening.* Accessed at www.rti4success.org/essential-components-rti/universal-screening on August 15, 2019.

Collins, C. (2011). *Progression charts: Common Core State Standards.* Accessed at https:// turnonyourbrain.files.wordpress.com/2011/07/progression-charts.pdf on February 22, 2019.

Colorado Department of Education. (2014). *Writing standards-aligned individualized education programs (IEPs): A supplemental guidance document for designing effective formal educational plans.* Accessed at www.cde.state.co.us/cdesped/guidance_ieps on August 15, 2019.

Conley, D. T., & Darling-Hammond, L. (2013). *Creating systems of assessment for deeper learning.* Stanford, CA: Stanford Center for Opportunity Policy in Education. Accessed at https://edpolicy .stanford.edu/sites/default/files/publications/creating-systems-assessment-deeper-learning_0.pdf on August 15, 2019.

Construction Financial Management Association. (n.d.). *The eight-step process for leading change.* Accessed at www.cfma.org/content.cfm?ItemNumber=2378 on August 8, 2019.

Council for Exceptional Children. (2008). *CEC's position on response to intervention (RTI): The unique role of special education and special educators.* Accessed at www.cec.sped.org/~/media/Files /Policy/CEC%20Professional%20Policies%20and%20Positions/RTI.pdf on December 8, 2016.

Council for Exceptional Children and CEEDAR Center. (2017). *High leverage practices in special education (HLPs).* Accessed at http://ceedar.education.ufl.edu/wp-content/uploads/2017/11/HLP -flyer-list.pdf on August 11, 2019.

Cowan, K. C., Vaillancourt, K., Rossen, E., & Pollitt, K. (2013). *A framework for safe and successful schools.* Bethesda, MD: National Association of School Psychologists. Accessed at www.school counselor.org/asca/media/asca/home/frameworkforsafeandsuccessfulschoolenvironments.pdf on April 16, 2019.

Davis, L. (2018). *Survey results: Top 10 barriers to student success.* Accessed at www.schoolplanner .com/2018/03/01/barriers-student-success on August 11, 2019.

Delaware Department of Education. (2019). *Curriculum development for English and language arts (ELA).* Accessed at www.doe.k12.de.us/Page/2425 on February 20, 2020.

Denton, C. A. (2012). Response to intervention for reading difficulties in the primary grades: Some answers and lingering questions. *Journal of Learning Disabilities, 45*(3), 232–243. Accessed at www.ncbi.nlm.nih.gov/pmc/articles/PMC3454349/#R50 on June 29, 2019.

Diply. (2016). *17 inspirational quotes from children's books.* Accessed at https://diply.com/childrens -books-that-inspire/4?publisher=funny-videos on August 15, 2019.

Direct/explicit instruction: Five essential phases for an instructional process. (n.d.). Accessed at https://education.ky.gov/school/stratclsgap/instruction/Documents/Direct%20Explicit%20 Instruction%20Model.pdf on August 11, 2019.

DuFour, R. (2015). *In praise of American educators: And how they can become even better.* Bloomington, IN: Solution Tree Press.

DuFour, R., & Eaker, R. (1998). *Professional Learning Communities at Work: Best practices for enhancing student achievement.* Bloomington, IN: Solution Tree Press.

DuFour, R., DuFour, R., & Eaker, R. (2008). *Revisiting Professional Learning Communities at Work: New insights for improving schools.* Bloomington, IN: Solution Tree Press.

DuFour, R., DuFour, R., Eaker, R., & Karhanek, G. (2010). *Raising the bar and closing the gap: Whatever it takes.* Bloomington, IN: Solution Tree Press.

DuFour, R., DuFour, R., Eaker, R., & Many, T. (2006). *Learning by doing: A handbook for Professional Learning Communities at Work.* Bloomington, IN: Solution Tree Press.

DuFour, R., DuFour, R., Eaker, R., & Many, T. (2010). *Learning by doing: A handbook for Professional Learning Communities at Work* (2nd ed.). Bloomington, IN: Solution Tree Press.

DuFour, R., DuFour, R., Eaker, R., Many, T. W., & Mattos, M. (2016). *Learning by doing: A handbook for Professional Learning Communities at Work* (3rd ed.). Bloomington, IN: Solution Tree Press.

Eber, L. (2008). Wraparound: A key component of school-wide systems of positive behavior supports. In E. J. Bruns & J. S. Walker (Eds.), *The resource guide to wraparound.* Portland, OR: National Wraparound Initiative, Research and Training Center for Family Support and Children's Mental Health. Accessed at https://nwi.pdx.edu/NWI-book/Chapters/Eber-5e.3-(school-wide -support-systems).pdf on December 15, 2019.

Ehren, B. J., Laster, B., & Watts-Taffe, S. (n.d.). *Creating shared language for collaboration in RTI.* Accessed at www.rtinetwork.org/getstarted/buildsupport/creating-shared-language-for -collaboration-in-rti on February 13, 2019.

Ellevate. (n.d.). *Quotes about the power of community.* Accessed at www.ellevatenetwork.com /articles/8538-quotes-about-the-power-of-community on June 26, 2019.

Ervin, R. A. (n.d.). *Considering Tier 3 within a response-to-intervention model.* Accessed at www .rtinetwork.org/essential/tieredinstruction/tier3/consideringtier3 on December 14, 2016.

Farley, C., Torres, C., Wailehua, C. U. T., & Cook, L. (2012). *Evidenced-based practices for students with emotional and behavioral disorders: Improving academic achievement.* Accessed at https:// elementaryemotionaldisturbance.weebly.com/uploads/1/4/7/3/14738022/farley_2012.pdf on August 11, 2019.

Ferri, B. A., & Connor, D. J. (2006). *Reading resistance: Discourses of exclusion in desegregation and inclusion debates.* New York: Peter Lang.

Ferriter, B. (2012). *The tempered radical.* Accessed at https://blog.williamferriter.com/2012/11/21 /are-you-a-what-if-guy-slide on March 16, 2020.

Ferriter, W. (2017, November 15). *Small schools and singletons: Structuring meaningful professional learning teams for every teacher.* Solution Tree Associate Retreat and Workshop, Salt Lake City, Utah.

Foegen, A. (2009). *Functions of progress monitoring.* Accessed at https://ies.ed.gov/ncee/wwc/Docs/PracticeGuide/wwc_mrti_pg_rec07.pdf on December 14, 2018.

Formative assessment & monitoring student progress: Focused instruction, guided practice, collaborative learning, independent learning. (n.d.). Accessed at https://schools.archmil.org/CentersofExcellence/DOCsPDFs/Learning-Support-Teams/2015-16/October-8-2015/Formative-Assessments/FormativeAssessmentandMonitoringStudentProgress.pdf on August 23, 2019.

Fountas, I. C., & Pinnell, G. S. (2012). *Benchmark assessment system 2nd edition: Executive summary.* Accessed at www.fountasandpinnell.com/shared/resources/FP_BAS_2ED_Research_Executive-Summary_v2012-08.pdf on August 15, 2019.

Fuchs, L. (n.d.). *How can Tier 3 intervention be conceptualized in the RTI approach?* Accessed at https://iris.peabody.vanderbilt.edu/module/rti05/cresource/q1/p03 on August 11, 2019.

Gage, N. A. (2015). *Evidence-based practices for classroom and behavior management: Tier 2 and Tier 3 strategies.* Accessed at http://ceedar.education.ufl.edu/wp-content/uploads/2015/11/Behavior-Management-tier-two-and-three-strategies.pdf on August 11, 2019.

George, J., & George, R. (2016). *10 strategies and practices that can help all students overcome barriers.* Accessed at http://inservice.ascd.org/10-strategies-and-practices-that-can-help-all-students-overcome-barriers on August 11, 2019.

Goin, D. (2012). Guiding coalition: A dream team to help you implement strategy quickly. *Forbes.* Accessed at www.forbes.com/sites/johnkotter/2012/02/08/guiding-coalition-a-dream-team-to-help-you-implement-strategy-quickly/#55a1b703b294 on August 8, 2019.

Goodreads. (n.d.a). *Antonio Machado quotes.* Accessed at www.goodreads.com/quotes/289625-xxix-traveler-there-is-no-path-the-path-is-made on August 23, 2019.

Goodreads. (n.d.b). *Charles Dickens quotes.* Accessed at www.goodreads.com/quotes/524147-a-very-little-key-will-open-a-very-heavy-door on August 15, 2019.

Goodreads. (n.d.c). *John P. Kotter quotes.* Accessed at www.goodreads.com/author/quotes/26977.John_P_Kotter on July 6, 2019.

Goodreads. (n.d.d). *Nelson Mandela quotes.* Accessed at www.goodreads.com/quotes/36606-it-always-seems-impossible-until-it-s-done on August 11, 2019.

Gooey Brains. (n.d.). *Growth mindset quotes for kids.* Accessed at http://gooeybrains.com/growth-mindset-quotes on February 25, 2019.

Haager, D., Klingner, J., & Vaughn, S. (Eds.). (2007). *Evidence-based reading practices for response to intervention.* Baltimore, MD: Brookes.

Hanover Research. (2013). *Effective programs for emotional and behavioral disorders.* Accessed at https://bigfivetech.com/upload/resources_guide/Self_Management_and_Effective_Interventions_for_EBD.pdf on August 23, 2019.

Hanover Research. (2014). *Improving student achievement and closing the achievement gap.* Accessed at www.rcoe.us/educational-services/files/2015/12/10c-Hanover_Improving_Student_Achievement_and_Closing_the_Achievement_Gap__12-2014.pdf on July 5, 2019.

Harlacher, J. E., Sanford, A., & Walker, N. N. (n.d.). *Distinguishing between Tier 2 and Tier 3 instruction in order to support implementation of RTI.* Accessed at https://idahotc.com/Portals/0/Resources/282/Distinguishing%20Between%20Tier%202%20and%20Tier%203.pdf on June 29, 2019.

Hartmann, E. (2015). Universal design for learning (UDL) and learners with severe support needs. *International Journal of Whole Schooling, 11*(1), 54–67. Accessed at https://files.eric.ed.gov/fulltext/EJ1061020.pdf on February 24, 2019.

Hattie, J. (2012). *Visible learning for teachers: Maximizing impact on learning.* London: Routledge.

Heick, T. (2019). *Why your students aren't learning: 10 silent disruptors of academic performance.* Accessed at www.teachthought.com/pedagogy/10-silent-disruptors-of-student-academic -performance on August 11, 2019.

Heritage, M. (2008). *Learning progressions: Supporting instruction and formative assessment.* Accessed at www.semanticscholar.org/paper/Learning-Progressions%3A-Supporting-Instruction-and-T -ASSESSMENT-Heritage/f9f3744dc76d1aea13b2190f0135b6f882e1668d on August 15, 2019.

Hess, K. K. (2008a). *Developing and using learning progressions as a schema for measuring progress.* Accessed at www.nciea.org/publications/CCSSO2_KH08.pdf on December 8, 2016.

Hess, K. K. (2008b). *Student profile: Science inquiry learning grades preK–4.* Accessed at www.nciea .org/publications/ScienceProfile_KH08.pdf on August 15, 2019.

Hess, K. K. (2013). *An educator's guide for applying Webb's Depth-of-Knowledge levels to the Common Core State Standards.* Accessed at https://education.ohio.gov/getattachment/Topics/Teaching /Educator-Evaluation-System/How-to-Design-and-Select-Quality-Assessments/Webbs-DOK -Flip-Chart.pdf.aspx on January 23, 2020.

Hess, K. K., Jones, B. S., Carlock, D., & Walkup, J. R. (2009). *Cognitive rigor: Blending the strengths of Bloom's taxonomy and Webb's Depth of Knowledge to enhance classroom-level processes.* Accessed at https://files.eric.ed.gov/fulltext/ED517804.pdf on February 23, 2019.

Hess, K. K., & Kearns, J. (2010). *Learning progressions frameworks designed for use with the Common Core State Standards in mathematics K–12.* Accessed at www.nciea.org/publications/Math_LPF _KH11.pdf on August 15, 2019.

Hierck, T., Coleman, C., & Weber, C. (2011). *Pyramid of behavior interventions: Seven keys to a positive learning environment.* Bloomington, IN: Solution Tree Press.

Hoff, N., Strawhun, J., & Peterson, R. L. (2015). *Examples of behavior screeners.* Accessed at https:// k12engagement.unl.edu/Examples%20Behavior%20Screeners%204-23-2015.pdf on February 27, 2019.

Israel, M., Ribuffo, C., & Smith, S. (2014). *Universal design for learning: Recommendations for teacher preparation and professional development.* Accessed at http://ceedar.education.ufl.edu /wp-content/uploads/2014/08/IC-7_FINAL_08-27-14.pdf on August 15, 2019.

Jackson, S. (n.d.). *Using data to inform instruction and personalize learning: A continuous improvement framework.* Accessed at www.edweek.org/media/071813_usingdata.pdf on August 15, 2019.

Johnson, E. S., Pool, J., & Carter, D. R. (n.d.). *Screening for reading problems in grades 1 through 3: An overview of select measures.* Accessed at www.rtinetwork.org/essential/assessment/screening /screening-for-reading-problems-in-grades-1-through-3 on December 14, 2016.

Jordan, L. (n.d.). *Cognitive strategies.* Accessed at www.specialconnections.ku.edu/?q=instruction /cognitive_strategies on July 25, 2019.

Joseph, G. E., & Strain, P. S. (2010). *Helping young children control anger and handle disappointment.* Accessed at http://csefel.vanderbilt.edu/modules/module2/handout7.pdf on August 27, 2019.

Juel, C. (1988). Learning to read and write: A longitudinal study of 54 children from first through fourth grades. *Journal of Educational Psychology, 80*(4), 437–447. Accessed at http://people.uncw .edu/kozloffm/learningtreadandwrite.pdf on August 15, 2019.

Kilgore, K. (n.d.). *10 steps to implementing effective inclusion practices: A guide for school site leaders.* Accessed at http://laspdg.org/files/10%20Steps%20Final%20Guide.pdf on August 15, 2019.

Knips, A. (2019). 6 steps to equitable data analysis: When analyzing data, educators should include students' identities and culture for a fuller picture of how they are doing. *Edutopia.* Accessed at www.edutopia.org/article/6-steps-equitable-data-analysis on August 23, 2019.

Kobrin, J. (2016). *How learning progressions can help with both monitoring progress and progress monitoring.* Accessed at www.pearsoned.com/learning-progressions-monitoring-progress on August 15, 2015.

Kohn, A. (1996). *Beyond discipline: From compliance to community.* Alexandria, VA: Association for Supervision and Curriculum Development.

Kosanovich, M., & Verhagen, C. (2012). *Building the foundation: A suggested progression of sub-skills to achieve the reading standards: Foundational skills in the Common Core State Standards.* Accessed at www.readingrockets.org/sites/default/files/Building%20the%20Foundation.pdf on August 23, 2019.

Kotter, J. P. (2006). Leading change: Why transformation efforts fail. *Harvard Business Review.* Accessed at www.academia.edu/13726263/Leading_Change_Why_Transformation_Efforts_Fail on August 8, 2019.

Lahey, J. (2014, February 13). Students who lose recess are the ones who need it most. *The New York Times.* Accessed at https://parenting.blogs.nytimes.com/2014/02/13/students-who-lose-recess-are-the-ones-who-need-it-most on December 17, 2019.

LeadershipNow. (n.d.). *Quotes about problem solving.* Accessed at www.leadershipnow.com/probsolvingquotes.html on August 15, 2019.

Lee, V. E., & Smith, J. B. (1996). Collective responsibility for learning and its effects on gains in achievement for early secondary school students. *American Journal of Education, 104*(2), 103–147. Accessed at www.researchgate.net/publication/240556015_Collective_Responsibility_for_Learning_and_Its_Effects_on_Gains_in_Achievement_for_Early_Secondary_School_Students on August 8, 2019.

Lewis, D., Madison-Harris, R., Muoneke, A., & Times, C. (n.d.). *Using data to guide instruction and improve student learning.* Accessed at www.sedl.org/pubs/sedl-letter/v22n02/using-data.html on August 11, 2019.

Loman, S., & Borgmeier, C. (n.d.). *Practical functional behavioral assessment training manual for school-based personnel: Participant's guidebook.* Accessed at https://assets-global.website-files.com/5d3725188825e071f1670246/5da4e87901ad6fcb1df7c8de_PracticalFBA_TrainingManual.pdf on January 19, 2019.

Mattos, M. (2016, October 26). *Certain access: How to create a mutitiered system of support.* RTI at Work™ Institute. Denver, Colorado.

McConnell, K., & Ryser, G. R. (2005). *Practical ideas that really work for students with ADHD: Preschool through grade 4* (2nd ed.). Austin, TX: Pro-Ed.

McCray, E. D., Kamman, M., Brownell, M. T., & Robinson, S. (2017). *High-leverage practices and evidence-based practices: A promising pair.* Accessed at http://ceedar.education.ufl.edu/wp-content/uploads/2017/12/HLPs-and-EBPs-A-Promising-Pair.pdf on August 11, 2019.

McFarland, J., Hussar, B., Wang, X., Zhang, J., Wang, K., Rathbun, A., et al. (2018). *The condition of education 2018.* Washington, DC: National Center for Education Statistics. Accessed at https://nces.ed.gov/pubs2018/2018144.pdf on January 5, 2020.

McLeskey, J., Barringer, M., Billingsley, B., Brownell, M., Jackson, D., Kennedy, M., et al. (2017). *High-leverage practices in special education.* Arlington, VA: Council for Exceptional Children & CEEDAR Center. Accessed at http://ceedar.education.ufl.edu/wp-content/uploads/2017/07/CEC-HLP-Web.pdf on August 11, 2019.

McLeskey, J., Maheady, L., Billingsley, B., Brownell, M., & Lewis, T. J. (Eds.). (2019). *High leverage practices for inclusive classrooms.* New York: Routledge.

Minahan, J. (2013). *Teaching self-calming skills.* Accessed at www.responsiveclassroom.org/teaching-self-calming-skills on August 23, 2019.

Minnesota Department of Education. (2013). *Developing standards-based IEP goals and objectives: A discussion guide*. Accessed at www.lcsc.org/cms/lib6/MN01001004/Centricity/Domain/21/MDE%20Discussion%20guide.April2013.pdf on August 15, 2019.

Moen, R. D., & Norman, C. L. (2010). *Circling back: Clearing up myths about the Deming cycle and seeing how it keeps evolving*. Accessed at www.apiweb.org/circling-back.pdf on March 8, 2019.

Muhammad, A. (2009). *Transforming school culture: How to overcome staff division*. Bloomington, IN: Solution Tree Press.

Muhammad, A. (2018). *Transforming school culture: How to overcome staff division* (2nd ed.). Bloomington, IN: Solution Tree Press.

National Center on Response to Intervention. (n.d.). *Transcript: What is progress monitoring?* Accessed at www.rti4success.org/sites/default/files/Transcript%20What%20is%20Progress%20Monitoring.pdf on August 15, 2019.

National Council of Teachers of English. (2013). *Formative assessment that truly informs instruction*. Accessed at www.ncte.org/library/NCTEFiles/Resources/Positions/formative-assessment_single.pdf on August 15, 2019.

National Governors Association Center for Best Practices & Council of Chief State School Officers. (2010). *Common Core State Standards for English language arts and literacy in history/social studies, science, and technical subjects*. Washington, DC: Authors. Accessed at www.corestandards.org/assets/CCSSI_ELA%20Standards.pdf on March 13, 2020.

New Hampshire Department of Education. (n.d.). *School-wide inclusive education best practice indicators: Self-rating survey*. Accessed at www.education.nh.gov/instruction/special_ed/documents/appendix_d.pdf on August 15, 2019.

New Jersey Department of Education. (n.d.). *Essential components for effective NJTSS implementation*. Accessed at www.nj.gov/education/njtss/comp/comp.pdf on August 11, 2019.

Northern State University. (2017). *Back to school workshop: High leverage teaching practices*. Accessed at https://northern.edu/sites/default/files/highleverage.pdf on July 15, 2019.

O'Connor, R. E., Harty, K. R., & Fulmer, D. (2005). Tiers of intervention in kindergarten through third grade. *Journal of Learning Disabilities*, *38*(6), 532–538.

Olson, C. B., & Land, R. (n.d.). *Cognitive strategies toolkit*. Accessed at www.ldonline.org/article/21573/ on July 25, 2019.

OSEP Technical Assistance Center on Positive Behavioral Interventions and Supports. (n.d.a). *Tier 1 supports*. Accessed at www.pbis.org/school/Tier1supports on February 27, 2019.

OSEP Technical Assistance Center on Positive Behavioral Interventions and Supports. (n.d.b). *What are student-level Tier 3 systems?* Accessed at www.pbis.org/school/Tier-3-supports/what-are-student-level-Tier-3-systems#Wraparound on February 26, 2019.

OSEP Technical Assistance Center on Positive Behavioral Interventions and Supports. (2019). *Positive behavioral interventions & supports* [Website]. Accessed at www.pbis.org on August 11, 2019.

PBIS World. (n.d.). *Check in check out (CICO)*. Accessed at www.pbisworld.com/Tier-3/check-in-check-out-cico on February 27, 2019.

Pierce, C. (2015). *Revised: RTI2 implementation guide July 2014—State of Tennessee*. Accessed at www.noexperiencenecessarybook.com/W85Wa/revised-rti2-implementation-guide-july-2014-state-of-tennessee.html on May 8, 2017.

Popham, W. J. (2007). All about accountability: The lowdown on learning progressions. *Educational Leadership*, *64*(7), 83–84. Accessed at www.ascd.org/publications/educational-leadership/apr07/vol64/num07/The-Lowdown-on-Learning-Progressions.aspx on August 15, 2019.

Powers, K., & Mandal, A. (2011). Tier III assessments, data-based decision making, and interventions. *Contemporary School Psychology, 15*(1), 21–33. Accessed at https://files.eric.ed.gov /fulltext/EJ934703.pdf on December 12, 2016.

Prasse, D. P. (n.d.). *Why adopt an RTI model?* Accessed at www.rtinetwork.org/learn/what/whyrti on January 5, 2020.

Rajan, R. S. (2011). Collaborative action research for professional learning communities. *i.e.: inquiry in education, 2*(1). Accessed at https://digitalcommons.nl.edu/cgi/viewcontent.cgi?article=1039 &context=ie on March 3, 2019.

Read Naturally. (n.d.). *Hasbrouck & Tindal oral reading fluency data.* Accessed at www.readnaturally .com/knowledgebase/documents-and-resources/26/386 on August 15, 2019.

Reading Recovery Council of North America. (n.d.). *Clay's observation survey.* Accessed at http:// readingrecovery.org/reading-recovery/teaching-children/observation-survey on August 15, 2019.

Reschly, D. J., & Wood-Garnett, S. (2011). *Response to intervention innovation configuration.* Accessed at https://gtlcenter.org/sites/default/files/docs/IC_RTI.pdf on July 15, 2019.

Robinson, K., & Taylor, G. (2016). *Arkansas Adolescent Literacy Intervention (AALI): The Strategic Instruction Model SIM—How does it relate to school improvement?* Accessed at www.arkansased.gov /public/userfiles/Public_School_Accountability/School_Improvement/School_Improvement _Conference_2016/SIM_Overview_ADE_School_Improvement_Conference_2016.pdf on August 11, 2019.

Rose, D. H., & Meyer, A. (2002). *Teaching every student in the digital age: Universal design for learning.* Alexandria, VA: Association for Supervision and Curriculum Development.

RTI Tier 3 intensive intervention. (n.d.). Accessed at www.hillsdale-isd.org/cms/lib/MI01001046 /Centricity/Domain/15/RtI_Tier_3_Intensive_Intervention.pdf on August 8, 2019.

Sagor, R. (2010). *Collaborative action research for professional learning communities.* Bloomington, IN: Solution Tree Press.

Shanker, S. (2019). *See a child differently and you'll see a different child.* Accessed at https://self-reg .ca/2019/02/05/see-a-child-differently-and-youll-see-a-different-child on July 11, 2019.

Simmons, D. C., Kame'enui, E. J., Harn, B., Coyne, M. D., Stoolmiller, M., Santoro, L. E., et al. (2007). Attributes of effective and efficient kindergarten reading intervention: An examination of instructional time and design specificity. *Journal of Learning Disabilities, 40*(4), 331–347.

Skiba, R. J., Poloni-Staudinger, L., Gallini, S., Simmons, A. B., & Feggins-Azziz, R. (2006). Disparate access: The disproportionality of African American students with disabilities across educational environments. *Exceptional Children, 72*(4), 411–424.

Snyder, T. D. (Ed.). (1993). *120 years of American education: A statistical portrait.* Accessed at https:// nces.ed.gov/pubs93/93442.pdf on December 16, 2019.

Sparks, S. D. (2016). *A Colorado leader taps teacher specialists to serve all students.* Accessed at https:// leaders.edweek.org/profile/steve-sandoval-executive-director-of-special-services-supporting-all -students on August 8, 2019.

St. Vrain Valley Schools. (2012). *Tier 1 instruction best practices: Student achievement and growth increase as a result of effective initial instruction.* Accessed at www.svvsd.org/files/Tier%201 %20Instruction%20Best%20Practices.pdf on August 11, 2019.

Stiggins, R. (2017). *The perfect assessment system.* Alexandria, VA: Association for Supervision and Curriculum Development. Accessed at www.ascd.org/ASCD/pdf/siteASCD/publications/books /PerfectAssessmentSystem_Stiggins.pdf on August 15, 2019.

Sugai, G., Lewis-Palmer, T., & Hagan-Burke, S. (2000). Overview of the functional behavioral assessment process. *Exceptionality, 8*(3), 149–160.

Sugai, G., & Todd, A. W. (2003). *Conducting leadership team meetings.* Accessed at www.pbis.org/resource/805/conducting-leadership-team-meetings on August 23, 2019.

SWIFT Center. (2016). *Identifying data-driven instructional systems.* Accessed at https://files.eric.ed.gov/fulltext/ED571845.pdf on August 15, 2019.

SWIFT Education Center. (2018). *Schoolwide integrated framework for transformation fidelity integrity assessment, version 2.0.* Accessed at www.swiftschools.org/sites/default/files/SWIFT-FIA%202.0%20Fillable_0.pdf on August 23, 2019.

TeachingWorks. (n.d.). *High-leverage practices.* Accessed at www.teachingworks.org/work-of-teaching/high-leverage-practices on August 11, 2019.

Texas Education Agency. (n.d.). *TSLP—K–5—Effective instructional framework—E4—Tier III intervention.* Accessed at www.texasgateway.org/resource/tslp%E2%80%94k%E2%80%935%E2%80%94effective-instructional-framework%E2%80%94e4%E2%80%94tier-iii-intervention on August 15, 2019.

Tomlinson, C. A. (2003). *Fulfilling the promise of the differentiated classroom: Strategies and tools for responsive teaching.* Alexandria, VA: Association for Supervision and Curriculum Development.

The University of Kansas. (n.d.). *The strategic instruction model.* Accessed at https://sim.drupal.ku.edu/lesson-organizer on August 11, 2019.

University of Nebraska–Lincoln. (n.d.a). *Behavior and discipline briefs by tier.* Accessed at http://k12engagement.unl.edu/behavior-and-discipline-briefs-tier on February 27, 2019.

University of Nebraska–Lincoln. (n.d.b). *Strategies related to behavior and discipline.* Accessed at http://k12engagement.unl.edu/strategies-related-behavior-discipline on April 3, 2017.

U.S. Department of Education. (n.d.a). *Instructional practices.* Accessed at https://osepideasthatwork.org/federal-resources-stakeholders/tool-kits/tool-kit-universal-design-learning-udl/practices on August 15, 2019.

U.S. Department of Education. (n.d.b). *Tool kit on universal design for learning.* Accessed at https://osepideasthatwork.org/sites/default/files/intro.pdf on August 15, 2019.

Vancouver Island University. (n.d.). *Ten metacognitive teaching strategies.* Accessed at https://ciel.viu.ca/teaching-learning-pedagogy/designing-your-course/how-learning-works/ten-metacognitive-teaching-strategies on July 25, 2019.

von Ravensberg, H., & Blakely, A. (2014). *When to use functional behavior assessment? Best practice vs. legal guidance.* Accessed at https://assets-global.website-files.com/5d3725188825e071f1670246/5d76c15b8d6d91e42180feba_when_to_use_functional_behavioral_assessment.pdf on February 27, 2019.

The W. Edwards Deming Institute. (n.d.). *PDSA cycle.* Accessed at https://deming.org/explore/p-ds-a on August 15, 2019.

Wees, D. (2012). 56 examples of formative assessment. *Edutopia.* Accessed at www.edutopia.org/groups/assessment/250941 on August 15, 2019.

What Works Clearinghouse. (n.d.). *Best practice for RTI: Small group instruction for students making minimal progress (Tier 3).* Accessed at www.readingrockets.org/article/best-practice-rti-small-group-instruction-students-making-minimal-progress-tier-3 on August 26, 2019.

Wisner, J. (Ed.). (2010). *PowerTeaching cooperative learning handbook.* Accessed at http://olms.cte.jhu.edu/olms2/6918/resource_id:41642/hash:be8b900b41f497e6970a77fb61691f66/resources_sub:rh/jsd:ajax on August 11, 2019.

Wolfe, P. S., & Hall, T. E. (2003). Making inclusion a reality for students with severe disabilities. *TEACHING Exceptional Children, 35*(4), 56–60. Accessed at www.cde.state.co.us/sites/default/files/documents/cdesped/download/pdf/ssn_article_makinginclusionareality.pdf on February 24, 2019.

Wright, J. (n.d.). *Extending learning across time and space: The power of generalization.* Accessed at www
.jimwrightonline.com/htmdocs/interventions/specialneeds/generalization.php on July 17, 2019.

Wylie, C., & Lyon, C. (2012). *Formative assessment: Supporting students' learning.* Accessed at www
.ets.org/Media/Research/pdf/RD_Connections_19.pdf on August 15, 2019.

Youn, M. (2016). Inequality from the first day of school: The role of teachers' academic intensity
and sense of responsibility in moderating the learning growth gap. *Journal of Educational Research,
109*(1), 50–67. Accessed at https://eric.ed.gov/?id=EJ1094013 on August 8, 2019.

Index

WOW!

I liked how I was given
an effective, organized plan
to help EVERY child.

—Linda Rossiter, teacher,
Spring Creek Elementary School, Utah

PD Services

Our experts draw from decades of research and their own experiences to bring you
practical strategies for providing timely, targeted interventions. You can choose from a
range of customizable services, from a one-day overview to a multiyear process.

Book your RTI PD today!
888.763.9045

Solution Tree